Criminal Justice
SELECTED READINGS

edited by

JOHN BALDWIN and
A. KEITH BOTTOMLEY

Martin Robertson

First published in 1978 by Martin Robertson & Company,
17 Quick Street, London N1 8HL

British Library Cataloguing in Publication Data

Criminal justice.
   1. Criminal justice, Administration of — England
   — Addresses, essays, lectures
   I. Baldwin, John II. Bottomley, Allan Keith
   345′.42′0508   KD7876.A75

ISBN 0—85520—234—3
ISBN 0—85520—233—5 Pbk

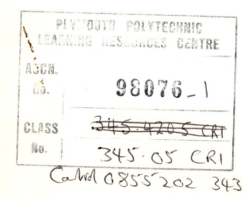
Typeset by Preface Ltd., Salisbury
Printed and bound in Britain at The Chaucer Press, Bungay

Contents

Contents   v

Preface

This collection of readings, devoted largely to the writings of English researchers and commentators in the 1970s, reflects the rapid progress that has been made in the study of the criminal justice system in England during the last decade. Indeed, we see the end of the 1970s as representing something of a watershed in the study of criminal justice policy and practice, perhaps with the search for a more mature identity and sense of direction only just beginning. Thus in this volume, we seek not only to show what has been achieved by research to date but also to indicate some of the questions still to be answered.

We have tried to select material that fairly reflects current writing on the subject, though we have deliberately excluded some of the better known work. In choosing the pieces for inclusion, we have not been much interested in particular schools of thought or in specific labels, or with the rifts within the subject that tend to characterise so much contemporary writing. Rather we see everything to be gained by complementary studies stemming from different disciplines (whether by sociologists, lawyers, historians, social administrators or others) of the structure and processes of criminal justice, instead of encouraging the development of narrow rivalries between particular factions. It is perhaps inevitable, therefore, that much of the empirical work we have included is typical of what Colin Low (in the first contribution in the book) has termed the 'social administration' approach, deriving as it does from the earlier traditions of criminological and penological work established in Britain in the 1960s. We are more concerned with examining how this work can be built upon and developed in the future.

Although we have compiled this collection of readings primarily from English sources, our indebtedness — indeed, the indebtedness of researchers in general in this country — to scholars elsewhere, especially in the United States, will be apparent. This has been acknowledged only inadequately in the suggestions for further reading that we make in the Introductions to each of the six sections in the volume. Furthermore, it goes without saying that our major debt is to the numerous authors and publishers who have given us permission to include their work in this

vii

collection and who have given much helpful advice to us. We offer our apologies to them for the savage editing to which we often had to resort in order to make the collection as comprehensive, yet concise, as our limits of space and cost would allow.

JOHN BALDWIN
Institute of Judicial
Administration, University
of Birmingham

KEITH BOTTOMLEY
Department of Social
Administration, University of
Hull

PART I

Approaches to the Study of Criminal Justice

Introduction

In recent years many different approaches to the study of 'criminal justice systems' have been adopted by criminologists and other social scientists. The choice of approach is inevitably influenced by a wide range of considerations including those of an academic and political nature, and every student of criminal justice is likely to have his own particular objectives. Various traditions of research have developed in England during the 1960s and 1970s, and rather artificial distinctions are now being drawn between traditional criminology and the emergent sociology of law. We do not see the present collection of material as defining our own perspectives on the subject, but an attempt is made in this Introduction to identify some of the main issues as we see them and to indicate the direction we favour for the continued study of criminal justice within the broad framework we have adopted.

The first issue to be faced must be that of the implications of the lack of agreement in society at large about the way those deemed criminally deviant ought to be dealt with. More specifically, we must recognise that this lack of consensus is to be found among agents of law enforcement and those who work within the criminal justice field, and the practical implications of this for the operation of social control must be confronted. It should come as no surprise to find that research confirms that the criminal justice system lacks any agreed objectives, or even justifications, of day-to-day practices of police officers, lawyers, judges or those professionally involved in the control and treatment of convicted offenders. A similar state of affairs is revealed in whatever part of the process is under scrutiny, raising hitherto unanswerable questions such as 'Who is right?', 'What is just?' and 'What is effective?'

One of the main elements that serves to aggravate these problems of internal conflict within society and between its agents of criminal justice is the 'low visibility' of so much that takes place. This applies not merely during the first encounters on the street and in the homes of suspected offenders, but also in the privacy of the police station, the solicitor's office, the magistrates' retiring room, the jury room or the meetings of boards of visitors and local review committees in penal institutions throughout the country. The freedom of researchers (or other observers) to study these areas of low visibility decision-making is severely limited in this country and there is still considerable defensiveness on the part of many official bodies to allow close investigation of what is, in essence, the administration of 'private' or 'informal' justice. Nevertheless, it is for researchers to urge greater openness, to engage in public debate and to draw attention to the misunderstandings and conflicts of interest still characteristic of so much of the criminal justice process. The exercise of discretion at various stages in the processing of suspects provides ample scope for acrimonious debate, criticism and self-justification. Who should have discretion and how it should be exercised are questions that cannot be answered successfully until overall objectives have been clarified. Some attempt must be made to consider the relationships between the various groups of decision-makers, and the nature of their accountability, not only within their own professional sphere but also in relation to other groups involved.

The last decade has witnessed a number of attempts to construct 'models' of the criminal justice system; perhaps the most important has been Herbert Packer's distinction between 'crime-control' and 'due-process' models of the process. Packer was much more aware of the limitations of the exercise in which he was engaged than many of those who have followed in his wake. In his view these models were neither accurate *descriptions* of what went on nor representations of what the criminal process *ought to be* like. He writes:

> The two models merely afford a convenient way to talk about the operation of a process whose day-to-day functioning involves a constant series of minute adjustments between the competing demands of two value systems and whose normative future likewise involves a series of resolutions, of greater or lesser magnitude, of the tensions between mutually exclusive claims. [Packer, 1969, p. 153]

When the 'model-building' exercise is regarded in this cautious way, it can clearly be valuable in understanding current reality and future options, especially if the academically imposed 'labels' are recognised by those to whom they are attached. The danger arises when competing models are not used in constructive debate but result instead in negative polarisations and distortions of the complexity of the reality they seek to illuminate. Further confusion has been added to the situation by the parallel developments of approaches to criminal justice which envisage it in terms of a 'system'. Not only does the colloquial use of the terms 'penal system' and 'criminal justice system' imply a degree of integration that does not in fact exist, but this usage has been used by academics and politicians as the basis for more elaborate conceptions of studying and manipulating the personnel and procedures of criminal justice agencies. It may indeed be desirable and legitimate to analyse the interconnectedness between the different stages of decision-making, but there is a risk of the 'systems approach' becoming so dominant in official thinking that it results in a total closure of other perspectives and creates an overall image that is misleading for researchers and policy-makers alike.

In the final analysis, once the boundaries of what society deems 'criminal' have been clarified (a task outside the scope of this present book), the major question that needs to be faced relates to the implications of the concept of 'justice' in this context. This is primarily a matter of *objectives* – attempting to decide whether offenders in general (or in particular categories) should be punished, deterred, segregated from society, reformed or used to deter other potential offenders; it is also a matter of the *procedures* that may culminate in the application of whatever sanctions are considered appropriate. Procedures on their own, however 'just' they may appear, cannot compensate for objectives that fall short of the ideals of justice; but neither can unjust procedures be justified by the ultimate objectives.

A just criminal justice process must fulfil certain minimum criteria: individuals (whether under suspicion or convicted) must know what is happening to them and why; they must be made aware of the options open to them to influence the course of events; the broad criteria that are taken into account in the exercise of discretion by decision-makers at all stages must be spelled out and more open to scrutiny; reasons for decisions should be made explicit.

Finally, one other general principle that should permeate the entire process is that of the *public accountability* of criminal justice, so that the criteria against which new procedures and policies should be measured are those of a criminal justice process responsive to society and answerable to it, rather than a more private kind of justice which revolves around concerns such as professional status and organisational efficiency, thereby elevating self-interest and bureaucracy above the ideals of a more truly social justice.

Further Reading

American Friends Service Committee, *Struggle for Justice* (Hill and Wang, 1971).

Blumberg, A. S., *Criminal Justice* (Quadrangle Books, 1967).

Bottomley, A. K., *Decisions in the Penal Process* (Martin Robertson, 1973).

—— 'Conflict and communication in criminal justice' *Howard Journal of Penology*, 15, 3 (1977) p. 3.

Bottoms, A. E. and McClean, J. D., *Defendants in the Criminal Process* (Routledge & Kegan Paul, 1976), Ch. 9.

Carlen, P., *Magistrates' Justice* (Martin Robertson, 1976).

Cole, G. F., *Politics and the Administration of Justice* (Sage, 1973).

Davis, K. C., *Discretionary Justice: A Preliminary Inquiry* (Louisiana State University Press, 1969).

Griffiths, J., 'Ideology in criminal procedure, or a third "model" of the Criminal Process' *Yale Law Journal* 79 (1970) p. 359.

Newman, D. J., *Introduction to Criminal Justice* (Lippincott, 1975).

Packer, H. L., *The Limits of the Criminal Sanction* (Stanford University Press, 1969).

Reiss, A. J., 'Citizen access to criminal justice' *British Journal of Law and Society*, 1 (1974) p. 50.

1. The Sociology of Criminal Justice: Progress and Prospects

by COLIN LOW

Previously unpublished paper, given at the Fifth National Conference on Teaching and Research in Criminology, Cambridge, July 1973.

Introduction: the Sociological Approach to Law

As Aubert has pointed out,[1] both as dependent and independent variable, law is an area of human activity that is particularly capable of repaying sociological study. As dependent variable, the law is potentially a particularly vulnerable target for what Berger has termed the 'debunking motif inherent in sociological consciousness'.[2] This is perhaps especially true of the criminal law and criminal justice systems, which offer the promise of a particularly rich harvest to the sociologist anxious to indulge his perennial preoccupation with irony, latent function and the overlap and interpenetration of vice and virtue.[3] For here are to be found society's most solemn proscriptions of unrighteousness on the one hand, and on the other its most formal procedural prescriptions as to how to deal with it. Yet the classical distinction between the law in books and the law in action[4] is now an axiom of the sociological study of the subject. Of course, informal subversion of formal prescriptions is universal and the sociologist's preoccupation is general. As Berger again puts it:

> The sociological frame of reference, with its built in procedure of looking for levels of reality other than those given in the official interpretations of society, carries with it a logical imperative to unmask the pretensions and the propaganda by which men cloak their actions with each other.[5]

7

Yet nowhere else is the gap between theory and fact, precept and practice, more acutely embarrassing than it is in the area of criminal justice.

The various wrinkles that grease the wheels of formal organisation are, as I have said, well known to every one of us. Two examples will therefore have to suffice from among an almost infinite number that could be given from the field under consideration. Grosman describes how over-burdened Canadian prosecutors, committed to maximising successes with limited time and resources, depart from the norm of judiciality and the zero-sum game known as the adversary system in favour of a series of arrangements or informal accommodations with defending counsel involving non-zero-sum bargains over things such as pleas, charges and disclosure. He concludes:

eg

overload

> it is not judicial or legislative theory which determines the prosecutor's discretion or mode of professional behaviour. Often it is the administrative demands made upon him and the informal social relationships which develop within his operational environment that control his decision-making processes. These informal factors, although crucial to any realistic appraisal of the criminal prosecuting process, have not in the past been acknowledged by legislation or by the judiciary.
>
> There are considerable and important differences between what the prosecutor does and what the legal literature and judicial decisions say he should do. In any legal structure there is a multiplicity of aims and values. Informal adjustments are continually made in order to cope with operational realities while at the same time lip-service is paid to officially stipulated means and required ends.[6]

Again, Maureen Cain notes the prevalence of 'easing behaviour' as a response to the 'endemic boredom, monotony and frequent cold, and to the impossibility of achieving the formally stated goals' of police work. This is defined as 'non-prescribed behaviour on the part of an employee designed to make his work or conditions more congenial', which 'can be either licit or illicit from the point of view of the senior members of the work organisation'.[7] Examples given include calling back to the station at least once in every half shift for tea, if possible on the pretext of having to write up a report or relieve the office, and calling at local cafés or pubs, especially after hours. A third means of

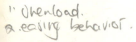

1. Overload.
2. easing behavior.

making a dull and cold eight hours more tolerable, reports Dr Cain, is to seek marginally legitimate arrests. This gives 'excitement, the opportunity to go off duty early or at least to return to the warmth and relative conviviality of the police station, as well as prestige',[8] Senior officers probably know in general terms that some of these activities take place, but patrolmen are concerned to ensure that they do not find out about a specific behaviour involving a particular man.

As an independent variable, men have long recognised that law is second to none as an index of societal values, and Aubert speaks of it as a 'diagnostic tool to uncover structural pre-conditions'.[9] Indeed, this insight scarcely requires a sociologist to give it birth. Churchill was making a similar point when as Home Secretary he told the House of Commons on 25 July 1910 that 'the mood and temper of the public in regard to the treatment of crime and criminals is one of the most unfailing tests of the civilisation of any country'.[10]

This observation of the structural interrelation of law and society indeed has served as the starting-point for much classical sociological speculation on the subject of law. According to Durkheim, for example: 'Since law reproduces the principal forms of social solidarity, we have only to classify the different types of law to find therefrom the different types of social solidarity which correspond to it.'[11] Sorokin, too, embarked upon his mammoth study of 104 actions designated criminal in the penal codes of five countries through the ages because, as he put it: 'the best source or social mirror of the ethical mentality and respective forms of conduct or of the mores is usually given by the totality of the official laws of a given group, plus its official moral prescriptions.'[12] He dismisses other sorts of material such as the testimony of contemporaries by saying:

> These cannot give even remotely as good, as reliable, as systematic material as that given by the codes. The testimonies and other material are almost always biased, fragmentary, uncertain, untypical and incidental, while the code, which has been law and been enforced and followed for decades and centuries is an objective and super-individual, super-factional epitome of the main aspects of the respective ethico-juridical reality of the period of the code's validity.[13]

The mode of expression is a trifle baroque, but the basic sentiment is unexceptionable.

The Contribution of Classical Sociology

After such favourable auguries, it is disappointing to report that a premise that offered such heuristic promise remained largely untranscended, but such unfortunately appears to have been the case. Durkheim's work on mechanical and organic forms of social solidarity with their legal correlates, criminal and civil law, remains at the very highest level of abstraction and generality. Marx had little to say about law as such, and Weber's work seems to be to a large extent jurisprudential in character. Sorokin as we have seen attempted more, but even so, for all his labours, he seems to have advanced the general proposition but little:

> These erratic fluctuations in the tendencies [humanitarian, anti-humanitarian, religious, secular, liberal, authoritarian, etc.] are not erratic however in their connection with the transformation of other main compartments of culture. . . . The tendency to erratic changes in criminal law well reflects similar tendencies of change in other compartments of culture. In this sense the outline dynamics of the tendencies of criminal law is harmonious with the tendencies in the other divisions of culture studied.[14]

At one and the same time, the methodology is pseudo-scientific and subjectively impressionistic: that is to say, it falls into the trap of attempting to quantify entities that themselves depend on highly problematical evaluations. At best Sorokin achieves a *tour de force* of analytical description which, however, pays no attention whatever to the structural roots of the values he locates.

Much of what he says is mere platitude.[15] At worst it becomes a monumental exercise in the banal.[16] Sorokin might possibly argue that he was merely using the codes as confirmation of his basic thesis about social values, and that as such we should not expect them to do more than reflect what already seems self-evident from the use of other indices. But it will be recalled that Sorokin was claiming the codes as the *best* index, so that one would expect him to be using them for diagnosis and prediction and not just for mere slavish imitation. Instead one finds law being treated almost exclusively as a secondary reflection of values whose primary characteristics are defined in completely different terms.

New Departures

I have chosen to focus upon Sorokin because he seems to me to represent more fully than anyone else both the promise and the disappointment of this kind of macroscopic sociology. The initial assumption is unexceptionable, but if the risk of providing not glimpses but, in Sorokin's case, epic portrayals of the obvious is to be avoided, there needs to be a good deal more middle-range spade-work before a grand theory can be constructed on such an all-embracing scale. It is perhaps not without significance that Sorokin is in fact much more illuminating when he limits his scope and concentrates on some much more precisely defined variable such as punishment.

Perhaps in reaction against such magnificent failures, general sociology seems to me to have abandoned its interest in the field of law somewhat in recent years, and what interest has been shown has largely had to come from the newly efflorescent sociology of deviance. Even here, attention seems to have been concentrated at the level of the microscopic case study, as in Becker's analysis of the passage of the Marijuana Tax Act,[17] Platt's history of the child-saving movement in Illinois[18] or Lemert's study of the change in the California juvenile court law in 1961.[19] In complete contrast to Sorokin all that one can descry here is a confused and complex web of groups and individuals jockeying for position and lobbying for their own definition of the situation, and law is the almost patternless outcome of countless accidents of local circumstance. I agree with Albert Cohen[20] that there is room for both the eagle and worm. We need the vantage points of both if we are to have a complete and rounded account of phenomena. Each has its contribution to make, whether in terms of pattern and perspective or detail and complexity. But if real progress is to be made, more work surely needs to be done in the middle range to bring the two levels of analysis together. At the moment this middle ground seems mainly to be occupied by the so-called conflict theorists,[21] who have probably still contributed more in the way of a seemingly promising organising hypothesis than actual data to substantiate it, and by scholars like Matza with their ideas concerning police use of the institution of localised suspicion[22] and the social construction of criminality and criminal statistics, which by now probably *can* be said to have received a substantial body of documentation.[23] One of the most encouraging things about this latest body of seminal work is the genuinely dialectical relationship that, unlike much theorising, it appears to enjoy with empirical research, both crystallising and synthesising what has already been done and providing a radical/critical frame of reference which acts as a spur to new endeavours.

But this is to anticipate somewhat. In the concluding part of this paper I shall suggest some other ways in which sociologists of the criminal justice process could attempt to occupy the middle ground of theory and research and provide alternative radical models, but in the meantime we must turn aside to examine the prevailing conservative and liberal models and the research that they have stimulated or not as the case may be, especially in this country.

Conservative and Liberal Models

An American judge and academic, Herbert Packer, has given an illuminating account in ideal type form of two contrasting approaches to the criminal process which may aptly serve as the background to official, professional and academic attitudes that may equally be seen to predominate in this country.[24] On the one hand he discerns the crime-control model, which accepts the elimination of crime as a self-justifying end which, in a situation of large magnitudes and limited resources, places primary emphasis on a managerial efficiency and uniformity of enforcement, in which considerations of speed and the informality of administrative fact-finding that is relatively final and immune from challenge in the courts are paramount. According to such a view, administrative fact-finding, efficiently done, creates a factual presumption of guilt for those not screened out at an early stage, and can safely be allowed to become official guilt determination through the agency of the guilty plea, if only the suspect can be persuaded to co-operate.

On the other hand, says Packer, there is the due-process model, which corresponds more to an obstacle course than an assembly line. This approach begins by accepting the aims of eliminating or at least reducing crime and convicting the guilty, but sees these as requiring to be qualified by alternative and competing, perhaps overriding, values such as a concern for individual freedom, an appreciation of the seriousness of loss of liberty as a sanction and an awareness of the need to limit state power. Such a view stresses the risk of error in informal procedures, and emphasises the need for formal adjudicative machinery and subsequent scrutiny independent of the investigative process. The risk that excessive concern with reliability will impair efficiency is accepted, and the official presumption of factual guilt is not regarded as something to be treated as sovereign and all-controlling. Instead, the presumption of innocence, something normative and legal, as opposed to factual and descriptive, requires that the State make its case in accordance with certain prescribed and potentially guilt-defeating forms in the adjudicative context. Finally, says Packer, having begun by accepting the official ends of state power, albeit in modified form and in such a way as to differ radically as to the means of implementing them, the due-process model is led by its disagreement over means to question even the ends.[25]

Although, as Packer himself recognises,[26] these models have their prescriptive as well as their descriptive aspects, which perhaps compromises their sociological integrity somewhat,[27] nevertheless they can I think be taken as delineating pretty faithfully the spectrum of attitudes to the criminal justice system to be found in this country as well as in the United States. Although, as we saw, the due-process model led its adherents to the edge of a radical model which questioned both ends and means, if the models are correct the overwhelming weight of opinion (including official, professional and academic opinion) both in this country and in America, save perhaps for those few sociologists of deviance already referred to, is either conservative or liberal in its orientation to the subjects of crime and criminal justice; it either accepts both ends and means more or less uncritically, or at most allows a concern with means and competing ends to qualify the official ends.

Not surprisingly, this has important consequences for the sort of research that has been done. The conservative approach has been relatively uninfluential; in so far as it accepts the prevailing order of things more or less without question, it has inevitably tended to be obscurantist and hostile to sociology or even to any kind of social research. But such an extreme position is difficult to maintain generally today, at least in the higher official circles where these matters are decided. The triumph of rational bureaucracy has effectively ensured that the research imperative has become irresistible, even for rational bureaucrats of a conservative disposition. As far as research is concerned, therefore, rational liberal values have prevailed. But the very fact of the liberal hegemony over the field of research has had a profound and, in my view, controlling influence on the form such research has taken. In a word, I should want to argue that liberalism has ensured that research in the criminal justice area has assumed a social administration rather than a strictly sociological character, at least as far as this country is concerned. Before considering what some of the consequences of this have been for research and theory, it is necessary first to survey briefly the British research effort in the field of criminal justice in recent years to see whether or not my assertion as to its character can be sustained.

The British Research Effort: Limitations of the 'Social Administration' Approach

Despite the presence of Cain's work on the police, already referred to,[28] Walker's work on the treatment of the mentally abnormal offender throughout the ages,[29] and the emergent interest in the sociology of criminal justice on the part of some members of the National Deviancy conference, few surely would doubt the basic assertion. If one looks at the considerable volume of work that has now been undertaken by Zander,[30] Bottomley,[31] Davies,[32] the Cobden Trust[33] and the Home Office itself[34] on bail; by Zander,[35] Borrie,[36] Dell,[37] Justice[38] and the Cobden Trust[39] on legal aid; and by Cornish[40] and the Penal Research Unit, Oxford,[41,42] on the jury, one cannot be left in any doubt that the overwhelming bulk of the research carried on in the criminal justice area in recent years in this country is primarily concerned with the rational and efficient functioning of the systems as relatively self-contained entities, and not, for example, with the structural basis of such systems, with their relation to any of the other systems that go to make up the complex of social institutions that is society, or with any of the other questions that have traditionally preoccupied mainstream sociology.

People are of course free, like humpty-dumpty, to use terms in whatever manner they please, and to insist that they *are* doing sociology even when I say they are not. But I would maintain that my use of the terms 'sociology' and 'social administration' to denote spheres of interest that are significantly different accords with a practice that is now virtually standard among practitioners of the two disciplines, and it should be clear from all that I have said about the traditional concerns of mainstream sociology that they are radically different from those of the body of research that I have not had time to do more than catalogue here. The distinction should become clearer a little later on when I try to indicate some paths that sociological research proper might usefully take in the years that lie immediately ahead. Let me stress that nothing I have said in this section is intended to depreciate the value of the work I have been discussing. Much of it is wholly admirable and necessary, and not without a critical cutting edge of its own. But I would maintain — as surely who would not? — that it has its limitations, to which I now turn.

Perhaps the first of these is an absence of perspective, of the relativising impact and cosmopolitan consciousness that Berger says sociological awareness gives.[43] Instead, the officially stated goals of the system are largely taken for granted, and the sole concern is with the means by which they are realised. This leads to the research having a pragmatic quality. The accent is everywhere empirical. Now there is nothing whatsoever wrong with empirical research, but when it lacks any properly articulated theoretical underpinning, as it does for the most part in the kind of work I am discussing, it tends to be somewhat abstracted.[44]

An example may serve to highlight the disadvantage of not having a critical or explicit theoretical standard. Without one, what are we to make of the Cobden Trust finding that a third of those who apply for bail in magistrates' courts have their applications rejected?[45] Is this a lot or a little? Is the criminal justice system being used as an instrument for the oppression of under-privileged groups and the maintenance in power of a 'ruling class', however indirectly and however loosely 'ruling class' may be defined, or is it on the contrary being used as an instrument for securing equality before the law? At best the answers to these kinds of question are implied by the sorts of work I am discussing, but in the main there is a total lack of principles by reference to which one might evaluate the data with which one is supplied in such lavish abundance. Or again, what are we to make of the Cobden Trust finding that magistrates uphold police objections to bail in 75 per cent of the cases[46] (the corresponding figure in Bottomley is 96 per cent)?[47] Does this mean that 'the police exercise a decisive influence over bail' as one writer has suggested,[48] or does it mean that the magistracy is free from influence by the police who, however, act in the main scrupulously in the matter of opposing bail? What would it mean if magistrates overrode police objections in more than 25 per cent of the cases? These are questions that the authors scarcely set out to answer.

Many of the factors making for British students' preference for the social administration approach will already have emerged. The English empiricist tradition is clearly one of them, and bureaucratic considerations, spurred on by rising crime rates and consequent pressure on the institutions of criminal justice, clearly represent another. A third is probably the gradual realisation that law is part of the social services and as such is something that requires to be studied from the vantage point of social policy. To give people paper rights, it is belatedly recognised, is not sufficient. Rather, it is necessary to study things such as the take-up of entitlements and the use made of legal facilities in order to see where if at all the system is breaking down, and how it can best be improved. All these tendencies can be seen to be closely interrelated when one considers the institutional sources from which most of these researches have emanated. The Home Office of course features prominently, either directly or indirectly, and so does the Cambridge Institute of Criminology, which itself enjoys substantial Home Office support. Finally, in a rather different tradition, there is the London School of Economics, one of the most illustrious fountainheads of latter-day English empiricism.

Some Options for Further Research

I can think of no finer specification of the essentials of the sociological inquiry than that given by C. Wright Mills at the beginning of his *Sociological Imagination* in the form of a series of interrogatories which all the great sociologists have posed to themselves:

(1) What is the structure of this particular society as a whole? What are its essential components, and how are they related to one another? How does it differ from other varieties of social order? Within it, what is the meaning of any particular feature for its continuance and for its change?

(2) Where does this society stand in human history? What are the mechanics by which it is changing? What is its place within and its meaning for the development of humanity as a whole? How does any particular feature we are examining affect, and how is it affected by, the historical period in which it moves? And this period — what are its essential features? How does it differ from

other periods? What are its characteristic ways of history-making?[4 9]

From all that I have already said on both sides of the argument, it will be clear that I believe that the best way forward lies in the middle range of theory and research. I have already referred to the promising essays of the deviance theorists in this area, so that all that remains for me to do is to try, as far as possible in obedience to Mills' promptings, to point to one or two other ways in which it seems to me the age-old sociological concerns could be pursued in the area of criminal justice. I need hardly add that these are just the very bare bones of ideas as to the *kinds* of research that might be done, not well worked out blueprints for research on any given topic.

Research on the Structural Basis of Legal Institutions

Uncovering the latent functions of social institutions is a difficult business at the best of times and one that is not without its methodological problems, yet it is a responsibility that no true sociologist worth his salt can shirk. Occasionally, however, the latent may suddenly be made manifest, and the sociologist must constantly be on guard to take every such opportunity of uncovering the basis in the social structure of the institutions he is studying. One such example is perhaps to be found in paragraph 48 of the Guthrie Committee's report on legal aid in criminal proceedings in Scotland, where the conclusion is reached that:

> The day in which the doctor and the lawyer were the rich men of the community and could afford to spend a fair proportion of their time on unremunerative work of a charitable nature is over. From the evidence we have received, we are fully satisfied that in present conditions, with high taxation and high overhead expenses, it is unreasonable to expect the legal profession to continue to act for accused persons in the criminal courts without remuneration.[5 0]

We can almost see the legal system responding before our very eyes to the needs of the professional classes, rather than those of the accused persons whose ends it is manifestly intended to benefit.

The sociologist who looks at matters in this way will not be short of problems to occupy him. To mention just one more with a rather topical ring, he would want to inquire not simply what changes had taken place in the law regulating the composition of the jury as the result of the Criminal Justice Act, 1972, but rather what were the changes in social conditions making for such a change? Did it represent a shift in the balance of power in society, or was it merely a piece of democratic window-dressing which is likely to be largely without effect?

Research on the Structural Basis of Legal Doctrine

An area that surprisingly seems to have been somewhat neglected is the social basis of legal doctrines themselves. Perhaps the easiest way to see the effect of social factors on legal concepts is to use a cross-cultural lens. If we do this, we can see even the same doctrinal vessels being filled with radically different content according to the social and cultural milieu in which they evolve. Take for instance the apparently infinitely elastic notion of reasonableness. Just how far the notion is capable of being stretched may be shown by reference to two cases from southern Africa.

The first is the case of a Rhodesian farmer who was convicted of culpable homicide rather than murder when he shot and killed one of his employees. Justifying his action in evidence, he said that the victim had been an unsatisfactory employee and had made him angry. He had had a provocative smile and tried to annoy him by the way that he spoke. After letting fly with a .22 rifle in order to frighten the man, he brought out a .303 because it would make more noise and frighten him even more. The farmer's wife confirmed that the man had been cheeky. The verdict probably resulted from the accused's lack of *mens rea*, but in contending for a verdict of guilty on the more serious murder charge, prosecuting counsel revealingly declared that 'a reasonable man would have stopped shooting after using the .22 rifle'.[51] How often indeed is it the case in sociology that the most significant things men say turn out to be those about which they entertain no question!

The second case concerns a South African cattle-herder who had been kicked and beaten to death by two whites. After taking what seems like a very short way with the facts, the court found that both accused 'had been provoked to anger because of the presence of cattle on the road, which was a hazard to approaching traffic'. In the circumstances, the judge said he would impose a very light sentence, and the accused were given a fine of 50 rand or two months each for common assault instead of being convicted of the crime of culpable homicide with which they were charged.[52] Evidently South African courts are somewhat indulgent to irate motorists.

But lest it be thought that such sharp divergences over something so straightforward as what constitutes reasonable behaviour occur only between widely differing cultures, it is worth reminding ourselves that similar disagreements, albeit usually on a somewhat less dramatic scale, are to be found in plenty even within our own society. Should anyone feel inclined to doubt this point, it is only necessary for him to consult Matza's extremely subtle and illuminating account[53] of the differences between the norms embodied in the criminal law and those of the delinquent sub-culture regarding the defence of self-defence for just one among many possible examples.

Historical Research on Legal Doctrine

Social comparisons, as Mills appreciated only too well, can of course (and should) equally be made over time. One area that is surely ripe for social and historical analysis is the development of police powers of search and seizure. A comparison of the celebrated case of Entick *v.* Carrington,[54] with the twentieth-century accretions such as those of Elias *v.* Pasmore,[55] Chic Fashions *v.* Jones[56] and Ghani *v.* Jones[57] cannot but leave one convinced that the concept of freedom of property is being used in radically different ways at different times. Macroscopic analysts would no doubt see this development in class terms – in terms of a rising bourgeois class at first affirming its immunity from arbitrary molestation by the executive but latterly defending itself against the incursions of the proletariat. Microscopic analysis would perhaps more modestly characterise the trend in terms of the 'climate' of the respective periods. However this may be, we cannot fail to note the dialectical relationship between notions like freedom and reasonableness and the social soil in which they germinate. Whether legal doctrines are taken as dependent or independent variables for study, in different times and in different places precisely the same idea may serve radically different ends.

Though it may not be part of the sociologist's function to do so, I would point out that all these models for research have their normative implications for law-makers; and for those beset by the difficulties of trying to determine what is the correct policy with regard to such matters as police powers, it may be worth observing that the sociologist can always take the easy way out by refusing to commit himself, preferring rather to use his discoveries descriptively rather than judgmentally, that is to say as a means of depicting the character of a particular time or place while refraining from any sort of ideological comment.

Postscript: Fact-Value Problems

But that would be to stray again too close to the path of social adminstration, and if anything I have said in this paper is correct, it is impossible anyway for the sociologist. As we have seen several times, research has pointed to the need for a radical/critical model within which to organise itself, and several lines of thought have pointed to the sort of models that might meet such a need. Inevitably I have laid myself open to the charge of mixing factual and evaluative considerations at several points, but I have done far too much lecturing to magistrates and policemen still to believe that there is any way of avoiding that. Inevitably, fact and theory and fact and values must co-exist dialectically, for such is the nature of life itself. The important thing is that we should always remain open to the possibility of their modifying one another. In the final analysis, the adoption of a frame of mind, which at the very least puts commitment to any particular set of official ends temporarily in abeyance — the essence of the sociological enterprise — is not something that readily can discharge the empiricist's onus of proof.

NOTES

1. V. Aubert (ed.), *Sociology of Law* (Penguin, 1969), p. 11.
2. P. Berger, *Invitation to Sociology* (Penguin, 1966), p. 51.
3. David Matza, *Becoming Deviant* (Prentice-Hall, 1969), Ch. 4.
4. The distinction seems first to have been articulated in this form by Pound (see R. Pound, 'Law in Books and Law in Action', *American Law Review*, 44 (1910), p. 12), but the idea probably derives originally from Ehrlich.
5. Berger, op cit., p. 51.
6. B. A. Grosman, *The Prosecutor: an Enquiry into the Exercise of Discretion* (University of Toronto Press, 1969), p. 3.
7. Maureen Cain, 'On the beat: interactions and relations in rural and urban police forces', in S. Cohen (ed.), *Images of Deviance* (Penguin, 1971), pp. 62—97, at p. 71.
8. Cain, op cit., p. 73.

9. Aubert, op. cit., p. 11.
10. Quoted in Rupert Cross, *Punishment, Prison and the Public* (Stevens & Sons, 1971), p. 40.
11. See Emile Durkheim, *The Division of Labour in Society* (Free Press, 1964), p. 68.
12. P. A. Sorokin, *Social and Cultural Dynamics* (Bedminster Press, 1937), Vol. II, Ch. 15, at p. 525.
13. ibid., p. 527.
14. ibid., p. 575.
15. See for example, his comments on the various ideological tendencies he divines, ibid., p. 574.
16. ibid., p. 575.
17. Howard Becker, *Outsiders* (Free Press, 1963), Ch. 7.
18. Anthony Platt, *The Child Savers: the Invention of Delinquency* (University of Chicago Press, 1969).
19. E. Lemert, *Social Action and Legal Change: Revolution within the Juvenile Court* (Aldine, 1970).
20. Albert K. Cohen, *Deviance and Control* (Prentice-Hall, 1966), pp. 35–6.
21. See Austin T. Turk, *Criminality and Legal Order* (Rand McNally, 1969); William J Chambliss, *Crime and the Legal Process* (McGraw-Hill, 1969); and Richard Quinney, *The Social Reality of Crime* (Little, Brown & Co., 1970).
22. See Matza, op. cit., pp. 180–95.
23. The best review of this literature known to me is to be found in Stephen Box, *Deviance, Reality and Society* (Holt, Reinhart & Winston, 1972), Ch. 6.
24. See Herbert Packer, *The Limits of the Criminal Sanction* (Oxford University Press, 1969), Part II, esp. Ch. 8.
25. Packer, op. cit., pp. 170–1.
26. ibid., pp. 149–50.
27. Whether it does or not is something to which I return later in the paper.
28. Cain, op. cit. See also her *Society and the Policeman's Role* (Routledge & Kegan Paul, 1973).
29. Nigel Walker, *Crime and Insanity in England* (Edinburgh University Press, 1968) Vol. I. Vol. II (Edinburgh University Press, 1973), written with Sarah McCabe, is more in the social administration mould, but there is nothing wrong with social administration; and indeed everything to be said for it, when set in its proper context as here.
30. Michael Zander, 'Bail: a reappraisal', *Criminal Law Review* (1967), pp. 25, 100 and 128; 'A study of bail/custody decisions in London magistrates' courts', *Criminal Law Review*, (1971), pp. 191–211.
31. Keith Bottomley, *Prison Before Trial* (Bell & Sons, 1970).
32. Clive Davies, 'Pre-trial imprisonment: a Liverpool study', *British Journal of Criminology*, 11, 1 (1971) pp. 32–48.
33. Michael King, *Bail or Custody* (Cobden Trust, 1971).
34. Evelyn Gibson, *Time Spent Awaiting Trial*, Studies in the Causes of Delinquency and the Treatment of Offenders, no. 2 (HMSO, 1960).
35. Michael Zander, 'Unrepresented defendants in the criminal courts', *Criminal Law Review*, (1969), pp. 632–44; 'Legal advice and criminal appeals: a survey of prisoners, prisons and lawyers', *Criminal Law Review* (1972), pp. 132–73;

'Access to a solicitor in the police station', *Criminal Law Review* (1972), pp. 342—50.

36. G. J. Borrie and J. R. Varcoe, *Legal Aid in Criminal Proceedings, a Regional Survey* (Institute of Judicial Administration, University of Birmingham).

37. Susanne Dell, *Silent in Court* (Bell & Sons, 1971).

38. Justice, *The Unrepresented Defendant in Magistrates' Courts* (Stevens & Sons, 1971). It is perhaps not without significance that a semi-official committee report features alongside the inventory of research studies cited here.

39. Alan Paterson, *Legal Aid as a Social Service* (Cobden Trust, 1970).

40. W. R. Cornish, *The Jury* (Allen Lane: The Penguin Press, 1968); see also LSE Jury Project, 'Juries and the rules of evidence', *Criminal Law Review* (1973), pp. 208—23.

41. Sarah McCabe and Robert Purves, *By-Passing the Jury: a Study of Changes of Plea and Directed Acquittals in High Courts* and *The Jury at Work: a study of a Series of Jury Trials in which the Defendant was Acquitted* , Oxford Penal Research Unit Occasional Papers nos. 3 and 4 (Basil Blackwell, 1972).

42. It will be observed that this list contains no counterpart to Lafave's imposing study of the use of police discretion in the making of arrests; see Wayne R. Lafave, *Arrest: the Decision to Take a Suspect into Custody* (Little, Brown, 1965), or to Grosman's study of the use of prosecutorial discretion (see Grosman, op. cit.), suggesting that with notable exceptions British researchers have not as yet succeeded in penetrating the comparatively sensitive regions of the process through which the accused has to pass before he reaches court. Nor have I cited any of the voluminous literature on the penal system, but with the possible exception of Roger Hood's work on sentencing, this too would be found to be largely imbued with the spirit of social administration. For a novel and original technique for studying the system as a whole, see Ruth Brandon and Christie Davies, *Wrongful Imprisonment* (George, Allen & Unwin, 1973).

43. Berger, op. cit., pp. 61, 66.

44. For a critique of this kind of empiricism, see C. Wright Mills, *The Sociological Imagination* (Penguin, 1970), Ch. 3.

45. See King, op. cit., p. 15.

46. Michael King, 'The bail decision' *New Society* (18 November 1971) p. 984.

47. Bottomley, op. cit., p. 59.

48. See Alec Samuels in *Criminal Law Review* (1971), p. 311.

49. C. Wright Mills, op. cit., pp. 6—7.

50. *Report of the Departmental Committee on Legal Aid in Criminal Proceedings in Scotland*, Cmnd 1015 (HMSO 1960), para. 48: the whole of this passage is worth looking at for the way the argument is spelled out with seemingly impeccable logic.

51. Judith Todd, *The Right to Say No* (Sidgwick & Jackson, 1972), pp. 25—6.

52. *The Friend*, Bloemfontein (December 1970).

53. See *Delinquency and Drift* (John Wiley & Sons, 1964), pp. 75ff.

54. (1765) 19 *St. Tr.* 1029.

55. (1934) 2 *K.B.* 164

56. Chic Fashions (West Wales) Ltd. *v.* Jones (1968) 2 *Q.B.* 299.

57. Ghani *v.* Jones (1969) 3 *W.L.R.* 1158.

2. False Dichotomies in Criminal Justice Research

by DOREEN J. McBARNET

Original contribution, specially prepared for this volume.

Sociological research into criminal justice has painted a detailed and fascinating picture of the day-to-day running of the law: the policeman on his beat seeing drunks home from carnivals or organising arrests around teabreaks; the lawyer negotiating and string-pulling in his chambers; the probation officer fitting people into stereotypes; the magistrate and advocate performing with language, gesture and ritual in court; the mystified defendant being processed willy-nilly on 'the conveyor belt of criminal justice', (Bottomley, 1973, p. 217).[1] Social administrators[2] have barraged us with statistics on how many people — or more accurately how few — are granted bail, legal aid, access to solicitors in police stations; how many choose to plead guilty, appear in magistrates' or crown courts, have a lawyer representing them; how many are convicted, sentenced in various ways or successfully appeal.[3]

These are two very different approaches, positivist and interactionist, theoretically at odds, yet neat corollaries to each other, one providing the skeleton of figures, the other the flesh of how people experience and construct criminal justice. And in one sense, this is a mass of valuable information and explanation. But in another it is severely limited. For both approaches have offered almost exclusively a picture of how the criminal justice system *operates*, showing how its alleged aims are reinterpreted or distorted in practice by the people who operate it. Neither has focused on the system itself, seen its aims as problematic rather than to be taken for granted, treated its rules as a significant factor in explaining its practices, or seen its assumptions and rhetoric, its concepts of necessity, fairness and civil liberty, as requiring

23

analysis and explanation too. The net result is that research into how criminal law works overlooks the most obvious element, the law itself.

Social administrators tend to shy clear of the task of analysing the system they are studying as a matter of policy. They are by definition less concerned with theory than practical information, less interested in structural change than increasing efficiency or fairness 'within a system whose broad parameters we endorsed', to cite the example of Bottoms and McClean (1976, p. xvi). Sociologists might more readily be expected to have turned their attention to this issue. Yet instead, they too have concentrated on behaviour within the system rather than on the system, have focused less on legal than on general social behaviour, showing how the informal rules of social interaction operate in legal institutions just as in any other. Thus the people who operate the law are studied either as *any people* or as *any occupational group*.

So their legal doings, arrests, strategies in and out of court, judgments, are explained by the fact that they are just human beings subject to all the biases, whims, ups and downs, vanities and self-interests of the human lot (Bottomley, 1973, p. 143; Box, 1971, p. 175). So judgments are related to the quality of the judge's breakfast, the organisation of the court list to golf matches (Carlen, 1976). Sometimes it is more explicitly a matter of the human element in a specific type of society. In a male-dominated society, the treatment of rape victims in court is explained by male bias (Holstrom and Burgess, 1974); in a capitalist or white society, differentiation in arrest, conviction and sentencing between black and white, working-class and middle-class people is explained by race and class stereotypes (e.g. Box, 1971).

Likewise law-enforcers are seen as subject like anyone else to the pressures of their occupational group. So the emphasis on speed rather than fairness in court cases is related to bureaucratic pressures (Bottoms and McClean, 1976), the arrest rate to career interests (Cain, 1973), negotiations over the defendant's fate to reciprocal obligations or professional practices (Blumberg, 1967), the isolation and degradation of the defendant to work routines (Carlen, 1976).

These are general social pressures, informal rules that you could find in any social situation. But this emphasis underplays two factors. First, criminal justice is a legal system, with not just informal rules of acceptable social behaviour to organise it but a massive volume of formal rules on how it may be, should be or must be organised. Second, there are the elements of power and structure in both society and law. The legal system is a hierarchy, and the petty administrators are not the only people engaged in constructing the operation of the law. There is a top to the hierarchy too, the élite of judges and politicians who make those rules; their activities in relation to law enforcement have been almost totally ignored.[4]

The reasons for this seem to lie in an interlocking series of questionable dichotomies, once useful analytical devices but now, arguably, straitjackets on research — dichotomies between the substance and administration of law (sometimes put in terms of 'the law in the books' and the 'law in action'), between macro- and microsociological theories, between the 'new criminology' and 'the old', between abstract theorising and empiricism.

Although the sociology of law has a long tradition in the classics, its current resuscitation is largely an outgrowth of the study of deviance in the 1960s, an outgrowth that took two forms to produce a bifurcated sociology of law. The sociology of substantive law grew out of the issue: who defines deviance and why? It took the criminal law as defining deviance and examined the people and processes of law-making. It led quite logically into questions of social structure, class, power, ideology and interests at the top of the hierarchy, in short into the politics and structure of law. The other fork grew out of the issue of defining at a different level: who defines *deviants* and why? The focus was on the labelling of particular individuals and particular actions as opposed to the broad categories of definition with which substantive law deals, defining at the level of the individual rather than the level of 'society', dealing quite deliberately in the areas of criminal justice where visibility is low and the scope for discretion high. Logically enough, the police and other agents of face-to-face social control were the subject matter, and the focus was on that face-to-face control, on interpersonal interaction and decision-making. Law enforcement therefore became the precinct of micro-sociology, separated off from concern with the structure of law *per se*.

This parallelled the bifurcation of theoretical development, one half highly abstract, relying heavily on Marxism, viz. the new criminology (Taylor, Walton and Young, 1973), the other very concrete and ethnographic, relying heavily first on interactionism then on phenomenology, really very empirical with the theory more terminological than explanatory. The result was macro- *or* micro-sociology, why questions *or* how questions, and no link between the two. Research into law enforcement, as though from some endemic appropriateness, but in fact by the historical accident of its own roots and the development of sociological theory, has remained almost exclusively the preserve of micro-sociological description within the legal system.

Bridging the gap, by linking analysis of the individual in the criminal justice system with 'society', was in fact theoretically pre-empted for micro-sociology, since its 'social construction of reality' perspective ruled out analysing 'social structure' as reification. 'Social structure' only existed and could only be analysed in the process of being built up Pisarro-like from the dots of individual action. Rules and roles could therefore be realistically described only as they were acted out not as they were prescribed.

This approach found a ready niche in traditional criminal justice research since it echoed an older dichotomy of the law from the legal realists of the 1930s. They argued that law was not the 'law in the books' (what the law should be according to statutes and authorities), but the 'law in action' (how it was actually interpreted, operated, acted out). It was not the legal reasons laid down in formal law that counted, but the real reasons—back to the human element—behind judges' decisions.[5] It also fitted with the lawyers' interest either in demystifying the law by showing the gap between the rhetoric of civil rights and the reality of legal practice, or in demonstrating the tension—yet another dichotomy—between the ideals of 'due process' in the law and the practical necessity for 'crime control' (Packer, 1964). So the law in law enforcement got lost in the fascinating analysis of human action; formal rules got lost in the unending informal methods of avoiding or redefining them; the intentions behind the law got lost in the unintended consequences of its operation; explanation got lost in micro-sociological description and indignant demystification.

Meantime macro-sociological research has stuck with analysis of substantive law rather than enforcement, or failed to operate at the level of empirical research at all. Any hope that the new criminology might provide a structural analysis of law enforcement has come to little. For although it has provided 'an immanent critique' (Taylor, Walton and Young, 1973) and raised vital questions, these questions remain at the level of abstractions. Indeed, if theory in the micro-sociology of law has been criticised as more terminological than explanatory, the same could be said, for all its grandiose claims to be bringing social theory to criminology, of the new criminology. Only the terms are different. What the new criminology has done, though, is create yet another unproductive split in the analysis of law, a split

between the old criminology and the new, blending into the resuscitation of a much older split between theory and empiricism.
Traditional criminology with its positivist approach has come in for hard criticism by the advocates of the new.[6] It has been characterised methodologically as empiricist, isolated from the concerns of sociological theory; ideologically as geared to the *status quo* via either correctionalism or liberal reformism. The social administrators for their part respond by embracing this description and explicitly dissociating themselves from the 'cynics and revolutionaries' of the new criminology (Bottoms and McClean, 1976, p. xvi). And so a classical, not to say clichéd, position is set up: two armed camps, theory versus empiricism, science versus policy, radicalism versus conservatism.

Much of the new criminology's criticism is quite accurate and its demands for change quite valid. Many books 'conceived in the older tradition', to draw on Bottoms and McClean again as the most recent and explicit work of this kind, sadly fail to do their own findings justice because they are just too cautious, too afraid of being seen as revolutionary, too empiricist, to give the necessary emphasis to the blatant indictment of the judicial system and structural explanation of the defendants' plight clearly there in their own data. But there are two problems in the particular way in which the new criminology's criticisms and demands have been presented.

First, there is a distinct danger that in their concern for total revision of what has gone before they are going to throw the baby out with the bathwater. For there is also a great deal in the old criminology that is of value. For a start there is a lot to be said for doing rather than talking. The old criminology concentrates on empirical research, and if it is sometimes ill-conceived and the resulting data affected by that ill-conception, it is equally often information that provides a useful, indeed *necessary*, basis for explanation. (So, for that matter, does the data provided by micro-sociological interactionism.) Bottoms and McClean's book is a veritable mine of valuable data on the processing of the defendant through the criminal justice system. In fact, although they do not themselves play up the theoretical implications, focusing conventionally on the petty administrators for their explanations, this includes vital pointers to how the legal structure itself actually shapes the way people operate and experience the law. There are the penalty clauses that emasculate real choices of plea, venue or appeal (Bottoms and McClean, 1976, pp. 103, 121, 181), limitations on legal aid (p. 165), failure to check out a guilty plea (p. 232), the unilateral power of the police in the absence of a solicitor at the police station (p. 188)—all the product of formal legal rules. The irony is that the old criminology is providing data on which the new could feed to answer very different questions.

The second problem is that demands and criticisms are not enough. But the danger is that the criticisms may pre-empt the fulfilment of the demands. So thorough has the new criminology been in its criticisms of existing empirical work — whatever is is wrong — that it is scarcely likely to encourage the lowly, lonely, fallible researcher to opt for the minefield of the real world when he could dabble instead in the ideologically safe territory of debating again what type of research might be acceptable to Marx, Gramsci, Lukacs, Taylor, Walton and Young, or Paul Q. Hirst. If the new criminology is taken too much as doctrine, it could quite plausibly produce not the stimulus to research it sets out to provide but a desert of non-problematic, non-explanatory tenets of faith never put to the test of empirical research. Research in the criminal justice field would then, ironically, be left quietly under the aegis of the old criminology, whose monopoly is exactly what the new criminology set out to destroy.

So the criminal justice field has been beset by a series of dichotomies which threaten to stultify rather than stimulate research. But they are questionable dichotomies and there are signs that these are not only being recognised as such but are being confronted and bridged. Indeed, given the dialectical development of knowledge with old analyses leading to new syntheses, that is exactly what one would expect.

That theoretical and empirical work need each other should hardly need repeating and it is a sad comment on the discipline that it does. However, there are signs of some movement towards a bridging of the two. Bottoms and McClean, for example, despite their own caution, argue for the accompaniment of 'fact-finding research' by 'explanatory research': 'for ultimately (as we have shown from our own study), administrative research raises important explanatory questions' (Bottoms and McClean, 1976, p. 242). They add a significant corollary: 'Unless we know more of the answers to some of those explanatory questions our effort at policy-making will be hindered by operating to change the system in ignorance of the true nature of the system' (p. 242). Theory is as necessary for policy aims as data is for explanation.

More important than such programmatic conclusions to research, however, is the fact that the starting-point and aim of some current research is precisely formulated to move beyond these dichotomies. Thus ethnomethodologists argue that the tendency for micro-sociology to stop at description rather than theory, appreciation rather than explanation of the subject's views and experience, is not inevitable. Recent work tries to make the study of interaction in situations like the courtroom more rigorous than the metaphorical explanation they see as all that has been offered so far. Thus Drew tries to relate information management, and specifically the build-up to an incontrovertible accusation, to the structure rather than just the content of court 'conversation'. Atkinson takes the degradation and mystification of defendants by the dock, the strange procedures or the constant sitting and standing, not as conclusion but as starting point. Why is this so? His approach is to examine the situation and purposes of the court to separate out ritual degradation from the methods necessary to produce order in court. Time-saving for example is seen as a product of the fact that time is not unlimited, and the issues involved not academic but practical. The court is not a way of adjudicating ideally but just a solution for the practical purposes of settling matters somehow. Finding a gap between ideals and practice is hardly a revelation but exactly what one would expect. The question from the policy point of view — for Atkinson tries to bridge the theory–policy gap — is rather how far the gap is inevitably tied up in the practical problems of the court and how far those problems could be met by alternative means without unacceptable side-effects, for example doing away with the dock as degrading and as fulfilling no necessary practical function anyway.

Of course Garfinkel's work or a day in court make one suspect the purpose *is* degradation and there is a distinct whiff in this approach of the old errors of functionalism, taking the aims of the system as given, focusing on the functions of existing situations rather than their historical purposes, on logical inevitability rather than social determinants. However it illustrates one current attempt to confront the empiricism–theory, theory–policy, law in the books-law in action dichotomies by moving micro-sociology beyond description to explanation, beyond demystification to practical policy recommendations.

The need to move beyond demystification is one of the changes Taylor, Walton and Young call for in *Critical Criminology* (1975, p. 6). The irony is however that few social administrators or sociologists have really succeeded in demystifying because they have only demystified practice not the legal structure itself. That formal legal rules are organised around civil rights is taken for granted by both the champions and the critics of the *status quo*. Thus those lobbying for wider police powers argue that the rights for the defendant built into the legal structure prevent the police from getting criminals behind bars. Due process prevents crime control. And the critics, rather than confronting this assumption, accept it, by focusing on police practices, not legal rules (Cox, 1975). Indeed, sociologists have endorsed the system by suggesting that, if only police practices could be brought into line with the law, the defendant and the citizen would be in a fairer position (Skolnick, 1966).

If, however, we question the dichotomy between due process and crime control, the substance of law and its enforcement, we are drawn to a rather different conclusion. Actually examining the rules of due process in statutes and precedents indicates that they are not dichotomies at all. Judges and politicians may deal in the rhetoric of civil rights and due process, but the actual rules they create for law enforcement and the policies they adopt on sanctioning police malpractices are less about civil rights than about smoothing the path to conviction, less about due process than *post-hoc* acceptance of police activities as justifying themselves. Thus a good many of the practices in criminal justice described as informal perversions of the formal rules are in fact allowed, facilitated or upheld in the formal rules of statute and precedent. There are inklings of this in earlier work, new and old research never falling into the neat categories overviews like this might suggest — in Bottoms and McClean, for example, or Greenawalt, or Green, in Skolnick's reference to the institutions of public prosecutor and defender facilitating plea-bargaining, or Stinchcombe's tying together of class differentiation in arrests and legal definitions of privacy and liberty. But one can go through the whole process of criminal justice and find the same systematic and pervasive pattern.

Thus arrest on suspicion is exactly what the Vagrancy Act, 1874, Prevention of Crimes Act, 1871, and local acts like the Glasgow General Powers Act, 1960, are about. Using a holding charge to arrest and question on suspicion of a different offence, quite contrary to the rhetoric of the Judges' Rules, is upheld in legal texts (Renton and Brown, 1972, p. 32) and judicial decisions (e.g. Christie *v.* Leachinsky). Search without warrant is accepted at law (Bell *v.* Hogg: Hay *v.* HM Advocate; Chic Fashions *v.* Jones; Jeffrey *v.* Black), while evidence obtained illegally is still accepted in court: 'It matters not how you get it; if you steal it even it would be admissible' [an opinion of 1861 cited in Kuruma 1955]. Access to a solicitor is quite legitimately refused if the police feel it might cause 'unreasonable delay or hindrance . . . to the processes of investigation or the administration of justice' (HO Circular 31), regardless of whether the lack of a solicitor might affect justice from the perspective of the defendant and due process rather than the police and crime control. The management and suppression of information in court is not just a product of informal techniques but is affected at the pre-trial stages by formal rules facilitating the preparation of the prosecution's case and limiting the preparation of the defence's, at the trial itself by the rules of evidence, all geared far less to civil rights and more to conviction than the rhetoric of justice suggests. In short, the dichotomies organising criminal justice research are false. The operation of the law is not a subversion of the substance of the law but exactly what one would expect it to produce; the law in action is only too close a parallel to the law in the books; due process is for crime control (McBarnet, 1976, 1977).

For a full explanation of how law is enforced then, substantive law, legal structure, the State must be added to[7] moods and bureaucracies and face-to-face interaction. It's a long way from the Law Lords to the Saturday night affray, from the corridors of power to the Monday morning guilty plea, but a clear chain links the two. Social structure and individual action are merely two sides of the same coin; macro-sociology has as much to contribute to the explanation of specific arrests or convictions as micro-sociology.

But bringing law in as an explanatory factor in the operation of criminal justice is not enough. We must examine the assumptions and purposes underlying criminal justice itself in terms of its social, historical and political basis, in relation to class, power, interests and ideologies; in short, we must apply the questions and concepts hitherto reserved for the analysis of specific laws to the legal system *per se*. We must do so not at the level of tautological assumption – taking it as unproblematic that in bourgeois society law will take bourgeois forms – but empirically, asking what this means, if it is quite so simple (is ideology only empty rhetoric or does it have some causal impact too? Thompson, 1975), and analysing how it is achieved. Systems do not operate themselves; people construct them. Exactly 'who' is important. So is 'how?' If law is an ideological tool, how is it operated? Douglas Hay's work on the apparent inefficiency of eighteenth-century criminal law enforcement — its 'inefficiency' was the key to its ideological strength — provides a fine example of the value of empiricising such questions. One might also ask how ideology is maintained in the face of blatant negations of it. How, for example do judges maintain the ideology of civil rights while satisfying in the same judgement the 'necessity' of conviction? Or more broadly, how is mystification achieved? Burton and Carlen's work on official discourse makes a start on just this type of problem. The implication is that, if macro-sociology has to be brought in to explain the operation of the local court, so micro-sociology must be brought in to explain the system, not to analyse the local bobby but the élite of the State, not the petty administrators but the creators of the criminal justice system, not to turn in scorn from abstract questions of power but to examine real people constructing and maintaining domination.

Bridging false dichotomies thus opens up a whole new level of problems for criminal justice research, combining the questions of macro- with the methods of micro-sociology, the critical insights of the new criminology with the dogged empirical work of the old.

Notes

1. See for example Blumberg (1967); Bordua (1967); Cain (1971, 1973); Carlen (1976); Chambliss (1969); Cicourel (1968); Garfinkel (1956); Hetzler and Kanter (1974); Newman (1966); Sykes and Clark (1975).
2. This is a broad term which includes lawyers and sociologists with a positivist approach (see Taylor Walton and Young, 1973, for an explication of positivism) as well as those who would label themselves social administrators. An overview of this kind necessarily if unfortunately (especially given the argument!) operates on broad categories and crude summaries.
3. For example: Bottomley (1968, 1973); Bottoms and McClean (1976); Dell (1971); Hood (1962, 1972); Justice (1971); King (1971); Zander (1969, 1972a, 1972b).
4. Chambliss and Seidman have analysed the Supreme Court, but in the conventional model, that is mainly for the purpose of demystifying its value-neutrality and showing how human and organisational factors influence judicial decisions at this level too. Even élite studies in sociology have curiously neglected the study of judges.
5. See how Chambliss and Seidman used this dichotomy as an organising model.
6. And of course, on some shared, some different grounds, by interactionists. See for example Cohen (1971), Introduction.
7. Note 'added to'. Structural analysis is a corollary to and context for, not a replacement of, interactionist analysis.

References

Bell *v*. Hogg 1967 *J.C.*

Chic Fashions (West Wales) Ltd. *v*. Jones 1968 1 *All. E.R.*

Christie *v*. Leachinsky 1947 *A.C.*

Hay *v*. H.M. Advocate 1968 *S.L.T.*

Jeffrey *v*. Black 1977 *Q.B.D. T.L.R.* 15.7.77.

Kuruma *v*. R. 1955 *A.C.*

Atkinson, J. M. (1976) 'Order in court: some preliminary issues and analyses', presented at the Conference of the International Sociological Association Research Group on Sociology of Law.

Blumberg, A. S. (1967) *Criminal Justice* (Quadrangle).

Bordua, D. (ed.) (1967) *The Police* (John Wiley).

Bottomley A. K. (1968) 'The granting of bail: principles and practice', *Modern Law Review*, 31. (1973) *Decisions in the penal process* (Martin Robertson).

Bottoms, A. E. and McClean, J. D. (1976) *Defendants in the Criminal Process* (Routledge & Kegan Paul).

Box, S. (1971) *Deviance, Reality and Society* (Holt, Rinehart & Winston).

Burton, F. and Carlen, P. (1977) 'Official discourse,' presented at the British Sociological Association conference.

Cain, M. (1971) 'On the beat' *in* S. Cohen (ed.) *Images of Deviance* (Penguin); (1973) *Society and the Policeman's Role* (Routledge & Kegan Paul).

Carlen, P. (1976) *Magistrates' Justice* (Martin Robertson).

Chambliss, W. J. (1969) *Crime and the Legal Process* (McGraw Hill).

———and Seidman R. B. (1971) *Law, Order and Power.* (Addison-Wesley).

Cicourel A. (1968) *The Social Organisation of Juvenile Justice* (John Wiley).

Cohen, S. (1971) *Images of Deviance* (Penguin Books).

Cox, B. (1975) *Civil Liberties in Britain (Penguin).*

Dell, S. (1971) *Silent in Court,* Occasional Papers in Social Administration no. 42 (Bell).

Drew, P. (1978) 'Accusations: the occasioned use of religious geography in describing events', *Sociology* (**January 1978**).

Garfinkel, H. (1956) 'Conditions of successful degradation ceremonies', *American Journal of Sociology,* **61**.

Green, E. (1961) *Judicial Attitudes in Sentencing* (Macmillan).

Greenawalt, K. (1973) 'Perspectives on the right to silence' in R. Hood, (ed.) *Crime, Criminology and Public Policy* (Heinemann).

Hay, D. (1975) 'Property, authority and law' in Hay *et al. Albion's Fatal Tree* (Allen Lane).

Hetzler, A. N. and Kanter, C. H. (1974) 'Informality and the court' in Sylvester S. F. and Sagarin E. *Politics and Crime* (Praeger).

Holstrom L. L. and Burgess A. W. (1974) 'Rape: the victim goes on trial' in Drapkin and Viano *Victimology* Vol. III (D. C. Heath).

Home Office Circular no. 31 (1964).

Hood, R. G. (1962) *Sentencing in Magistrates' Courts* (Stevens); (1972) *Sentencing the Motoring Offender* (Heinemann).

Justice (1971) *The Unrepresented Defendant in Magistrates' Courts* (Stevens).

King, M. (1971) *Bail or Custody?* (Cobden Trust).

McBarnet, D. J. (1976) 'Pre-trial procedures and the construction of conviction' *in* P. Carlen Sociological Review Monograph on *The Sociology of Law* (Keele University) (1977); 'The police and the state: arrest, legality and the law', presented at the British Sociological Association Conference.

Newman, D. J. (1966) *Conviction* (Little, Brown).

Packer, H. (1964) 'Two models of the criminal process' *University of Pennsylvania Law Review*, 113. p. 1.

Renton, R. W. and Brown, H. H. (1972) *Criminal Procedure According to the Law of Scotland* 4th edn (Green).

Skolnick, J. (1966) *Justice without Trial* (Wiley); (1967) 'Law and conflict resolution', *Journal of Conflict Resolution*, XI.

Stinchcombe, A. (1963) 'Institutions of privacy in the determination of police administrative practice', *American Journal of Sociology*, 59. p. 150.

Sykes, R. E. and Clark, J. P. (1975) 'A theory of deference exchange in police-civilian encounters', *American Journal of Sociology*, 81. p. 584.

Taylor, I., Walton, P. and Young, J. (1973) *The New Criminology* (Routledge & Kegan Paul); (1975) *Critical Criminology* (Routledge & Kegan Paul).

Thompson, E. P. (1975) *Whigs and Hunters* (Allen Lane).

Zander, M. (1969) 'Unrepresented defendants in the criminal courts', *Criminal Law Review*; p. 632 (1972a) 'Legal Advice and Criminal appeals', p. 132 *Criminal Law Review*; (1972b) 'Access to a solicitor in the police station', *Criminal Law Review*, p. 342.

PART II

Police: Gatekeepers of the Criminal Process

Introduction

To describe the police as 'gatekeepers of the criminal process' highlights the importance of their role in the detection of crime and the prosecution of offenders. The ways in which they operate with certain fixed expectations and stereotypes of the nature and location of 'criminals', and the manner in which they exercise discretion in making arrests or else in deciding whether to prosecute, continue to be the major interests of researchers. In Britain, research of this kind is still in its infancy compared with the United States, and we still await definitive published work on these major aspects of police activity, particularly with regard to their role in the charging and prosecution processes.

The police not only have an obvious and major filtering role in the selection of those individuals who may ultimately appear in court, but they also have a powerful influence upon the subsequent stages of the criminal process in ways that are rather less obvious: thus, decisions that may appear on the surface to be relatively simple matters concerning the police alone have repercussions that go far beyond the confines of the local police station. It is necessary to recognise the wider implications of decisions on the deployment of police patrols in different urban localities; the typical ways in which reported crimes are initially followed up; techniques of questioning suspects and collecting physical or verbal evidence and the like. The more formal actions such as the granting of police bail and decisions about charges or pleas, which have similar implications, are considered more fully in Part III.

Internal and external pressures upon the police to get results in the 'crime control' terms of court convictions can partly account for many traditional police practices. Increased public awareness and police sensitivity in this area, however, may serve to increase their sense of isolation and alienation within the wider field of criminal justice and penal policy, being conscious of criticisms from all sides for being out of tune with the public, the sentencing courts and 'treatment' agencies alike. This trend can only contribute to increased conflict and frustration within the criminal justice system and in public attitudes towards the work of the police and the other agencies involved. Ways need to be explored of engendering a new climate of opinion within which the complex relationships among criminal justice and law enforcement personnel can be recognised for what they are, and new solutions attempted to enable them to work towards common objectives on the basis of agreed procedures which maximise the freedoms of individuals and further the cause of social justice.

Finally, having recognised the central importance of the police role in filtering 'offenders' through to later stages in the criminal process, one needs to ask how far the police are in fact the sole or main gatekeepers of the process. Once a distinction had been drawn by researchers between 'reactive' and 'proactive' police work, it was realised that much of the early work on the exercise of police discretion in crime control among juveniles, drug-takers and in vice squads tended to distort the extent to which the police took the initiative in general law enforcement and hence the nature of alleged 'bias' in such work. Research in America, particularly by Black and Reiss, is being confirmed by ongoing work in Britain by Chatterton, Steer, Bottomley and Coleman, which emphasises the role of the *public* (as witnesses or victims of crime) in taking the first steps to report crime to the police. The attitudes and expectations of victims of crimes determine in a critical way the scope of criminal justice in virtually all crimes, not just those such as rape and 'wife-battering', which have recently been a special focus of attention in this respect. Seven out of every eight indictable crimes officially recorded by the police are reported to them by the victims or other members of the public, and are not discovered or detected as a result of police initiative.

Apart from the 'incidental' role of members of the general public (as victims or witnesses), there are several other 'intermediaries of social control' whose role is of special significance in the production of official crime rates, though this has largely been neglected by researchers. These include the store detectives and security firms responsible for actions against suspected shoplifters; headmasters and others in educational institutions who have wide discretion in the way they handle vandalism, theft or personal violence on their premises; the works managers who deal with offences within the firm — all these, and many others in comparable positions, exercise discretion which *in toto* is probably more extensive and significant than that of the police in a large number of often quite serious crimes. Therefore there are major problems not only of defining what is crime in legislative terms, but equally of recognising how so much criminal behaviour is unreported and largely unknown outside the confines of particular establishments or social groups. This should be of as much concern to those who favour more open and public justice as are the practices of the police with respect to the minority of individuals who are processed through rather different channels after they have been suspected of criminal behaviour.

Further Reading

Alderson, J. C. and Stead, P. J., *The Police we Deserve* (Wolfe, 1973).

Banton, M., 'The keepers of the peace', *New Society* (5 December 1974) p. 604.

Belson, W. A., *The Police and the Public* (Harper and Row, 1975).

Black, D. J., 'Production of crime rates' *American Sociological Review* 35 (1970) p. 733.

Black, D. J., 'The social organisation of arrest' *Stanford Law Review* 32 (1971) p. 1087.

Black, D. J. and Reiss, A. J. 'Police control of juveniles', *American Sociological Review* 35, (1970) p. 63.

Bottomley, A. K. and Coleman, C. A., 'Criminal statistics: the police role in the discovery and detection of crime' *International Journal of Criminology and Penology* 4 (1976) p. 33.

Box, S., *Deviance, Reality and Society* (Holt, Rinehart and Winston, 1971), Ch. 6.

Cain, M. E., *Society and the Policeman's Role* (Routledge & Kegan Paul, 1973).

―― 'An ironical departure: the dilemma of contemporary policing' in *The Yearbook of Social Policy 1976* (1977).

Cicourel, A. V., *The Social Organisation of Juvenile Justice, rev. edn (Heinemann, 1976).*

Coleman, C. A. and Bottomley, A. K., 'Police conceptions of crime and "no crime"' *Criminal Law Review* (1976) p. 344.

Criminal Law Revision Commitee, *Eleventh Report: Evidence (General)* Cmnd 4991 (HMSO, 1972).

Dickens, B. M., 'The control of prosecutions in the United Kingdom' *International and Comparative Law Quarterly* 22 (1973) p. 1.

Ditchfield, J. A., *Police Cautioning in England and Wales* Home Office Research Study No. 37 (HMSO, 1976).

JUSTICE, *The Prosecution Process in England and Wales* reprinted in *Criminal Law Review* (1970) p. 668.

Holdaway, S., 'Changes in urban policing' *British Journal of Sociology* 28 (1977) p. 119.

Lambert, J. R., *Crime, Police and Race Relations* (Oxford University Press, 1970).

Manning, P. K., 'The police: mandate, strategies and appearances' in J. D. Douglas (ed.) *Crime and Justice in American Society* (Bobbs-Merrill, 1971).

Mark, Sir R., *Policing a Perplexed Society* (Allen & Unwin, 1977).

Miller, F. W., *Prosecution: the Decision to Charge a Suspect with a Crime* (Little, Brown, 1969).

Price, C. and Caplan, J., *The Confait Confessions* (Marion Boyars, 1977).

Punch, M. and Naylor, T., 'The police: a social service' *New Society* (17 May 1973), p. 35.

Rock, P., *Deviant Behaviour* (Hutchinson, 1973), Ch. 4.

Steer, D., *Police Cautions — A Study in the Exercise of Police Discretion* (Blackwell, 1970).

Wilcox, A. F., *The Decision to Prosecute* (Butterworths, 1972).

Williams, D. G. T., *Keeping the Peace: The Police and Public Order* (Hutchinson, 1967).

Wilson, J. Q., *Varieties of Police Behaviour* (Harvard University Press, 1968).

Zander, M., 'Access to a solicitor in the police station' *Criminal Law Review* (1972) p. 342.

3. Police in Social Control

by MICHAEL CHATTERTON

Reprinted with permission, in abridged form, from J. F. S. King (ed.) *Control Without Custody* (Institute of Criminology, Cambridge, 1976), pp. 104–22.

Introduction

This paper concentrates on the work of those persons who are frequently the first members of police organisations to be mobilised in response to the great variety of demands which members of the public make upon the police. It has been argued that their decisions and actions largely determine the type and the quality of police work which we receive in this country. They may also be described as critical gatekeepers in the process which provides most of the human and statistical material with which the rest of us, involved practitioners and academics alike, work.

I refer, of course, to the uniformed constables on the beat and their sergeants and to their counterparts in the CID. . . .

A discussion of the police in social control could be much wider ranging than will be attempted below and there are important aspects of police work such as the operations of specialist departments, community relations and juvenile liaison departments, drug, vice and serious crime squads etc., as well as other decisions and stages in the policing process, like the decisions of senior police officers about prosecutions and cautions, which will not be considered.[1] On the other hand, by focusing upon the discretionary decisions and actions of patrol personnel and their arrests (and to a lesser extent upon detectives' arrests), it will be possible to introduce several ideas from the literature on police work and to discuss these with reference to some data from my own research on the work of such officers in a force in Northern England (the section covered is hereafter referred to as the 'Research Division').[2]

In previous studies of the police a good deal of attention has been devoted, for example, to police discretion. However, even in the studies which have examined arrest data in their investigations of this topic, little work has been done on the question of how the policemen and the persons whom they arrested or reported for offences were brought into contact in the first instance. Research interest has tended to focus exclusively upon the discretionary decisions of policemen once they were in the situation of encounter, i.e. on what happened *after* the suspect or 'trouble-maker' and the policeman confronted each other. Although these *police* decisions are of critical importance, I shall suggest, using certain arrest data from my research, that *the public* play a far more crucial role in the policing process than has previously been portrayed, particularly in studies of the police in Britain. These findings will underscore the more general point that we need more comparative data on arrests and on the various ways in which the situations of encounter resulting in arrests are produced, if only because they enable us to assess the relative importance of the public's role in the control process.

A second and related point to be discussed below turns on the idea that 'enforcing the law', in the sense of arresting someone, may be only one of several resources available to policemen for handling incidents. From this point of view an arrest is not adequately explained by the evidence presented by the arresting officer to justify his use of the resource, i.e. his use of his powers of arrest. For on other occasions when this power might have been invoked, an alternative resource may have been used to deal with the incident. Not only does this perspective on arrests lead us to seek out the non-statutorily referable grounds for electing to take someone into custody, (i.e. the reasons which are not obvious in the officer's evidence nor in the legislation), but it also requires us to identify the range of alternatives which are available and are used on occasions in preference to an arrest. One of the aims of the paper is to stress the need for more data on these other policing outcomes than are currently available.

The Roles of Police and Public in the Arrest Process

Descriptions in novels and in several research reports of policemen at work portray them in a manner which might easily tempt us to infer that most of the arrests they effect result from their own information-gathering activities. In this literature policemen are depicted as *investigators* and police organisations are consequently seen as *proactive* systems.

We learn that when he is out on patrol, for example, the ever-vigilant uniformed patrolman is attuned to notice anything which does not fit into the context of familiar appearances and activities which define the normal state of order on his beat. His training in the classroom and on the beat has taught him to notice the unusual, to become an expert at 'inferring the probability of criminality from the appearances of persons present in public places'.[3] His superiors direct him to leave the patrol car, to police *from* wheels and not just *on* wheels and to spend a period of his shift patrolling his beat on foot, inspecting the front and rear of vulnerable property and checking on persons who arouse his suspicions.

His colleague the detective uses forensic scientists and computer systems, cultivates a network of informants, visits places of entertainment frequented by known criminals and even mixes in their company in order to acquire the information which, we are told, 'is the life blood of the good detective'.[4]

In other words, there is a substantial body of work which indicates that policemen working in specialist departments spend a good deal of their time endeavouring to obtain information about crime upon which they may be able to act subsequently. Even the uniformed patrol-man engages in proactive policing activities which are designed to catch the perpetrators of offences in the act or soon afterwards. However, one research team working in the USA has challenged this prevailing conception of police work and has provided an alternative model which, the researchers argue, corresponds more closely to the reality of police work in urban areas today. In this model, police forces are described as *reactive* units which await the input of information from the public as the source of much of their activity and consequently for most of their results.[5]

These researchers found, for instance, that of 5,360 mobilisations of the patrol branch, 81% originated from citizens telephoning the police for service whereas only 14% originated in the initiative of the policeman while he patrolled his area. The patrol branch made most of the arrests and the detectives, whom, the researchers argue, many people would expect to have a more proactive style of working, relied extensively upon members of the public being able to identify the perpetrators of offences, in order to make their arrests.

This research by Reiss and his associates is important because it

TABLE 1. *Sources of information and types of investigation
leading to arrests:* distribution of arrests for crime showing the
branch of the arresting officer and the source of information
and type of investigation leading to the arrest of the prisoner.

Mode of detection	*CID*		*Uniform*			
	No.	*%*	*No.*	*%*	*Total*	*%*
Named	155	25	50	7	205	15
Search	10	2	85	12	95	7
Enquiries	126	20	28	4	154	11
Implicated	91	14	51	7	142	10
Fingerprints	24	4	–	–	24	2
Other unit	71	11	19	2	90	7
Radio call	10	2	74	10	84	6
Police-initiated	47	7	272	38	319	24
Detained	95	15	143	20	238	18
Total	629	100	722	100	1,351	100

indicates that, despite the evidence from other studies, police attempts
at proactive police work are less productive of apprehensions than the
calls which police organisations receive from their publics. Hence what
have traditionally been interpreted as the products of police discretion
may in fact be largely attributable to citizen discretion, by virtue of the
control members of the public exercise over the input of information to
the police and the relative failure of the attempts of the police to
achieve results on their own initiative. [6]

Using material available in the official records, I attempted to
investigate the part played by members of the public in arrest processes
of the Research Division by examining the ways in which the situations
of encounter between the arrested person and the arresting officer had
been produced.

During the period of the survey of arrests on the Research Division,
there were 1,558 arrests for crime by members of both the CID and
the uniformed branch. Table 1 provides a breakdown of these arrests
according to the department of the arresting officer and the source of
information and type of investigation leading to the arrest of the
prisoner, i.e. the mode of detection. [7] If the prisoner had actually been
detained by the victim or witnesses when the police officer arrived on
the scene, the arrest was classified accordingly as 'Detained'. Unless

there was a statement to that effect in the files, however, this designation was *not* applied to the case, even though the prisoner may still have been at the scene of the incident when the policeman arrived. Such incidents were classified as the result of a 'Radio-call'. The cases in the 'Named' category are those where someone at the scene of the offence was able to provide the attending officer with some information identifying the prisoner, usually his name and/or address or, less frequently, a nickname, car registration number etc. The important point to note in connection with this category is that the information about the identity of the prisoner was provided *when the matter was reported to the police*. If persons who were in a position to identify the prisoner had only been discovered during the course of the subsequent investigation then the case would have been recorded in the 'Enquiries' category, which applied to those arrests which were the products of investigation and detection work (e.g. house-to-house enquiries), after the police had been provided initially with very little information with which to work. (Information from regularly used informers also came into this category, therefore.) If the police had been supplied with a description of the offender and had mounted a search of the immediate vicinity and had caught the accused in that way, then the arrest was classified in the 'Search' category. (In a few cases the search was conducted for several days, visiting premises in the area etc., and if these cases had happened frequently it would have been necessary to introduce a different category for those arrests, because they were sufficiently distinct from the searches of the immediate vicinity to warrant a separate classification. However, there were too few of these to make that worthwhile.) In those cases where the arresting officer was not following up a complaint or a request from a member of the public, e.g. a radio call or a crime complaint, but had initiated his involvement in the incident and the encounter with the prisoner himself, the arrest was classified as 'Police-initiated'. The category 'Fingerprints' was used to classify those arrests where fingerprint evidence left at the scene of the crime provided the information about the person who was subsequently arrested. The 'Implicated' category was used for those cases where information about the prisoner's identity was provided by another person who was already in police custody. Occasionally this category was used to refer to those cases where an arrest had provided the police with an opportunity of searching the prisoner's premises and someone else was discovered living there who could not have failed to know about the crime and the stolen property and became a prime suspect through association. Finally, if the prisoner had been *apprehended* by some other police unit and brought to the Division to be *charged* by a member of the Research Division, the arrest was classified in the 'Other Unit' category.

The data in Table 1 enable us to compare the relative contribution of each style of detection, to establish whether there were any differences between the CID and Uniformed branch, and to assess the relative significance of the public's role in these arrest cases.

Six hundred and twenty-nine (47%) of these arrests were effected by members of the CID who were stationed on the Research Division. Of these detective-arrests, 155 (25%) were cases where someone had been able to provide the identity of the accused and in 95 (15%) of the cases the prisoner had been detained by a member of the public. In 91 (14%) of the cases information leading to the arrest had come from persons who were already in custody, having been arrested for an offence, and who implicated their accomplice(s). In only 197 (31%) cases had the detectives produced the arrest through police-initiated work, their own enquiries or through the use of fingerprint evidence left at the scene of the crime. The arrests made by members of the uniformed patrol branch reveal a different pattern. In 300 (42%) of cases the arrest resulted from police-initiated activity or enquiries. In 143 (20%) of cases the prisoner had been detained by a member of the public and in 74 (10%) cases the arrest was the product of a radio call which, in another 85 (12%) cases, was followed by a successful search of the area for the prisoner.

Combining the totals of these arrests by the members of both departments which were clearly cases in which members of the public played an active part in the process leading to the arrest, i.e. the cases in the 'Named', 'Implicated', 'Radio Call' and 'Detained' categories, we are provided with a grand total of 669 arrests (49%) of all arrests for crime. Almost half of all arrests for crime were cases in which the public had provided the police with a prisoner. Inasmuch as this excludes the cases in the 'Search' and 'Other unit arrest' categories, where members of the public may have played a critical role in the apprehension of the accused, this figure may, in fact, underestimate the extent of public participation in the arrest process. Examining the total of arrests for both departments combined where the mode of detection was unequivocally *police initiated*, i.e. the arrest cases in the 'Enquiries', 'Fingerprints' and 'Police-initiated' categories, we get a total of 497 cases, representing 37% of all crime arrests on the Research Division.

Even in these cases, however, the role of the public may have been more significant than at first appears.

For example, as part of the analysis of the background features of the offence, it was discovered that in a large number of cases where the officer had reported that the arrest resulted from his enquiries, there had been some kind of pre-existing relationship between the accused and the victim.[8]

It is important that the reader appreciate the difference between the arrests which have already been examined and those which I shall now move on to discuss, although economies of space do not permit a detailed explanation of the point.[9] Of the crime arrests it is possible to state that they occurred in circumstances where the arresting officers would have considered it unreasonable and irregular to take any action other than apprehending any suspect and taking him to the police station for further questioning and perhaps to be charged. In their terms these were 'good prisoners', they were arrests which they were gratified to have made. Consequently, in so far as the decisions of the *arresting officers* are our concern here, we can assume, from the type of charge, that the question of *why* the officer apprehended the accused does not arise in these cases. For *these* arrest cases the pertinent question is *how* the apprehension was made possible.

On the other hand, there are arrest cases which a police officer would recognise as involving a type of charge which which he uses less frequently than he might when dealing with incidents encountered on the beat. When we consider arrests involving these charges therefore, whilst we must still examine *how* the arrested person and the policeman were brought into contact, we have also to consider *why* the officer decided that an arrest was the most reasonable and appropriate way of dealing with the incident. . . .

The Uses of Arrest Powers as Resources in Peace-keeping

One of the most extensively documented facts about police work is that the police underenforce certain laws and jealously protect the discretion which that implies. The reasons why there is less than full enforcement of certain pieces of legislation have been suggested and discussed at some length in the literature.[10] The debate indicates that discretion may be either delegated or non-delegated. The realisation that it is difficult to control the exercise of discretion of both kinds at the lower levels in police organisations, raised the question for researchers of how police officers in the lower ranks decide to invoke laws which they enforce less frequently than they might. What is it that distinguishes the occasions of use from those when the alternatives are preferred? And what are those alternatives? . . .

A useful starting point is to take another look at the charges themselves, suspending the conventional idea that laws are things to be enforced, and thinking of them instead as resources to be used to achieve the ends of those who are entitled or able to use them. If we do not explore the meanings which policemen build into the framework of charges supplied in legislation we run into the danger of making inferences from the law as it is written in the books which may have little, if any, relevance to the way control processes operate in practice. For example, legislation such as the various Acts relevant to public order discussed above has been described as presenting problems for police officers because it is so vaguely worded. To the practical policeman, however, viewing these pieces of legislation as the sources from which he derives his arrest powers, the vagueness of the legislation is an advantage. The more precisely worded the legislation the more narrowly defined are the grounds upon which he may invoke the powers of arrest it provides, and consequently the more circumscribed his room for manoeuvre. He will feel more cautious about not arresting someone, because the ingredients of the offence are less ambiguously defined and because it is therefore easier for someone to argue subsequently that he should have taken the action which was so unambiguously prescribed in the law. Conversely he will feel confident in arresting someone whom, on his own grounds, he considers he should arrest, knowing that it will be difficult for anyone to argue later that he could have known there was insufficient evidence to justify the arrest.

On the Research Division, the operational ranks shared certain routine understandings about several of the public order charges which have already been discussed above, e.g. drunk and disorderly behaviour, and another which has not been mentioned, namely Section 47 of the Offences Against the Person Act 1861, which deals with assault occasioning actual bodily harm and common assault. It was recognised that the legislation was vague and ambiguous but it was routinely understood that the evidence provided by the arresting officer to his station sergeant and to the courts would follow a well-tried and tested format and it was expected (correctly as the analysis of the court material indicated) that the majority of persons charged under these sections (with the exception of the assault cases) would plead guilty in any case.

When these officers referred to there being 'a story' behind these cases which was not discoverable by inspecting the legislation, they were referring to the fact that such a charge was used as the legal vehicle for conveying someone to the police station and that the grounds for the *decision to use it* were to be found elsewhere than in the reasons provided to *justify* its use to the courts. If we view these charges as resources used in peace-keeping, therefore we are directed to search out the interests which policemen are concerned to protect and promote in such work. Predominant among these interests, my experiences suggest, is the concern with 'trouble'.

Trouble as a Practical Concern in Peace-keeping

Broadly speaking there were two kinds of 'trouble' about which policemen on the Research Division were particularly concerned. The first kind I have called 'within-the-job trouble', which is bound up with the relationships between the patrol personnel and their superiors in the organisation. The second kind relates to their concern to control relationships between themselves and their various publics on the division, to maintain their capacity to intervene authoritatively in any incident and to preserve their own and others' beliefs that they are 'on top of the area', as they put it. For want of a better term this type of concern could be described as 'on-the-job trouble'. In some situations both types of trouble were relevant to how the policeman dealt with those situations.

The first kind of trouble is based upon policemen's appreciation of one of the basic facts about police-work, which is that one can never be absolutely certain that the action taken in a particular situation will later prove to be the most appropriate way of handling that situation. This important element of uncertainty stems partly from the fact that the police mandate is so widely defined that a certain course of action which may be deemed reasonable with reference to one of the aims of police work can be defined differently if it is viewed from another. For example a sergeant who directed his men to patrol their beats more 'aggressively' and engage in street stops and checks of persons, might be seen as contributing to the capacity of the police as a crime-prevention and thief-catching agency. But if complaints were made by persons living in and frequenting the area, and if the actions of his men destroyed the good relationships which his superiors were trying to build up between the police and local populace, then his actions and those of his men could be criticised as poor police-work.

Another source of uncertainty arises from the fact that policemen can rarely be certain that they have correctly assessed the circumstances of an incident and the parties to it. Through their inability to identify something which, it transpires, was of considerable relevance, the solution they may have proposed and worked to achieve may be rendered ineffective, and proved by the turn of events to have been inappropriate.

Although these sources of uncertainty are not unique to police-work, they take on a greater significance when subordinates appreciate how easily they can make mistakes and when they are also uncertain how such errors will affect their promotion and other job opportunities. It is this combination of factors which motivates policemen in the lower echelons to attempt to control the information about themselves which passes up the communications system to their superiors. Every attempt is made to ensure that only information which cannot damage their reputations is allowed to reach the higher echelons.

Hence, to the men on the Research Division, trouble in its mildest form meant allowing themselves to become involved in anything which could result in their superiors having to do more than routinely endorse a report which they had submitted on an incident. If the report 'bounced', i.e. was returned with comments requiring more details about the incident, that was seen as the fault of the report-writer. For controlling information also required the development of skills in report-writing, so that a report always provided a retrospective justification of the action which was reported to have been taken. Whenever possible the submission of a report was avoided. Instead one of several standard brief references was usually entered against the original entry in the station journal or in the radio-log, for example, 'parties advised', 'not a police matter', 'all quiet on arrival', 'unsatisfactory business transaction'. These observations on the concern to avoid 'within-the-job' trouble, by controlling information and handling of incidents and writing reports with the concern in view, will be particularly relevant to our subsequent discussion of incidents which result in no one being arrested or reported for an offence.

What I have called 'on-the-job trouble' requires an investigation of policemen's conceptions of the area where they work, their knowledge about types of premises and their conceptions of the types of persons who live upon or frequent the area. The use of this background knowledge is revealed in their responses to radio calls. Certain calls are guaranteed to produce a 'good turn-out': more than one officer will attend the incident even if one patrol-man only was directed to it by the communications officer. The response to these types of call is based upon an expectation that the officer dispatched to the scene might encounter difficulties and be exposed to a certain amount of danger in handling it alone. Those expectations are in turn inferred from the details provided in the radio message – details which are relevant to their *conceptions of significant locations and relationships*.

On the Research Division, '999' calls reporting trouble in a public house provided a good example of one type of significant location. When they heard the call, the patrolmen would interpret it in the light of their conceptions of the typical sequence of events leading up to the call (the trouble-maker will have been given more than one chance by the landlord), the types of persons likely to be present in the pub when they arrived (persons who will have a go at a policeman in difficulties and who will learn from how we deal with this one how much *they* can get away with in the future), and the likely outcome (if he is still there and he gives any trouble then he will be arrested).

In these kinds of location policemen are sensitive to the threat which the incident presents to their capacity to control the area, not only on the specific occasion but in the future. Taking an accused into custody who is defying their authority in such situations has to be interpreted in the context of those understandings. Behaviour of which they might be more tolerant in different circumstances consequently implies a high probability of arrest when it occurs in these significant locations.

The same observation applies in circumstances where the relationships between the complainant and the accused, and the situation of the complainant, were such that the police again considered that the incident in question threatened their control over the area. For example, there were certain occupations which exposed those who practised them in the area covered by the Research Division to a degree of personal risk from certain others who lived in the area. The policeman judged their success in keeping the area under control with reference to the confidence these people had that they could pursue their occupations without the fear of being victimised. In these incidents it was regarded as vital to prove, both to the complainant and the other party, that the police had the situation under control. If the trouble-maker was not prepared to co-operate with them, thus enabling them to resolve the issue in a way they thought appropriate, the power of arrest would be utilised, to teach him a lesson and to provide the complainant with the display or show of strength necessary to reassure him. In many circumstances their control was displayed without recourse to an arrest, by the compromise which they were able to negotiate once the person complained about accepted the legitimacy of their intervention and complied with their demands. Thus a taxi client would be taken to his home to obtain the money to pay the fare knowing that the alternative, which had been spelled out to him in no uncertain terms, was a night in the cells and an appearance at court the next day charged with 'D and D'. An ambulance driver would receive an apology for the insults he had received because, in the view of the offending party, he had not arrived quickly enough. The dissatisfied customer would pay for the main course of the meal he had not enjoyed and contribute half of the cost of the meal his companion had eaten before running out of the restaurant without paying. The patient in the casualty department who had been blaspheming and threatening the medical staff would allow them to treat his wound without continuing the disturbance he had been creating.

The arrest powers given by the resource charges were therefore used as a threat and invoked when the other alternatives failed. This seems to answer the question posed at the beginning of the paper. Policemen appreciated the power which the resource charges provided, for they strengthened the probability of a settlement being achieved without resorting to an arrest and thereby made their interventions more effective. For these reasons, it has been suggested that policemen on the Research Division were particularly sensitive to the kinds of behaviour which threatened both their control over the specific incident in hand and their control over the area generally. Certain significant locations and relationships highlighted this concern and although an arrest in these situations was not inevitable, the probability of such a response was higher in these incidents than in others. Even in other incidents, however, failure to resolve the altercation by negotiating a satisfactory outcome might necessitate recourse to the arrest powers in order to retrieve the controlling position of the police. . . .

Notes

1. For an interesting study of police cautioning at this level see D. Steer, *Police Cautions — a Study of the Exercise of Police Discretion* (Oxford, Blackwell, 1970).

2. A grant from the Social Science Research Council enabled me to spend a year observing the work of the patrol branch and other relevant departments. I was free to choose the officers with whom I wanted to work and spent between 48 hrs and 60 hrs per week in the field. During 1969 and 1970 these observations were supplemented during university vacations and at weekends and some time was spent observing the work of the Divisional CID. An analysis was made of arrests which occurred on the Research Division between 1st June 1968 and 31st August 1969. Only arrests by uniformed and CID officers who were posted on the Research Division were included in the analysis. Prisoners arrested and brought to the Division to be charged by members of other Divisions were not included (including dog-handlers, members of the Traffic Department, officers working overtime at football matches who were not members of the Research Division, policewomen and special constables.) Arrests of persons who were charged with prostitution, drugs and kindred offences were not included nor were arrests for non-payment of fines.
   I would like to express my thanks to the Social Science Research Council and to the Chief Constable of the Force for making the study possible.

3. H. Sacks, *Methods in Use for the Production of a Social Order: A Method for Warrantably Inferring Moral Character*, p. 4., cited by C. Werthman and I. Piliavin, 'Gang members and the police', in D. J. Bordua (ed.) *The Police: Six Sociological Essays* (Wiley, 1967), p. 75. See also J. Rubinstein, *City Police* (New York, Ballantine, 1974).

4. W. A. Westley, 'The police: A sociological study of law, custom and morality', in J. H. Skolnick, *Justice Without Trial* (New York, Wiley, 1966), p. 124.

5. This team was provided with the resources enabling it to undertake what is probably the most systematic and comprehensive study of the work of mobile and foot patrol units yet conducted. Thirty-six observers rode with the police in three cities, spending about seven weeks in each city. They recorded their observations on every single encounter which the officers had with the public during their tours of duty. Predictably the research generated a tremendous amount of data which it would be impossible to summarise here, but one point which is repeatedly documented by their data is the fact that the police in these cities relied heavily upon the public presenting them with work, calling them to incidents, making complaints etc. rather than initiating their work and their enquiries themselves. See for example Albert J, Reiss. *The Police and the Public*. (Hew Haven, Yale University Press, 1971); D. Black and A. J. Reiss, 'Police control of juveniles' *Amer. Soc. Rev.* 35 (1970), pp. 63–77: D. J. Black, 'Production of crime rates', *Amer. Soc. Rev.* 35 (1970), pp. 733–48.

6. As Reiss concludes 'They have considerable influence over what becomes a police matter and what is processed as crime, based on their decisions to mobilise the police or not, their demands and complaints for police

intervention, their preferences for arrest, and their willingness to aid the police as complainants." Reiss. op. cit., p. 88).

7. The reader will note that this table includes 1,351 crime arrests only, because arrests of shoplifters and arrests of persons on warrant for not appearing at court on a previous occasion are excluded. The shoplifters were the product of the 'detained by a member of the public' mode of detection and were cases which would have been included in the CID totals.

8. These 1,351 arrests for crime do not include arrests of persons charged with assault contrary to the Offences Against the Person Act, 1861. Also excluded are arrests of persons charged with indecent assault. Had these been included the dependence of the police on the involvement of members of the public would have been proved to be even greater than it appears in Table 1.

9. These and other points in the paper are developed in my unpublished PhD thesis: *'Organisational relationships and processes in police work: a case study of urban policing.'* (Department of Sociology, University of Manchester, 1975).

10. See especially W. R. LaFave, *Arrest: The Decision to Take a Suspect into Custody* (Boston, Little, Brown and Company, 1965).

4. Perspectives on the Right to Silence

by KENT GREENAWALT

Reprinted with permission, in abridged form, from R. G. Hood (ed.) *Crime, Criminology, and Public Policy.* (Heinemann, 1974), pp. 235–68.

The 'right to silence' embraces the right of suspects not to respond to police questioning and the right of defendants to be free from testifying at their own trial. . . . A suspect or defendant would have a 'perfect' right to silence if no one could draw any adverse inference from his decision to remain silent, if he were free from any other pressures to speak except those produced by his own conscience and by the possibility that speaking would help establish his innocence, and if he could make an informed decision whether speaking would be likely to help or hurt him. Such a person would speak only if he freely wished to confess his guilt and expose himself to punishment or if he intelligently concluded that speaking would be likely to help him. A 'perfect' right to silence is unrealizable in practice. First, most persons feel strong social pressures to be polite and cooperative, to speak when spoken to and no one likes to appear guilty.[1] Second, the police will focus special investigative attention on a suspect who declines to answer relevant questions, and it is hard to see how any rule could prevent this, even were it thought desirable. Thus, the suspect's natural feeling that his chances of appearing innocent may depend on his explaining himself are reinforced by the predictable police response to silence. Third, jurors sometimes will draw adverse inferences from a defendant's failure to testify, even if they are told not to, since they will suspect that the defendant's decision not to speak was based on a wish to hide his guilt. Damaging inferences may also be drawn, despite judicial comment, when jurors are made aware that a defendant has refused to answer police questions.

Because the law is powerless to guarantee a perfect right of silence,

55

considerable pressure to speak must remain on the best advised suspects and defendants whatever the applicable rules.[2] But in neither England nor the United States does the law go as far as it might to create an effective right to silence. Instead it compromises between protecting silence and satisfying competing interests, namely the usefulness for determinations of guilt of having suspects and defendants make statements and of allowing silence to be given its natural evidential significance. In both England and the United States the major impetus for change is now towards diminution of the existing right to silence, an impetus that is largely the result of acute fear of rising crime. . . .

In England the major debate now is over proposed legislative alterations of the right to silence, and particularly the influential proposals of the Criminal Law Revision Committee. The Committee would permit broader adverse inferences than are now allowed when suspects and defendants remain silent; it would eliminate the present caution of a right to silence, and it would relax the standards for inadmissibility of confessions obtained by threat or inducement. The Committee argues that these changes would enhance the accuracy of the process of guilt determination, without having an undesirable effect on police practices or directly violating any fundamental individual rights. The improved pursuit of the guilty is a common theme of those who wish to curtail individual rights; those who defend existing rights or propose their expansion are most likely to emphasize fundamental individual rights, protection of the innocent, and the need to prevent unacceptable police practices. . . .

Silence and the Determination of Guilt and Innocence

The major argument in the *Eleventh Report* for its proposed changes in the right to silence is that they will contribute to the conviction of the guilty, and particularly to the conviction of sophisticated professional criminals.[3] Opponents of the changes emphasize the danger that they will lead to the conviction of the innocent, a danger the Committee does not believe is real. . . .

Under existing practices, the level of confessions is fairly high. The ordinary willingness to respond initially to police questions is largely a consequence of 'natural' pressures to appear innocent and cooperative. But often it is also a consequence of ignorance; ignorance, despite a warning, of the full significance of the right to silence, or ignorance of the significance of some kinds of admissions. The latter may occur when a suspect wrongly supposes that oral statements can not be used against him or fails to understand that one who drives the getaway car for armed robbers is as culpable as those who commit the robbery.

Some suspects remain silent. Increased pressures to speak to the police would result in fewer instances of silence, and, therefore, in more damaging admissions and confessions; and since those who admit their guilt typically plead guilty in the hope of a lighter sentence, the percentage of cases resolved without a trial, already over 70 per cent, would probably rise. If juries were invited to draw broader adverse inferences the conviction rate of those who did not speak and went to trial would increase somewhat. . . .

All this is non-controversial. The real debate is over the percentage of cases in which admissions of the guilty are needed for conviction, and are obtainable. Though this is an empirical questions, it is rarely possible to answer with certainty whether any particular conviction would have been lost without a confession or whether any silent suspect not prosecuted or not convicted was in fact guilty and would have been induced to confess by now-impermissible tactics. General statistics on convictions and acquittals are by themselves not very revealing, either about how many guilty people escape conviction[4] or about how often their silence contributes to that escape. . . .

How much protection the innocent get from the right to silence is even harder to estimate than its probable effect on the guilty. Some few innocent defendants still must refrain from testifying for fear they will make a bad showing. Assuming that they are now receiving sound advice from counsel, the effect of more substantial inferences from silence and the resulting increase in pressure to testify is more likely to be hurtful than helpful. . . . In England, where adverse comment on a defendant who does not testify is still a possibility, there must be very few innocent defendants who do not testify, and fewer still whose acquittals would have turned into convictions had they testified.

Silence in response to police questioning or at the time of charge may prevent an innocent person from being cleared as fast as he might and it may result in unnecessary detention, but it will rarely increase the chances of his conviction.[5] If initial silence rarely leads to convictions of the innocent it need not follow that innocent persons really require silence; perhaps earlier statements would do them no substantial harm. Bentham and others have assumed that innocent persons will want to establish their innocence as soon as possible. No doubt this is usually true. But in a fair number of cases the line between guilt and innocence is not clear.[6] A suspect who kills in response to an attack by an angered acquaintance or one who is peripherally involved in some fraudulent scheme may not know whether he has committed a crime. Though in fact innocent of a crime, he may reasonably fear that responding fully to police questions will make prosecution and conviction more likely. The danger that this may happen is increased by the possibilities that under intensive questioning he will make some slightly inaccurate but very damaging admission whose significance he does not understand, or that he may even come to believe his degree of guilt was greater than it actually was. Further risks are that the police will understand him to have admitted something he has not, or that believing him guilty, they will fabricate an admission of guilt. Since silence may be quite important for uncounseled suspects who have come close to the borderline of criminal activity, a contraction of the pre-trial right to silence might do them considerable harm. By allowing broader adverse inferences to be drawn from silence, the Committee would make silence evidentially much more significant than it is now. This change would amplify the existing opportunities for inaccurate evidence resulting from police misunderstanding of what a suspect has or has not said. A genuine failure of communication might lead an officer to think a suspect unresponsive when in fact he failed to understand a question. Or, a suspect might make cryptic mention of a fact that is passed over by the officer because it seems unimportant. Later in the investigation when the significance of the fact emerges, the officer might forget the suspect's earlier mention of it and mistakenly recall that nothing had been said about it.

A minority of the Committee were concerned enough about inaccurate versions of what transpires during police questioning to suggest that the Committee's proposals should not be put into effect until a general system of station-house recording exists.[7] This change, despite the reservations of the Committee majority about its feasibility,[8] would be a substantial protection for the innocent that might well be worthwhile whether or not the law governing silence is altered. . . .[9]

We can tentatively conclude that limits on the right to silence will increase the numbers of guilty persons convicted but will also increase to a much smaller extent convictions of the innocent. That leads to the crucial and non-empirical question of what the acceptable 'trade-off' is between the two kinds of convictions. The Committee's comment, that 'It is as much in the public interest that a guilty person should be convicted as it is that an innocent person should be acquitted',[10] fails to give due regard to the deep belief that acquittal of the guilty is more tolerable than conviction of the innocent. Given the rather limited effect at best these proposals are likely to have on the commission of crimes, the possibility that they might prejudice some innocent suspects counts heavily against them, at least in the absence of some substantial offsetting protections for the innocent such as those proposed by the Committee minority for recording station-house questioning.

The Right to Silence and Basic Individual Rights

.... In ordinary social relationships between family members, friends and business associates, a person who has a substantial basis for thinking that another has caused unjustifiable injury often asks the 'suspect' whether or not he has done so, and the questioner expects a response. Suspicion does not confer a right to coerce an acquaintance by physical force or extreme browbeating, but if he declines to talk without giving a persuasive reason why he remains silent, it is ordinarily inferred that he is 'guilty'. . . .

If in ordinary relationships there is no 'right to silence' in response to substantial charges, do the state – individual relationship and the penalties of the criminal law change the moral assessment? By the time one has been committed for trial, a substantial basis for the charges against him has been demonstrated; compelling trial testimony is not inherently wrong unless it is made so by some special aspect of the administration of criminal justice. . . . The simple fact that state prosecution for crime is involved is not a sufficient basis for establishing a right to silence in the face of substantial charges which does not exist in ordinary social relationships. There is, however, very good reason for giving legal recognition to the moral right to remain silent in the absence of substantial charges. . . .

Pressure on suspects to respond to police questioning may violate this moral right to silence. The matter is complicated somewhat if one accepts, as I believe any thoughtful person must, the notions that people have a social duty to aid the police in solving crimes and that they should ordinarily respond helpfully to police inquiries, even if they are effectively free of legal obligation in this respect. In many cases initial police questioning of relevant persons is part of a general investigation of what happened. By the time the police treat someone primarily as a suspect rather than a possible witness, that is are questioning him primarily to establish his own guilt or innocence, they usually have a substantial basis for thinking him guilty. Unfortunately, however, if adverse inferences could be drawn from silence as the Committee proposes, there would still be circumstances in which a person might be under pressure to incriminate himself or respond to charges before there is a substantial basis for thinking him guilty. When a person is being questioned as part of a general investigation and realizes that a true answer to a particular question will incriminate him, he now has the right not to answer it, although he has received no warning of his right to silence. The Committee would allow juries to draw adverse inferences from a refusal to answer questions in this context. Also, the police sometimes treat people as suspects well before there is substantial evidence against them. The jury could draw adverse inferences from a suspect's failure at this early point to answer questions designed to elicit his guilt or innocence. . . .

Even if silence at preliminary stages can sometimes count against a defendant, a particular defendant may, of course, try to persuade a court or jury that no inference is proper in his case because he felt strongly he should not respond to insubstantial charges. But a judge or jury might view with scepticism the suggestion that a defendant against whom substantial evidence exists at the time of trial first remained silent because of the absence of such evidence. Moreover, persons questioned often do not know what information the police have, so even if silence in the face of insubstantial accusations were never harmful, suspects would sometimes overestimate the case against them and feel under pressure for that reason.

In summary, the Committee's proposals about silence in response to police questions contain nothing approximating the 'probable cause' safeguard of search and seizure law. Persons may be later penalized by a jury for refusing to answer questions before probable cause of guilt exists. In practice the addition of this pressure to speak may be slight in comparison with the natural and inevitable pressures to do so, but this legally approved pressure would conflict with the moral right to remain silent in the absence of substantial charges. . . .

Conclusion

I have considered a variety of arguments about the right to silence primarily in relation to changes proposed by the Criminal Law Revision Committee, but most of these same arguments are, with little transposition, relevant to other proposals to contract or expand existing rights. On many of the relevant issues empirical research could make some contribution, but any particular study is unlikely to resolve clearly even one of those issues, much less the broader questions of the overall desirability of a proposed change in the existing law. That answer depends on a whole host of non-empirical and sharply contested judgements of value. Realistically, it is doubtful if any empirical studies in the near future will change very many minds about the proper scope of the right to silence. My own conclusions on the basis of existing data follow.

The argument that it is inherently wrong to put pressure on a defendant to testify is not persuasive; such pressure would harm very few if any innocent defendants as long as prior convictions are not routinely introduced to impeach their testimony; and there appears little possibility of abuse if such pressure is introduced upon a counseled defendant in the public setting of a trial. Therefore, I see no major objection to the Committee's basic proposal to allow broader adverse inferences to be drawn from a defendant's silence at trial.[11] My reservation about that proposal, standing alone, concerns the slightness of its likely effect on present practices, since most defendants now testify and juries probably draw adverse inferences from silence even despite contrary instructions. Perhaps the actual change would be too insignificant to justify the symbolic fallout.

Because of the danger to the 'borderline' innocent of damaging distortions in memory and slips in answer to police questions; because the police may misconstrue what a suspect has or has not said; because of the moral right not to respond to insubstantial charges; and because juries may wrongly draw adverse inferences from justified silence at pre-trial stages, the Committee's proposals regarding silence before trial raise much more serious problems. Some of these could be cured by an accurate recording system safeguarded against manipulation but not all.

Present rules governing silence and pre-trial interrogation are defective in both England and the United States because there is more danger than there need be that an inaccurate version of what transpired between a suspect and the police will be accepted, and because the rules shield the intelligent and emotionally strong much better than the ignorant and weak. While recordings could remedy the accuracy problem in large part, only the advice and continuing support of a non-hostile participant can help the ignorant and weak if persistent police questioning of suspects is to be permitted. The participant might be a specially trained layman rather than a fully fledged solicitor. If interrogation of suspects could be carried on only in the presence of counsel, the right to silence that now exists would be genuinely protected, but perhaps the price of fewer admissions and confessions would be considered too high. If so, some combination of effective counsel and legally authorized pressures to speak, such as adverse inferences from silence, would be fairer than the grossly uneven effect of the pressures under existing practice, since these legally authorized pressures would call for the exercise of rational choice and fall with rough equality on all suspects. Perhaps the fairest procedure of all would be to have police questioning of suspects in front of magistrates, with those questioned represented by counsel who would be provided for by the government if necessary. The magistrate might have the responsibility of protecting the moral right to silence by ensuring that no one would be 'penalized' for refusing to answer questions unless there were already some substantial reason for thinking him guilty.

Entirely apart from government payments to provided counsel, a system such as this would involve a considerably greater drain on manpower and monetary resources than does the present form of police questioning. But fairness to criminal suspects and accurate determination of guilt are important enough social goals to warrant great efforts to improve the criminal process. . . .

Notes

1. See E. D. Driver, 'Confessions and the social psychology of coercion', *Harvard Law Rev.* 82 (1968), pp. 42, 57–8.
2. Perhaps a perfect right could be realized if police never questioned suspects at all, if no admissions or confessions could be presented in evidence, and if defendants could not testify, but such drastic changes in the criminal process are beyond the realm of suggested alterations. Cf. L. Levy, *Origins of the Fifth Amendment* (New York, Oxford University Press, 1968), pp. 433–41, describing the Talmudic rule that even voluntary confessions are inadmissible.
3. Criminal Law Revision Committee, *Eleventh Report* (1972) § § 21(vi), 30.
4. See General Council of the Bar of England and Wales, *Evidence in Criminal*

Cases, Memorandum on the Eleventh Report of the Criminal Law Revision Committee, § 67; A. Muir, 'The rules of the game' *Crim. L. R.* (1973) pp. 341–2.

5. With respect to cases where the crime itself or the suspect's possible involvement is minor enough to make non-prosecution a serious option, the police may be more inclined to drop a case against someone who has made a plausible assertion of his innocence than against someone who remains silent; in that context an initial decision to remain silent might conceivably lead to a conviction.

6. In *The Jury at Work,* Occasional Paper Number Four of the Oxford University Penal Research Unit (1972), Sarah McCabe and Robert Purves concluded, after observation of jury trials at selected courts of Quarter Session and Assize, that 80 of the 115 defendants who were acquitted admitted 'being involved in something which could have been interpreted as criminal activity' but claimed that 'this involvement did not amount to a crime' (p. 41). Some of these factual settings were ones in which the line between innocence and guilt was murky and an innocent defendant might have hurt himself by talking to the police, but more typical were cases in which the issue was quite clear and an initial explanation to the police by an innocent person would not have been likely to have been harmful. For example, in a shop-lifting case one would not suppose that a shopper who had actually forgotten that she had unpaid goods under her arm would be led into making slips or damaging admissions if she told that to the police when accused by the store-owner.

7. *Eleventh Report,* § 52.

8. ibid. at § § 50–51.

9. See C. J. Miller 'Silence and confessions – what are they worth?' *Crim. L. R.* (1973) pp. 343, 350.

10. *Eleventh Report,* § 27.

11. Its subsidiary proposals on the failure to testify are more subject to attack. Calling the defendant to take the stand even when he wishes to remain silent would be a demeaning ritual not fully consistent with the Committee's comment that in some circumstances adverse inferences from silence may not be warranted. *Eleventh Report,* § § 110,112; Council of the Bar Memorandum, § 82. Allowing silence to count as corroboration is of doubtful consistency with the premise that the state should have to make out a substantial case against the accused before he should have to answer it.

5. Do the Police Make Decisions?

by RUTH FINNEGAN

Reprinted with permission, in abridged form, from the Open University publication *Decision-making in Britain II: Public Order* (1976), pp. 182–95.

In the present essay I want to argue that, even if the police try *only* to enforce the law and to act as mere administrators, they nevertheless inevitably have to make decisions, and that these decisions have, cumulatively, a significant effect on that most important aspect of the law: how it is actually implemented. I will say something first about the sorts of spheres in which police discretion is exercised in Britain; then I will discuss the various factors influencing the decisions which are thus made.

Police Discretion

The first area in which discretion has to be exercised is in which laws to enforce — or at least which laws to enforce rigorously. The *theory* may be that all laws are enforced and enforced with equal rigour. But this does not accord with actual practice. This is partly a matter of shortage of police. Clearly somewhere a decision has been made — or has emerged — that the enforcement of certain laws shall have a lower priority either in general or on particular occasions than the implementation of others.

Who takes this decision, or series of decisions? A number of factors come in here but in the last analysis it is a matter of the deployment of the police force in any given area, and the decision-making process is thus located not in Parliament nor in the judicature but within the police forces themselves. . . . Decisions are sometimes made at a very

64

local level, an unspoken agreement among a group of policemen that certain offences will generally be winked at. Sometimes the practice is well-known among a number of police forces. For instance the practice about obscenity has often been that the police will not go round looking for offences but will take up specific complaints by members of the public.[1] They give a fairly low priority to enforcing laws about obscenity without totally refusing to act in this sphere. . . .

Decisions about which laws to enforce are thus partly determined by the extent of available police resources and the consequent constraints on the police which lead them to make choices about priorities in the enforcing of the law. But it is not just a question of resources.

This becomes evident in the question of discretion in prosecuting.[2] Even supposing there is the opportunity to enforce a particular law in the sense that a policeman is in fact on the spot when an offence is committed or has it it brought to his notice, the offender may still not be prosecuted. A decision must be made on whether or not to prosecute — and this decision is made not by Parliament, nor (generally) by the judiciary but by the police.[3] There are various levels at which this may take place. A police officer may come across some offence — a traffic offence for instance — and decide on his own authority not to take the matter any further (or to do anything beyond informally warning the offender to be more careful). Or the matter may be reported to a more senior police officer who (within various constraints) may decide on one of three courses: to take no further action; to issue a formal caution as an alternative to prosecuting; or to institute proceedings to prosecute the offender. Even after arrest, the police still have discretion. . . .

Even when the police do decide to prosecute an offender this is not the end of the decisions they must or can make. They also have to decide for which specific offence to prosecute him. There is a particularly wide range of possibilities in the sphere of public order. . . . Someone whom they deem worthy of prosecution under a head for which there is insufficient evidence may well be prosecuted on a different charge which in other circumstances the police might consider only a technical offence. . . .[4]

There are, then, a number of ways in which the police not only do exercise discretion (and thus make decisions) but must do so in order for the system to work. Their primary duties are to maintain public order and enforce the law. They cannot even *try* to do so without the exercise of discretion and therefore the making of decisions. If the actual implementation of the law is what is in question (as distinct from its mere enunciation in law books), then the police emerge as important decision makers in the whole sphere of law and order.

Factors in the Exercise of Police Discretion

If the police do take decisions of this kind, what factors influence the nature of these decisions?

First, there is the nature of the law itself. There are a number of laws on the Statute book which are not, by now, supported by public opinion. They are obsolete but have not been formally repealed. In examples like this the specific decisions not to enforce the law may in each case lie with the police, but this is with the support of public opinion generally. . . .

In the large sphere of police decisions about whether or not to prosecute a known or suspected offender, one common factor is whether the police consider the prosecution likely to be successful. They may themselves be convinced of his guilt, but have insufficient evidence to convince a court of law. Or the evidence may be sufficient, but considering all the circumstances, the likelihood of a conviction or (at best) anything more than a technical penalty may be small. In such cases the cost and effort involved in prosecuting may not be thought worthwhile. Again the complainant may decline to prosecute or help with the prosecution, and even if the the police have sufficient evidence for a successful prosecution they may decide, particularly in cases involving husbands and wives or close neighbours, that a reconciliation is more likely without a court case. . . .[5]

Another factor which often seems to influence the police in their decision on whether or not to prosecute is the nature of the offender. Sometimes it is thought that the wrongdoer has suffered enough or is too ill to stand trial with impunity, or, in the case of a juvenile who is a first offender, will react more favourably if not taken to court. Again the police, with full knowledge of the situation, may decide that another participant whom it is not feasible to charge, was equally responsible.[6] In cases like this, it seems that both the general state of public opinion and the likely reactions of the judiciary if the case were brought to trial have an indirect influence on the decisions made by the police.

Questions of public policy are also sometimes relevant. It is difficult to say how important this aspect is, for it is not a principle that is lightly acceptable to either the police or judiciary; the law is, or should be, no respecter of persons or politics. Nevertheless there do seem to be cases when the effect on public morale or order is considered, or when the risk of making the offender a martyr is felt to be too high. . . .

Factors of the kind just discussed which lie behind the exercise of police discretion are relatively well known. But there are some other factors involved which are much more difficult to pin-point, and of which the actors themselves may not be fully conscious.

First it is illuminating to look briefly at the complex of influences which could be termed the locally enforced norms and the local interactions of police both with each other and with the public. . . . These local norms not surprisingly sometimes involve accepted practices about bending or even breaking the formal rules. This may be of a relatively minor kind, like the 'easing behaviour' mentioned by Cain.[7] In other cases, the accepted practices of at least a significant number of members of the group may result in behaviour, which, if brought to light, would be regarded by senior officers and the general public as serious infringements of the official rules.

The actual *content* of these locally accepted norms among a group of colleagues probably vary widely. But the basic *process* of the development and reinforcement of local norms about accepted behaviour among a group of colleagues is the same, and is something one can expect to meet everywhere. This is not something that can be found in official reports – but it certainly seems that it often plays a part in actions and decisions by individual policemen at the local level. Since it is at the local level that so much law enforcement in practice takes place, this factor is likely to have a significant effect on decision making in the *actual* implementation of the law in this country.

The 'marginally legitimate arrests', also mentioned by Cain, are another instance where remembering the human qualities of individual policemen helps us to understand the influences which may lie behind such acts. In some respects these perhaps shade into the 'easing behaviour' but are worth mentioning separately since to most people the decision to make an arrest seems (rightly) to be a weighty aspect of a policeman's responsibilities in upholding the law. It is clear from Cain's account that other factors in addition to the general aim of law enforcement may be present: the policeman's short-term interests (he gets the excitement of making an arrest and the opportunity to go back to the comfort and company of the police station) as well as the reputation he may gain in the highly valued 'crime work' aspect of police duty.

Social interaction with members of the public can also affect decisions by the police. This comes out in Cain's discussion of relationships with the community generally and in particular the practice in the rural areas she studied. Even in urban contexts there are understandings with members of the public. There is sometimes a tacit agreement that certain technically illegal practices (like hawking, i.e. selling goods without a licence) will not be officially taken note of in a given area provided they are conducted discreetly. Again the reliance of detectives on informants means that a price often has to be paid in return for the information. This may involve a mutual bargain between police and offenders (or potential offenders) who have been arrested or are liable to be arrested, and give information to protect themselves. . . .[8]

A further factor which influences the way police enforce the laws relating to public order (in the wide sense) is the differential visibility of different groups in the community. . . . The rate of 'commission' of the kind of 'crimes' mentioned in studies like that by Stinchcombe in America[9] may well appear — to the police, to the compiler of statistics, to the general public — to be higher for those of lower than those of other social classes. This in itself is significant. For though this factor may not be fully recognised by the police and could not be said to lead to a conscious decision about apprehending individuals of one group rather than of another, nevertheless it can be seen as a *constraint* on police decision making that they are in a position to notice the 'crimes' of certain groups far more readily than those of others.

There is also a further point here. The greater visibility of 'crimes' by members of certain social classes leads to the forming of general expectations about which individuals are the most likely to commit crimes. One of the common stereotypes of conventional wisdom is that more crimes are committed by members of the lower classes in society. Whether or not this is true in fact will not be argued here[10] — the relevant point is that just because of this stereotype a policeman (like anyone else) tends to expect more trouble from individuals in this category, and perhaps unconsciously to devote more attention to such individuals. The expectation can then easily become a self-fulfilling prophecy — for the more attention is given to a particular group the more offences are likely to be detected there. As well, the expectations of the police in these respects sometimes at least lead them to adopt a type of behaviour themselves in dealing with such groups which, in turn, may encourage certain behaviour in the suspects. . . . . It is in fact inevitable that the police should develop certain images and expectations of the likely behaviour of certain individuals and groups. This is, after all, a necessary part of human life and activity everywhere. Police work, furthermore, would be impossible without such images. For when not every crime can be investigated nor every avenue followed up, individual policemen must have some canons (albeit unspoken ones) to guide them in the likely directions to look and the sorts of expectations about likely criminals which will be held by the courts and the public (and so lead to successful prosecutions by the police). . . .

This leads on to the final factor to be discussed here: the classification and explanation of certain behaviour as 'crime'. It has, for instance, been suggested that in some circumstances *who* performs an act and *where* may be as important as the act itself for whether or not it is classified as a 'crime' and acted upon by the police. . . .[11] Considering the number of unreported and unrecorded offences, which crimes policemen decide to notice and which not could clearly be a significant factor in the way the law is actually administered. If it is true that the actions of certain sections of the community are commonly classified as 'crimes' less often than those of other sections this could be said to involve a series of decisions by policemen which radically affects the nature of law enforcement in our society. . . .

Conclusions

According to the argument of this essay the straight answer to the question posed at the outset of this essay is 'Yes'. The police *do* make decisions. This is an inevitable part of the fact that they do, and in practice must have, discretion in administering the law. When one studies the reality as distinct from the ideal, this fact is inescapable. In the sphere of law and order as in so many other spheres 'administration is politics' — if by this well-known tag is meant that even those who are ideally intended 'only' to administer do in fact make decisions and these either directly or cumulatively can amount to policy decisions. Evidence about the *facts* cannot, of course, falsify prescriptions about what *ought* to be. But at the same time, it must be said that this ideal bears very little relation to the reality on the ground.

Notes

1. See the example quoted in G. Williams, 'Discretion in prosecuting' *Criminal Law Review* (1956). p. 2.
2. For further details on this see Williams, op. cit.
3. With the limitation that some decisions about prosecutions are in the hands of the Director of Public Prosecutions, and certain prosecutions require his sanction.
4. On the wide range of crimes which can be relevant to public order and the many uncertainties of the definition of offences see D. G. T. Williams, *Keeping the Peace: Police and Public Order* (London, Hutchinson, 1967)
5. See the example in D. Steer *Police Cautions — a Study in the Exercise of Police Discretion* (Oxford, Blackwell, 1970) p. 28.
6. See again Steer, op. cit. p. 34.
7. M. E. Cain, 'On the beat: interactions and relations in urban rural police forces' in S. Cohen (ed.) *Images of Deviance* (Harmondsworth, Penguin, 1971); also her later *Society and the Policeman's Role* (London, Routledge, 1973).
8. For a vivid account of this aspect see P. Laurie, *Scotland Yard: A Personal Inquiry* (London, Bodley Head, 1970) pp. 188 ff.
9. A. L. Stinchcombe 'Institutions of privacy in the determination of police administrative practice' *American Journal of Sociology* 69 (1963) p. 157.
10. For a recent discussion see S. Box and J. Ford, 'The facts don't fit: on the relationship between social class and criminal behaviour' *Sociological Review* 19 (1971).
11. For example, see D. Chapman, *Sociology and the Stereotype of the Criminal* (London, Tavistock, 1968) p. 56.

PART III

Negotiated Justice
Before Trial

Introduction

Researchers in this country have tended to focus on specific aspects of the criminal process and have largely ignored, or minimised, the importance of the interrelatedness of the different stages from arrest to conviction and sentence. It is usually the case, however, that what happens immediately after a suspect is arrested dominates subsequent decisions that are taken both by the defendant himself and by others involved in his processing. Thus, the fact that a suspect agrees to make a statement of admission to the police (and a suspect will almost certainly be put under pressure to do so) may well increase his chances of obtaining bail; may mean that he can be tried by magistrates (thus avoiding the delay, risk of a heavier sentence and other personal costs of Crown Court trial); will considerably reduce the likelihood of a not guilty plea; may well, directly or indirectly, affect the sentence that is imposed; and may even influence his chances of succeeding with an appeal. Similarly a decision taken either by the police or by the courts to withhold bail will in many cases have a critical bearing on a defendant's thinking about plea and where he should be tried and may well exert a decisive and independent influence over the likelihood of acquittal (should he decide to contest the matter) and the sentence imposed on conviction.

It is, then, misleading to treat any single stage in the penal process as independent of other stages. When one examines the most important decision a defendant has to make — whether to plead guilty or contest the case — one finds that it is a decision determined not so much by the straightforward question of guilt or innocence of the accused, but rather by a host of complex factors, many of which may be completely unrelated to legal culpability. The truth is that the resources of the system require a very high level of guilty pleas and there are, at almost all stages of the criminal process, pressures on defendants to plead guilty. Whether the defendant is threatened by a police officer if he refuses to sign a statement, or is strongly advised to plead guilty by his own lawyer, or even (as happens more commonly in this country than is often supposed) involved in a 'full-blown' plea bargain, or perhaps merely promised that the police will 'go easy on him' if he pleads

73

guilty, the fundamental problem is the same: pressures exist within a system that is simply unable to deal with more than a small proportion of contested trials. This is why there is in this country so much pre-trial haggling, not only about plea (which is a subject that has preoccupied American commentators for years), but also about bail; and it is now being increasingly realised that plea bargaining and bail bargaining may be merely different sides of the same coin.

The extent of pre-trial negotiation between defendants on the one hand and police officers and lawyers on the other remains very much a matter of speculation, although it is probably true to say that the more closely researchers have examined the question, the more they have uncovered evidence of such negotiation. Writers in this country, as in the United States, have tended to disagree about whether these informal discussions, whatever the undoubted administrative benefits, have served broadly the interests of justice. Nevertheless, the fact remains that there exists in this country on a wide scale a system of covert and informal justice which operates largely unregulated and without adequate safeguards to defendants. Furthermore, pre-trial discussions are often conducted at the very time most defendants feel at their most vulnerable (a situation that is no doubt often exploited) and it is not surprising if many defendants soon regret decisions taken at that stage. This is not to say that informal negotiation will inevitably give rise to injustice. It is rather that the standard of justice which such negotiation creates may well be arbitrary or else be seen to be so by defendants themselves.

Further Reading

Alschuler, A. W., 'The prosecutor's role in plea bargaining' *University of Chicago Law Review* 36 (1968) p. 50.
——'Defence attorney's role in plea bargaining' *Yale Law Journal* 84 (1975) p. 1179.
Ares, C. E., Rankin, A. and Sturz, H. 'The Manhattan bail project: an interim report on the use of pre-trial parole' *New York University Law Review* 38 (1963) p. 67.
Baldwin, J. and McConville, M. J., *Negotiated Justice* (Martin Robertson, 1977).
Blumberg, A. S., *Criminal Justice* (Quadrangle Books, 1970).
Bottomley, A. K., *Prison Before Trial* (Bell, 1970).
Cooper, H. H. A., 'Plea bargaining: a comparative analysis' *New York University Journal of International Law and Politics* 5 (1972) p. 427.

Davies, C., 'The innocent who plead guilty' *Law Guardian* (March 1970) pp. 9–15.
———'Pre-trial imprisonment: a Liverpool study' *British Journal of Criminology* 11 (1971) p. 32.
Davis, A., 'Sentences for sale: a new look at plea bargaining in England and America' *Criminal Law Review* (1971) pp. 150, 218.
Enker, A., 'Perspectives on plea bargaining' Appendix A in President's Commission on Law Enforcement and Administration of Justice, *Task Force Report: The Courts* (US Government Printing Office, 1967).
Ferguson, G. A. and Roberts, D. W., 'Plea bargaining: 'directions for Canadian reform' *Canadian Bar Review* 52 (1974) p. 497.
Home Office Working Party, *Bail Procedures in Magistrates Courts* (HMSO, 1974).
King, M., *Bail or Custody* (Cobden Trust, 1971).
McCabe, S. and Purves, R., *By-Passing the Jury* (Oxford University Penal Research Unit: Blackwell, 1972).
Melvin, M. and Didcot, P. J., *Pre-trial Bail and Custody in the Scottish Sheriff Courts* (Scottish Office Social Research Study) (HMSO Edinburgh, 1976).
Newman, D. J., 'Pleading guilty for considerations: a study of bargain justice' *Journal of Criminal Law, Criminology and Police Science* 46 (1956) p. 780.
——— *Conviction: The Determination of Guilt or Innocence Without Trial* (Little Brown, 1966).
Rankin, A., 'The effect of pre-trial detention' *New York University Law Review* 39 (1964) p. 641.
Rosett, A. and Cressey, D. R., *Justice By Consent* (Lippincott, 1976).
Simon, F. and Westheritt, M., *The Use of Bail and Custody by London Magistrates Courts Before and After the Criminal Justice Act 1967* (Home Office Research Study No. 20) (HMSO, 1974).
Thomas, P., 'An exploration of plea bargaining' *Criminal Law Review* (1969) p. 69.
University of Chicago Law Review, Note, 'Official Inducements to Plead Guilty: Suggested Morals for a Market-place' *University of Chicago Law Review* 32, p. 167.
Zander, M., 'A study of bail/custody decisions in London magistrates courts' *Criminal Law Review* (1971) p. 191.

6. Bail and the Judicial Process

by A. KEITH BOTTOMLEY

Reprinted, with permission, from A. K. Bottomley, *Decisions in the Penal Process* (Martin Robertson, 1973), pp. 88–93.

One of the main targets for attacks on the bail system by criminologists, especially in America, has been the evidence that defendants who are refused bail are much more likely to be convicted than are persons granted bail, and much more likely to receive custodial sentences. This evidence needs careful scrutiny, for if these claims are substantiated then the bail decision plays a central rather than merely peripheral role in the progress of a defendant through the penal process. Assuming the accuracy of the statistical association between bail and conviction/ sentence, the crucial question is whether this is in any sense a *causal* association, or whether the same factors independently influence both the bail decision and the subsequent ones. Unfortunately the available evidence does not allow firm conclusions either way, despite some suggestive indications from various research studies.

In America in the 1950s the University of Pennsylvania Law School carried out two important studies of the operation of the bail system, which seemed to provide strong evidence that defendants who were granted bail were more likely to be acquitted than those remanded in custody before trial, but a closer examination of these studies shows that the authors were usually much more cautious in interpreting their data than were many subsequent commentators. In the first study of 946 cases remanded before trial in Philadelphia during October — November 1953, Foote and his colleagues found that 48 per cent of bailed defendants were not convicted compared to 18 per cent of defendants remanded in custody: however, one reason for this difference was that in a greater proportion of bail cases the prosecution withdrew the charges before trial ('nol prosse'), so that when these 'nol prosse' cases were discounted only 25 per cent of bail cases going to trial were acquitted, compared to 16.5 per cent of cases remanded in custody.[1] A second study, of 3,223 felony cases in New York in 1956, found that 20 per cent of the defendants in custody were acquitted at their trial, compared to 31 per cent of those on bail, but the authors were cautious in the conclusions which they drew from these statistics:

The figures tend to support the propositions advanced earlier that jail in itself is likely to produce a guilty plea and that incarceration impairs a defendant's ability to defend himself. But the differences are not large and could be due in some measure to the fact that magistrates often set higher bail and thus keep the defendant in jail, in cases where they realize that the weight of evidence is against him.[2]

This New York study was careful to restrict analysis of acquittal/conviction rates to those cases where there was a plea of not guilty, as only 10 per cent of persons remanded in custody pleaded not guilty, compared to 25 per cent of bailed defendants.[3] Friedland's study of 6,000 cases in Toronto magistrates' courts in 1961–2, is perhaps the most detailed study of this aspect of the problem. He analysed the acquittal rate in indictable cases where there was a plea of not guilty, and found that 55 per cent of those on bail were acquitted, compared to 43 per cent of those in custody; this difference remained, even when he took into account other relevant factors differentiating between bail and custody cases.[4]

The two English studies which have provided some information on this question broadly support the evidence from America and Canada, although they were on a much smaller scale. Davies' Liverpool study of 418 men, remanded on charges of 'breaking and entering', found that in a partially matched subsample of 191 defendants 12 per cent of those remanded in custody before trial pleaded not guilty, compared to 31 per cent of those released on bail, and that only 14 per cent of those in custody were acquitted at their trial, compared to 47 per cent of those on bail.[5] Bottomley's study in a North of England city, in 1964, found that 39 per cent of those committed in custody for trial to a higher court pleaded not guilty, compared to 64 per cent of those committed on bail, although the eventual acquittal rate was 46 per cent of those in custody and only 43 per cent of those on bail; the importance of taking the plea into account is shown by the fact that if the simple acquittal rate of those committed for trial by the urban court had been used, it would have showed that 18 per cent of those committed for trial in custody were acquitted, compared to 27 per cent of those on bail.[6]

On the basis of this evidence, there seems little room for serious doubt that more persons who are refused bail by magistrates plead guilty at their trial, and, without needing to impute any kind of improper coercion upon defendants to make such a choice of plea, it is easy to understand how defendants in custody might reach their decision, on purely personal terms preferring their trial to be over as quickly as possible, and perhaps even with the knowledge that almost half the 'untried prisoners' in English and Welsh prisons are not subsequently given a custodial sentence by the courts![7] Nevertheless, the general problem of guilty pleas . . . and the possible extent to which defendants' pleas may not exactly reflect the 'truth' of the situation, but result from various pragmatic considerations, is clearly one which needs closer examination in relation to the pre-trial bail/custody decision, which itself adds an extra (and possibly crucial) dimension to the situation. Similarly, although the crude conviction rates should not be taken as an accurate guide, yet the evidence points to the fact that, when account has been taken of the different proportions of remanded offenders pleading not guilty and of those cases withdrawn before trial, there is still a difference of some 9—12 per cent between the proportion of defendants on bail who are acquitted and that of those in custody before trial. Clearly some of this difference may well be due to the fact that defendants on bail are in a much better position to consult with solicitors and prepare their own defence, but part of the explanation is also likely to be due to the fact that the initial decision by magistrates to grant bail is sometimes influenced by their assessment of the strength of the case against the accused and the likelihood of his guilt.

Moving from the question of pleas and acquittal to a consideration of the sentences passed on remanded offenders, the evidence for an association between the granting of bail and receiving a non-custodial sentence seems even stronger. Thus, in America, the Philadelphia study found that 22 per cent of those convicted after being on bail received a prison sentence, compared to 59 per cent of those who had been in custody before trial.[8] and in the New York study it was found that 45 per cent of those convicted after being on bail were imprisoned, compared to 84 per cent of those appearing for trial in custody.[9] In Toronto, Friedland found that only 15 per cent of indictable offenders on bail were sentenced to imprisonment, compared to 61 per cent of those in custody before trial.[10] Finally, in England, the Home Office Research Unit study in 1956 showed that 40 per cent of persons committed for trial on bail to higher courts were given custodial sentences, compared to 78 per cent of those committed for trial in custody; and, in summary cases, 14 per cent of those remanded on bail were given custodial sentences compared to 39 per cent of those in custody.[11] Davies found that, in his matched subsample, 69 per cent of those remanded in custody were sentenced to imprisonment, compared to 51 per cent of those on bail; and in Bottomley's urban and rural study, of those committed for trial to higher courts, 23 per cent of those on bail were given a custodial sentence, compared to 48 per cent of those in custody, and, in cases tried summarily, 11 per cent on bail were sentenced to imprisonment compared to 87 per cent of those remanded in custody.[12]

These statistics consistently show great differences between the sentences passed on defendants who have been in custody before trial, compared with those passed on defendants who have been released on bail; the differences are greater than those found in the previous analysis of choice of plea and acquittal rates and yet, on the face of it, there would seem to be more valid 'common-sense' explanations of the relationship between bail and the chances of acquittal, than between bail and the chances of a non-custodial sentence, if convicted. An obvious explanation of the statistical *associations* that have been found would seem to be simply that many of the factors associated with the chances of receiving custodial sentences are in practice found more frequently among those defendants refused bail by magistrates, but we still await a definitive study to confirm or reject this 'explanation', in view of the fact that different researchers have reached somewhat different conclusions on this matter. For example, the most detailed examination so far of the relationship between pre-trial detention and sentence was the analysis of 732 felony cases in New York City carried out by Rankin during 1961–2; in this sample, 64 per cent of the offenders in custody before trial were sentenced to imprisonment compared to only 17 per cent of those who had been remanded on bail.[13] A complex analysis of the data was carried out, controlling many different factors likely to be related to custodial sentences, but none of the factors, individually or in combination, was found to account for the large proportion of custody cases sentenced to imprisonment: for example, controlling the effect of previous criminal record, Rankin found that 59 per cent of first offenders who were in custody were sentenced to imprisonment, compared to only 10 per cent of the first offenders who were on bail, and conversely, 81 per cent of those with previous records who were in custody were sentenced to imprisonment, compared to 36 per cent of those who were on bail.[14] Bottomley's analysis of his sample, according to similar factors, revealed a rather different finding with regard to the influence of previous criminal record on the bail decision and the eventual sentences passed on remanded offenders: the effect of controlling the influence of the previous criminal record was to reduce considerably the gap between the proportions on bail and in custody who received custodial sentences and in one instance (although involving small numbers) to reverse the association, so that only 25 per cent of persons committed for trial in custody with *no previous convictions* were sentenced to imprisonment, compared to 47 per cent of persons committed on bail, with no previous convictions.[15]

Until a more definitive study is carried out, judgement about the possible reasons for the refusal of bail having a direct impact upon the chances of a convicted offender receiving a custodial sentence must be based on a balanced assessment of the available statistics set against the reasons which have been put forward to provide a possible *causal* link. The main suggestions from researchers in the United States have been (a) the detrimental effect that a loss of employment (during a remand in custody) might have on an accused's chance of being put on probation, and (b) the likely prejudice created by the defendant's appearance in court in the custody of police or prison officers.[16] These suggestions do not seem particularly convincing, at least in an English context, and it seems much more likely that when magistrates decide to grant or refuse bail to particular defendants they take into consideration very similar factors to those which will be taken into account in the sentencing decision, thus 'explaining' any statistical association which may be found in subsequent analyses. This guarded scepticism about some of the statistical studies carried out in America is not intended to detract from the impressive achievements of the bail reform movement in the United States during the 1960s, which derived much impetus from these same studies, but it is believed that much needed reform can equally derive from a consideration of the personal and social harm caused by unnecessary remanding in custody before trial, as from an apparently more objective statistical approach to this particular problem.

Notes

1. C. Foote *et al*. 'Compelling appearance in court: administration of bail in Philadelphia' *U. Pa. L. Rev.* **102** (1954) p. 1031 and Table 1 at 1052.

2. J. W. Roberts and J. S. Palermo 'A study of the administration of bail in New York' *U. Pa. L. Rev.* **106** (1958) pp. 685, at 727 and Table 16.
3. ibid., p. 726 and Table 15.
4. M. L. Friedland, *Detention Before Trial.* (University of Toronto, 1965) pp. 112ff.
5. C. Davies 'Pre-trial imprisonment: a Liverpool study' *Brit. Jo. Crim.* **11** (1971) p. 32.
6. A. K. Bottomley *Prison Before Trial* (Bell, London, 1971) p. 33. The Home Office's estimates for the proportion of persons committed for trial in England and Wales during 1957 who pleaded not guilty were 29 per cent of those on bail, of whom 46 per cent were acquitted, and 19 per cent of those in custody, of whom just 21 per cent were acquitted: see E. Gibson *Time Spent Awaiting Trial* (H.M.S.O. London, 1960) p. 13 and Table 11.
7. *Report on the Work of the Prison Department for 1970* Table C1: of the untried prisoners received in 1970, 45 per cent were not returned to custody after conviction, including 5 per cent who were acquitted.
8. Foote *et al.* op. cit., pp. 1031ff. at 1053.
9. Roberts and Palermo op. cit. p. 727.
10. Friedland op. cit. Table XIII.A p. 120.
11. Gibson, op. cit. Table 8. p. 11 and Table 28. p. 28.
12. Bottomley, op. cit., Table 6 p. 37.
13. A. Rankin 'The effect of pre-trial detention' *N. Y. U. L. Rev.* **39** (1964) p. 641.
14. ibid., Table 3 at p. 647.
15. Bottomley, op. cit., Table 6 p. 37.
16. See Foote *et al.* op. cit. p. 1053; see also the comments by Patricia Wald in her introduction to Anne Rankin's New York study, 'Pre-trial detention and ultimate freedom: a statistical study' *N. Y. U. L. Rev.* **39** (1964) pp. 631 at p. 635.

7. Bail Bargaining and Plea Bargaining

by A. E. BOTTOMS and J. D. McCLEAN

Reprinted, with permission, in abridged form, from *Defendants in the Criminal Process* (Routledge & Kegan Paul, 1976), pp. 118–30, 200–3.

'Innocent' Guilty Pleas?

Much public concern is rightly aroused when a man or woman is found to have been wrongly convicted through mistaken identification, etc. Equally, many in high places have become alarmed at the number of professional criminals who are not being convicted because, it is said, the rules of criminal procedure are weighted in their favour.

Another group where the outcome of the trial may be unjust, but which has occasioned little public discussion, are those who plead guilty although they claim innocence. In the nature of the case, this group – having pleaded guilty – is in a weak position to make subsequent protest; but if it exists, we should clearly know about it.

In the academic literature there are at least two previous examinations of this issue. In the USA, Blumberg (1967, pp 90–4) examined the statements made by guilty plea defendants in response to the probation officer's opening question (in a social inquiry interview), namely, 'Are you guilty of the crime to which you pleaded?' According to Blumberg's classification of the answers (and assuming, as he is unprepared to do, that 'fatalistic' answers represent guilt), then no fewer than 51.6 per cent declared their innocence after pleading guilty. Subsequent questioning indicated that the defence lawyer, and not the police, was the agent most responsible for this astonishing result.

As we shall discuss shortly in relation to plea bargaining, there are special features of the American criminal justice system which make 'bargain justice' more probable, and we certainly cannot transplant Blumberg's findings to England without careful investigation. The only

English work to consider 'innocent guilty pleas' systematically is Dell's (1971) rather special study of inmates of Holloway Prison. She found 56 cases, or 12 per cent of women in the prison who had been tried at magistrates' courts, who were 'inconsistent pleaders' in the sense that they pleaded guilty while believing themselves innocent of all the charges preferred against them. But one would be unwise to generalise from this sample: apart from the special features of the population (female, incarcerated, with a high proportion there on remand for psychiatric reports), one-third of the 'inconsistent pleaders' were charged with soliciting, a rather special offence against which (as Dell notes) it is peculiarly difficult for a professional prostitute to defend herself, however innocent she may be.

In our sample we separated off those who had pleaded guilty to any offence for which their statement of the facts in the interview seemed to us to raise a credible possibility of a not guilty plea. This is a wider definition than Dell's since she excluded both (i) 'those who denied some offences while admitting to others', and (ii) all those who believed themselves (even if wrongly) legally guilty although morally innocent. It is arguably also a wider definition than Blumberg's, since his defendants seem (he is regrettably unclear on the point) definitely to have asserted innocence, and some of ours did not go as far as this.

We have to make clear that we have excluded those cases where the defendant's statement rules out any hope of a legal defence (e.g. taking milk off a step and drinking it, where the defendant knew it was wrong but didn't think it was theft). We must also make plain that we are not saying we would ourselves, as legal advisers, have counselled a not guilty plea in all these cases, e.g. where the defendant had signed a confession which he now disowned, or where police and complainant's evidence seemed to be heavily against the defendant. We are saying, however, that these are cases which, if the defendant's post-trial version is correct, are quite possibly mistaken convictions.

Using this definition, 18 per cent of our guilty plea defendants had at least one charge which came into the category of 'possibly innocent'. This is well below Blumberg's figure, but higher than Dell's. . . .

Dell found that lack of legal representation was associated with 'inconsistent pleading', but our results give no support to that view — it will be seen that the only unrepresented category have the lowest rate of 'possibly innocent'. It may be thought surprising that lawyers will acquiesce in this kind of plea, but the following cases illustrate the kinds of reasons why they do:

Case 1043 (handling charge) 'I didn't know the goods were stolen — the evidence showed I should have known. It wasn't till later I knew they were stolen, though I suppose looking back I realised they were cheap — cheaper than they should have been. On solicitor's advice I pleaded guilty.'

Case 1069 B's brother had bought a house, and they went to look at it together. A three-piece suite had been left behind in it, and B's brother said B could have it. He took it, and then the police came round and accused him of stealing it from the original owners. Frightened, he denied having the suite, and later hid it, though it was found. The solicitor strongly advised a guilty plea — he said hiding it would look as if B had stolen it, and this couldn't be explained away.

We calculated the reasons why our 'possibly innocents' had pleaded guilty to the particular charges in question, and these are shown in Table 1. It will be seen that the foremost reason is legal advice, and in this respect our findings are similar to Blumberg's. It is apparent that English lawyers like American ones sometimes consider that the best interests of their clients are to be served by submission to a guilty plea rather than by fighting the charge; and in doing so they are undoubtedly partly motivated by the knowledge that heavier penalties may follow an unsuccessful plea of not guilty based on relatively weak foundations. By this deterrent threat, the bureaucracy of the legal system is enabled to keep not guilty pleas to an administratively acceptable level.

It will be recalled that those pleading guilty are on the whole younger and of lower social class than the not guilty pleas. We hypothesised that among our 'possibly innocents' there would be an unusually high proportion of young and of lower social class, and that the difference between them and those who actually pleaded not guilty was one of greater social confidence in pressing their innocence. The data showed no support whatever for this hypothesis; the 'possibly innocents' were not significantly different from other guilty plea defendants on either variable, and what trends there were were not in the direction hypothesised. We also found no difference between the groups in the proportion previously convicted; our negative findings in all these respects are similar to Dell's (at p 31). . . .

TABLE 1. *Reasons for pleas of guilty among 'possibly innocent' defendants.*

	% of defendants
On lawyer's advice	34
Thought it was legally wrong	16
Get it over/avoid delay	14
Police pressure/induced confession, etc.	9
Not worth challenging police	8
Too trivial to fight	5
Would be found guilty, get heavier sentence	5
Others	12

Plea Bargaining and Plea Changing

. . . The only study of the plea-bargaining phenomenon in England is that by the Oxford University Penal Research Unit (McCabe and Purves, 1972). This was a study of 90 cases, involving 112 defendants, in which the defendant had been sent for trial in the higher court and had been listed as likely to plead not guilty but at the last moment changed his mind and entered a guilty plea. Of the 112 defendants, 48 pleaded guilty to all charges, and 64 'had an arrangement of pleas accepted by the court'. In these cases there would be discussions with prosecuting counsel and usually with the judge, but the study gives no indication of the extent of such discussions. Its finding is that in most, if not all cases, a change of plea:

> followed after the defendant received 'certain good advice' from his legal representatives. This is especially the case with late or last-minute changes of plea where counsel, after reviewing his brief and assessing the evidence, speaks urgently to solicitor and defendant in a conference held, in all too many cases, immediately before the trial is due to start [McCabe and Purves, 1972, p. 9]

The Oxford study did not interview defendants, but felt able to say from its data (mainly prosecution papers) that the typical defendants involved were those with previous criminal experience, who 'generally approach plea-bargaining with much the same spirit of realism and practicality which characterises the approach of the police, the lawyers and the judge' [McCabe and Purves, 1972, p 45].

Our definitions of terms, and our scope of study, differ a little from those of McCabe and Purves. They distinguished two kinds of plea-bargaining: (i) involving a judge's intimation as to sentence, which they regarded as virtually dead since R. *v.* Turner, and (ii) 'discussions and negotiations which culminate in the defendant's decision to plead guilty . . . defence counsel, having examined his brief, conferred with his instructing solicitor and sometimes with the prosecution, gives the defendant the advantage of his advice'. We prefer to distinguish between 'plea bargaining', embracing their first category and such of their second category as involve bargains or negotiations with the prosecution; and on the other hand 'plea changing', or late changes of plea, usually but not always induced by the lawyer, but without apparent consultation with the prosecution. All our data in both these respects are restricted to the interview sample.

In considering 'plea bargaining', we excluded cases of 'alternative charges', for example theft and handling stolen goods in which charges are of approximately equal gravity, and represent different interpretations of the same facts. In such cases the defendant minded to plead guilty will usually select the lesser charge, and the prosecution is very ready to accept that plea and the not guilty plea to the other alternative. This is not a situation in which the double charge puts any pressure on the defendant to bargain; it seems not to require further examination in that connection. That leaves us with 3 cases of apparently 'real' plea-bargaining in our interview sample, but only in the first of these was the defendant openly offered a bargain by his counsel:

Case 7034   T was a company director, aged 47. He was active in his social life, a Freemason (he complained that one prosecution witness gave evidence 'in Masonic form, to lend more credibility to his answers'), and lived in a comfortable suburb. He faced 15 counts alleging theft, forgery of cheques and falsification of records, part of a complicated series of steps involving tax evasion, false accounts, deception of shareholders in his company, etc. His first interviews with the police were five months before his first appearance in court; he was not tried in the Crown Court until a further eleven months had elapsed. On the morning of the Crown Court appearance he was offered what he described as a 'deal': if he would plead guilty to 2 counts, 13 would be dropped. He refused — 'I wasn't prepared to do any deal and I told my counsel so.' He was convicted (after a five-day trial) on 13 charges, and received a total of 21 months' imprisonment; he subsequently thought that if he had accepted the deal he might have got a suspended sentence.

Case 4042   W was charged with (i) burglary, (ii) assault occasioning actual bodily harm and (iii) an alternative charge of assault. Right up to the morning of the Crown Court trial (i.e. ten weeks from his first appearance) he had every intention of pleading not guilty to the second and third charges on the grounds of self-defence. Just before the trial, his barrister came into the cell and according to W said he 'had to' plead guilty: 'Your statement says you are technically guilty and there's no point in pleading self-defence.' W agreed, reluctantly; the prosecution then dropped the 'actual bodily harm' charge and W pleaded guilty to the lesser charge of common assault.

Case 4041   The defendant was charged with theft of steel, and obtaining by deception, both charges being in respect of mismanagement of his own business affairs. His barrister came to see him a week before the trial and said he would make a bad witness, there was not enough evidence, and he should plead guilty and 'cut his losses'. He saw him again just before the trial and said, 'If you plead guilty you will get 18 months, if you plead not guilty you're bound to be found guilty and will get 3 years.' In sentencing the defendant to a total 18 months' imprisonment, the judge said, 'You are a wise man to plead guilty and have been soundly advised. If you had been convicted by a jury you would serve your suspended sentence (12 months) plus 2 years. But I take heavily into account your plea of guilty. . . . ' The defendant noted that the barrister's and the judge's statements were identical and strongly believed that his trial was 'a charade, with plea and sentence already decided'. He noted that although he had not finally decided on a guilty plea until 10 a.m. on the morning of the trial, no prosecution witnesses seemed to be available, and one such witness who had previously been his employee said that he had not been called.

TABLE 2. *Reasons for plea-changing (higher court cases).*

	%
Barrister's last-minute advice	68
Solicitor's advice during remand	14
Own last-minute decision	11
Influence of girlfriend or probation officer	7
Total	100

In none of the 3 cases do we have firm proof of plea-bargaining, but in each case there seems to be strong hints of the phenomenon.

Turning then to plea-changing, we could monitor this matter only at the higher court level (there are formidable difficulties in doing so at the magistrates' court level in view of the small time involved in many cases). Unlike McCabe and Purves, we did not have access to lists of court business specifying cases as 'likely not guilty pleas'; we must therefore construct the plea-changing sample from retrospective interview material. This we may not have done with complete success. . .

Making appropriate allowances for the differential sampling fraction, we get a pattern of reasons for plea-changing as shown in Table 2.

. . . These cases illustrate the decisive effect of legal advice in most plea changing. In this connection, we noted one feature of special interest. Fifty-four per cent of the plea change defendants (as reweighted) were represented by one particular barrister, who had only 16 per cent of the total caseload of the Bar in our interview sample. This barrister often seemingly gave last-minute advice in very strong terms: cases 4041 and 4042, above, are examples of this, while in another case he is said to have told a defendant that if he struck out for a not guilty plea he could get 7 years' imprisonment and his family (who were to give evidence for him) could be convicted of perjury. It is true that leading cases have stressed that counsel's duty is to press a plea change on his client in strong terms if he deems this necessary (see R. *v.* Turner, (1970) 54 Cr. App. R.352; R. *v.* Hall [1968] 52 Crim. App. R. 528); but it is obvious from the Sheffield experience that different counsel may interpret this duty in different ways. It may be relevant to record that the particular barrister in question had a 100 per cent record in contested trials during the research period, i.e. he won all those cases where he did not persuade the defendant to change his plea.

Finally, we have to record that defendants – including defendants with previous convictions – do not always respond to plea changing advice as happily and as 'realistically' as McCabe and Purves have suggested from their documentary study. True, in the majority of the cases the defendants were satisfied with having accepted the advice. But in just over a quarter of the cases they remained in one way or another unhappy about it, and in one or two cases felt very bitter indeed. Nor is this particularly surprising. Remembering the figures on the delay in handling Crown Court business, one realises that these defendants have for many weeks expected to plead not guilty. This intention has been supported by their solicitor – after all, a trained professional. Then, out of nowhere appears a barrister, usually on the morning of the trial, strongly suggesting a change of plea. It is hardly surprising if defendants acquiesce, faced with this predicament; it is also hardly surprising if some of them subsequently resent having acquiesced to last-minute pressure. The Bar could do its image some good if it resolved to see defendants some time in advance if any question of plea changing arises, so that a calmer decision may be made by the defendant. . . .

Bail or Custody before First Court Appearance

[It] emerged with disturbing clarity and consistency in quite a number of the interviews that the natural police wish to secure a conviction apparently very much enters into the bail-granting process. What we can legitimately call 'bail bargaining', that is the bargaining of the police power to release against the defendant's reluctance to capitulate, certainly exists, as a considerable number of cases made clear.

Case 1001   E was arrested at 10 p.m. on a Saturday night, having been found in a warehouse by a police-dog patrol. He said he was then interrogated until 3 a.m. on the Sunday morning, and held in custody until court on the Monday morning (when he was dealt with straight away and sentenced to imprisonment). During this interrogation period, 'They told me if I told them of anyone who had "knocked off stuff", they would release me on bail.'

Case 1093   A police constable saw two men pushing an old pram; it contained lead. At the police station: 'They said, if you don't tell us the truth you can't have bail. Then I made a statement admitting it, then I got bail.'

Case 6044 D, a scrap metal dealer, accustomed to a middle-class life-style, was charged with 4 counts of handling stolen metals. He was interviewed by the police, made a statement, and was then released on bail: 'They only released me when I made a statement, and they weren't going to release me until I did. The police wrote the statement for me.

One could multiply case examples, but there is little point in doing so. Quite clearly this kind of 'bail bargaining' is important in some cases, and we were able to identify a specific complaint of it in a total of 7 per cent of all the cases, without having asked a direct question about it. In a considerable number of other cases, other threats of custody (not allied to a specific bargain) were identified; and from some of these cases it would seem that even where the police have in fact no real intention of using custody, they will nevertheless use the threat of custody in a veiled way, by light-heartedly joking about it, to establish mastery over the defendant in the charge office situation. One defendant was able to see through this strategy and deal with it: 'they kidded me about keeping me in custody, but I told them to stop acting like Morecambe and Wise.'

Obviously ours is a very indirect study of the bail bargaining phenomenon, and for an adequate piece of research one needs to get inside the charge room itself. The police view and the legal view of bail may be poles apart in many cases, but it is the police view which in practice tends to dominate in the courts. This adds weight to the argument against courts' attaching importance to the objection that 'further inquiries have to be made'; at worst, this could degenerate into 'further pressure needs to be put on the defendant to get him to sign a statement'. . . .

References

Blumberg, A. S. (1967) *Criminal Justice* (Quadrangle Books).
Dell, S. (1971) *Silent in Court* (Bell).
McCabe, S. and Purves, R. (1972) *By-Passing the Jury* (Basil Blackwell).

8. Negotiations Between the Defendant and the Police

by P. LAURIE

Reprinted, with permission, from *Scotland Yard* (Penguin Books, 1972) pp. 215–19.

Plea of Guilty

Although the courts are central to the detective's life, he does not particularly want to have to fight his cases there. He prefers the accused to plead guilty, the procedure in court to be amiable and automatic. The layman tends, perhaps, to think of the typical trial as a contest, a forensic battle between good and evil. In reality, the situation is rather different. In terms of figures, not-guilty pleas are rare, and it becomes apparent that the smooth — or indeed any sort of — working of the police and the courts is completely dependent on a high rate of guilty pleas.[1]

The argument is this. The CID in London initiate some 70,000 prosecutions a year for indictable offences. All but three per cent are heard in Magistrates' Courts,[2] and it is thought that ninety per cent or more of these are settled by a plea of guilty, though the exact figure is not known. In the higher courts — Sessions and Assizes — the rate of guilty pleas falls to seventy-five per cent, but even so, the police have only to fight some 7,000-odd cases a year. It is difficult to say how much work these cause. A recent study of police manpower was unable to separate the work involved in preparing cases from that needed to detect criminals[3] but it would not be unreasonable to say that every contested case involves a detective in an average of two weeks' extra work.

This is not surprising when one considers that he has to find and

91

persuade witnesses, take two sets of statements from them – one for police use, one for committal proceedings – write a report on the case, complete some thirteen forms on the prisoner, complete legal aid forms, take charge of recovered property and eventually return it to the owners, appear three or four times in court to ask for remands. And against the large number of easy cases, one also has to set, say, the gang trials, which each occupied 100 detectives for over a year.

To see how the not guilty plea rate affects detective's work load, let us suppose that the rate in *all* courts rises to twenty-five per cent. To cope with the extra work, some 200–400 more detectives are needed. Since none of these are forthcoming, each existing detective's work is increased by one-seventh to one-third. Bearing in mind that detectives in London already work 116 hours a week,[4] it is evident that a *small* increase in the not guilty plea rate imposes a very *large* burden on them.

This analysis is so crude that it can only illustrate a qualitative relationship. It is none the less real for that. One might imagine that, as in all living systems, some sort of dynamic equilibrium exists, that the actual level of not guilty pleas is set by a process of give and take, of tacit bargaining between accuser and accused – which the courts abet. It is almost too much to dignify this process with the name 'negotiation'. Experienced criminals and experienced detectives know the factors involved so well that there is probably seldom any need for formal, verbal bargaining, but the understood object is to find a level at which the seriousness of the charge, the punishment to be expected, the burden on the detective, balance out to produce a solution acceptable to all parties, expressed as a guilty plea.

As one experienced detective sergeant said:

'You're supposed to report all conversations with the prisoner – well, who does? This is your moment. I have long chats with them about all sorts of things. He might have someone he wants to hand the poison to – if I treat him right he could ring up when he gets out. I'll willingly do deals if he'll be a man and plead – it saves me days of desk-work, writing reports, doing legal-aid forms, rounding up witnesses, going to court every week until the trial comes up – and I'll not put in the poison about him when I'm asked. This may sound very shocking, but what's more use to society: me tied down for a couple of weeks getting him a couple of months more on his sentence, or the whole thing over in a day, a happy informant, me out catching more thieves, and perhaps a string of arrests in the future?'

The elaboration of the law means that almost any criminal action can be 'interpreted' to the court as one of several named crimes. Thus a man arrested for attacking another could be charged with either attempted murder, causing grievous bodily harm, or common assault. Each is easier for the detective to prove, but each carries a lower sentence. He might feel doubtful about attempted murder, but confident of proving grievous bodily harm, and ask the prisoner to plead guilty to that. The prisoner, on the other hand, might feel that it was too good a bargain as it stood. He might insist on being paid something extra in the small change of these negotiations — that the detective should speak well of his character. So perhaps a deal is made.

From the layman's point of view, an unexpected corollary of the high guilty plea rate is that the *contested* trial which we have come to know from innumerable representations in courtroom dramas, on film and television, is completely atypical. In the vast majority of cases, the real trial is conducted privately and informally between the detective and the accused in the privacy of a cell, or crouched in the court hall; the decision which they come to is then quickly rubber-stamped by the court, whose only real function is to pass sentence. Some courts encourage this by tacitly giving lower sentences to those who cooperate. The bonus can be impressive — one of the Great Train Robbers who pleaded guilty got fifteen years as against his colleagues' thirty.

Even when the charge is of murder, the 'trial' following a plea of guilty consists of no more than a brief résumé of the circumstances of the offence and the passing of sentence. In less serious cases the whole business can literally be over in five minutes. One begins to see why it is important to policemen that their villains should plead. The investigation has often been hard enough work and the large amount extra needed to ensure conviction is to them so much unnecessary effort. In the long run, every plea of not guilty is a threat to the detective's precariously balanced work-load.

Then the detective's *amour-propre* is involved. A guilty plea recognizes the rightness of his case, the soundness of his judgement. The detective knows that the man is guilty — or else he wouldn't have arrested him — and a guilty plea shows a proper recognition of the fact. It gives the detective the initiative in his dealings, he can be lenient, agree to bail, put in a good word — and the prisoner becomes to some extent a collaborator. The detective is as much a prisoner of the judicial process as the man he arrests. A guilty plea unties his hands, and helps create a good relationship between them.

As well as saving him a great deal of physical work, the guilty plea relieves him of a lot of worry and thought. His witnesses may be weak — perhaps a feeble-minded girl, the victim, is his only witness of a sexual assault. She could be useless in cross-examination. It is like entering a horse for a race, and being given the blue rosette before you've saddled up.

Also, a plea pulls down the curtain on all past transactions. No questions can arise about the information that led to the arrest, about the arrest itself. There can be no complaints about the arresting officer's behaviour and no haggling over the Judges' Rules.

Notes

1. See also J. Skolnick *Justice Without Trial* (Wiley, 1966).
2. *Time Spent Awaiting Trial,* Home Office (HMSO, 1960).
3. J. P. Martin and G. Wilson, *The Police: A Study in Manpower* (Heinemann, 1969), p. 147.
4. Martin and Wilson, op. cit.

9. Plea Negotiation in England

by J. L. HEBERLING

Reprinted, with permission, from 'Conviction without Trial',
Anglo-American Law Review (1973), pp. 439–47.

The English Approach

Guilty pleas comprise between 80 and 90 per cent of total convictions
in both England and America. Thus the differences in Anglo-American
process lie not in the quantity of guilty pleas but in the manner of
securing them. Within the English system there are sharp differences in
the guilty plea process as it occurs before the crown court and the
magistrates' courts.

Crown Court Practice

Because almost all defendants before the crown court are represented,
and because there is a high incidence of negotiated pleas of guilty, it
may be said that the guilty plea process in the crown court resembles
that of the American courts. Still, two basic differences emerge. First,
the bargaining between English prosecution and defence counsel tends
to be episodal, rather than the result of considerable manoeuvring and
negotiating as in the United States. Secondly, plea agreements in
England do not focus on direct sentence commitments, because the
prosecutor by convention does not directly influence the sentence.
Instead, reduction of the level of the charge is the aim. For most major
offences there is a lesser included offence to which the defendant can
enter a plea, avoiding the consequences of conviction of the more
serious charge. Alternatively a lesser charge may be expressly joined to
the major charge. If the charge is one of causing grievous bodily harm
with intent (OAPA 1861, s.18), the defendant may plead to malicious
wounding (OAPA 1861, s.20). Similarly, dangerous driving when tried

summarily may be reduced by substituting a charge of careless driving; stealing may be reduced to handling, and indecent assault may be reduced to simple assault.

Plea negotiations tend to occur in the hallway outside the courtroom on the day set for trial.[1] The trial judge is informed of the result in court, the prosecutor proposing to offer no evidence on the major charge. Occasionally the discussion may be carried to the judge's chambers.[2] The court is not bound by an agreement between the prosecution and the defence,[3] but if the court accepts the plea to the lesser offence the sentence imposed must be appropriate to this offence, not the greater offence originally charged.[4] The defendant is technically acquitted on his plea of not guilty.[5] Alternatively certain charges or counts may be left to lie on the file. The defendant is not required to answer these charges. Theoretically they may later serve as the basis of proceedings against the defendant, but this is rarely done.

In spite of the fact that there is considerably less delay between arrest and trial in England, plea arrangements tend to be delayed until the day of trial because barristers often are not briefed until shortly before trial. In this sense the English division of the legal profession hinders the efficiency of criminal justice, because each time a calendared case is settled on the day set for trial court time goes idle.[6] A mechanism for settlement of criminal cases before final calendaring would result in considerable savings.

The fraternal nature of the English bar creates an atmosphere conducive to plea negotiations. There is generally more reasonableness in attitude towards a given case, since both sides retain barristers from a common pool. English plea bargaining has been described as a 'delicate mutual back scratching system'.[7] As in America there is the danger that counsel will settle cases in furtherance of their own interests, especially where the case is not a particularly lucrative one for one or both sides. A survey of 160 appeals conducted by Michael Zander revealed considerable superficiality of treatment by counsel in advising defendants on guilty pleas, and few of the defendants polled said they would recommend the services of the attorneys who had represented them.[8]

During plea negotiations English counsel have before them much more of the relevant case evidence than their American counterparts. In crown court cases, the prosecution evidence has already been presented at committal. Additional evidence is not admissible at trial unless the defence has had prior opportunity to examine it.[9] Similarly, if the defence intends to present an alibi it must notify the prosecution in advance.[10]

Another subject of charge bargaining between the prosecution and the defence is offences 'taken into consideration'. By convention, the defendant may offer to have other criminal transactions of a similar nature 'taken into consideration' at sentencing. An offence 't.i.c.' does not rank as a conviction,[11] but does constitute an admission of guilt in the offence.[12] 'T.i.c.'s' provide the police with solutions to crimes; they avoid trial, and even avoid the necessity of preparing formal charges against the defendant. It is clear from reported cases that 't.i.c.'s' may be the subject of plea negotiations.[13] But the extent to which this occurs, like so many questions in the guilty plea practice, remains speculative.

Guilty Pleas in the Magistrates' Courts

The represented defendant. Whether or not the defendant's solicitor intends to contact the prosecutor with a view toward a negotiated plea, the basic strategy in English guilty plea representation lies in keeping trial of the case at the magistrates' court level. Only a select few indictable offences are not triable summarily (e.g., murder, rape and aggravated burglary).[14] All other indictable offences may be tried summarily with consent of the accused and (in practice) the prosecution. In the vast majority of cases, the defence can succeed in keeping the case at the magistrates' court level through the defendant's consent to summary trial. Only 13 per cent of all defendants proceeded against in the magistrates' courts for indictable offences in 1971 were committed for trial before the higher courts.[15] The defence objective in obtaining summary trial is to limit the range of penalties the defendant may receive. Regardless of the statutory limits of the offence for which the defendant is convicted, the sentencing powers of the magistrates are limited (in the case of indictable offences tried summarily) to the imposition of two consecutive six-month terms of imprisonment for two separate offences.[16] More importantly, disposition of the case at the magistrates' level secures a *de facto* sentence-discount for the defendant. For any given offence, the defendant is likely to receive a significantly more lenient sentence from a magistrates' court than from the crown court. In the case of a first offender there is a further benefit from summary proceedings. Except where conviction is for violence to the person,[17] the magistrates may not imprison a first offender unless the magistrates commit the defendant for sentencing to the crown court.[18] The risk of committal for sentence is even lower than that of committal for trial. In 1971 only four per cent of all defendants convicted of indictable offences in the magistrates' courts were committed for sentence to the higher courts.[19] It is likewise in the prosecution's interest to keep the case at the magistrates' court level. The cost and complexity of a case before the crown court is avoided and the likelihood of conviction is substantially increased if the case is heard before the magistrates. The aquittal rate in contested cases before the crown court has been observed as 43 per cent,[20] whereas the acquittal rate in contested cases before the magistrates' courts may be estimated at between 7 and 14 per cent.[21] Thus we see that just as the defence strategy in guilty plea representation is keeping the case at the magistrates' level, often defence strategy in a contested case is to elevate the case to the crown court level to take advantage of the presence of the jury and the greater likelihood of acquittal.

If the defendant's solicitor wishes to reduce further the defendant's risk of imprisonment, at some time before the magistrates' hearing he will contact the police officer or prosecuting solicitor in charge of the case with a view toward a negotiated plea. The general procedure is that already stated for the crown court.

One disability for the defence in negotiating a plea at the magistrates' court level is that the prosecution's evidence has not yet been publicly examined. The defendant is not entitled to see the information before committal, and the defendant's right to notice is limited to 'such particulars as may be necessary for giving reasonable information of the nature of the charge'.[22] Occasionally there is an exchange of evidence if the defendant's solicitor has the favour of the prosecutor, but generally the defence must bargain in the dark.

Sometimes the magistrates' clerk is notified of a plea agreement between the prosecution and the defence, but the justices themselves receive no advance notice.[23] This has led to the charge by one magistrate, Dr E. Anthony, that 'the police are using magistrates merely to endorse a pre-made conviction without letting the court have any powers of adjudication'.[24] However, it would appear from my own observation of the Cambridge magistrates' court that the magistrates are often aware of the case settlement process, and concur in it. When a defendant appears before the magistrates represented by a solicitor, and the prosecutor offers no evidence on certain of the charges, the signal is fairly clear that a plea agreement has been reached. To a significant extent Dr Anthony is right, since the magistrates have little control over the settlement process which takes place before the case ever reaches the courtroom. Neither the plea agreement nor the fact of its existence is mentioned at the hearing.

The unrepresented defendant. Only about a quarter of defendants who appear before magistrates' courts are professionally represented.[25] The absence of a defender who knows the sequence of events in a criminal prosecution and who understands the informal rules of local practice has a profound effect on the manner in which the guilty plea process operates. One of the most interesting aspects of legal assistance in England is that the defendant usually must carry his case forward to the point of pleading not guilty before a magistrates' court before legal assistance is afforded. If an unrepresented defendant pleads not guilty, the hearing is often adjourned so that the defendant may apply for legal aid. Such applications are usually granted. However, if the unrepresented defendant enters a plea of guilty before the magistrates, and then applies for legal aid before being sentenced, he is usually denied.[26] Only about 10 per cent of defendants are represented at their first appearance before the magistrates.[27] This first hearing may or may not proceed beyond the question of bail to a reading of the charge and the defendant's plea, depending on whether the prosecution is ready to try the case. Mrs Dell found that where the hearing proceeded to the point of the defendant's plea, only 14 per cent of the defendants who pleaded guilty were represented.[28] Among defendants who pleaded not guilty 50 per cent ultimately obtained legal assistance. Mrs Dell did not divide the represented defendants who pleaded not guilty into those who were represented when they first entered their pleas and those who were not at first represented but were subsequently granted legal aid for their summary trial or committal proceeding. But from two other analyses prepared by Mrs Dell the substantial effect of prior representation upon the defendant's plea can be seen. Of the 106 defendants in the Holloway study who denied guilt at their interviews, 78 had had no legal aid before entering their pleas.[29] Of this group two-thirds entered pleas of guilty. Of the 22 defendants who had had attorney assistance before pleading only three entered pleas of guilty. The unrepresented defendants were six times as likely to plead guilty as the represented ones. In a separate survey of defendants appearing before the London magistrates' courts, Mrs Dell found that 60 per cent of the represented as compared with 6 per cent of the unrepresented pleaded not guilty.[30] From the above it may be concluded that the plea has an effect on representation, since defendants who plead not guilty are more likely to be granted aid, and that representation has an effect on the plea, since defendants with aid are more likely to plead not guilty.

The defendant who appears before the magistrates unrepresented is pretty helpless. He does not know what to expect, nor does he fully appreciate the significance of what does occur. He stands as the magistrates enter, yet he is addressed not by them but by someone sitting below and in front of them (the magistrates' clerk). Defendants often do not pay full attention to all that is said, and rarely do they interrupt the proceedings for a repetition of words that were inaudible or whose meaning was not understood. Most defendants have little education, are scared and are unable to express themselves in the kind of language they believe is expected in court.[31] With little active participation by the defendant, the magistrates' hearing can proceed from stage to stage rather quickly. At the close, after the defendant has pleaded guilty or been convicted, he is usually asked, 'Have you anthing to say?' At this critical point, when mitigating circumstances should be put before the court, the defendant often seems to think that the response expected is a short statement like 'I'm sorry'. Few defendants are encouraged to talk about the circumstances of their lives or the crime they committed. Many defendants simply want to 'get it over', and are allowed or encouraged to do so by the police and the courts. The whole arrest to conviction process can take place in 24 hours. The defendant has a right to bail or traduction before the magistrates within 24 hours after arrest,[32] and often if the police have obtained a statement from the defendant beforehand they can get a guilty plea conviction at this single magistrates' hearing[33]. The fact that most English defendants who plead guilty are unrepresented means that there is little real adjudication in the guilty plea process. The ideology of the common law pre-supposes an adversary proceeding, with each side presenting its case before a Judge who is more an arbiter than an active participant in the proceeding. At many points the onus is on the defendant to move affirmatively in his own defence. It takes a strong-willed defendant to make the truth-seeking process work. If the defendant surrenders and consents to conviction, there is little inquiry into the facts of the crime.

To some extent the police negotiate guilty pleas with defendants. The 1962 Royal Commission on the Police accepted the evidence presented by the Law Society and the National Association of Probation Officers that occasionally the police advise defendants to plead guilty, or offer to 'put in a good word' before the court, or otherwise suggest that leniency will follow co-operation with the authorities.[34] Of Mrs Dell's 56 'inconsistent pleaders' (those pleading guilty but later denying guilt), 17 said their guilty pleas were the result of police advice or pressure, 8 said there was no point in defending the case where it was only 'my word against the police', 5 said they entered pleas to avoid remands, and another 5 pleaded guilty in fear of a harsher sentence after trial.[35] Often such advice is given in fatherly tones, and the pressure to co-operate is more subtle than threatening.[36] Studies of police inquiries show a high degree of informality between the police and defendants, and much dialogue between them.[37] Where the defendant is unrepresented and has questions concerning what will take place in court, or what will be the probable consequences of his plea, it is natural that he address these questions to the police, especially where he is in the process of co-operating with them. It is not surprising that the police should hint that leniency will follow a plea of guilty, since this is what generally happens. It may seem only fair to the officer that the defendant should know this. It is also rather natural for the police to advise defendants to plead guilty, since they feel that evidence sufficient to charge is sufficient to convict. The police tend to be more interested in solving crimes than running the legal gauntlet to conviction. Their investigatory resources are limited, and the guilty plea is tailored to their needs. Even better suited to the investigatory needs of the police is the offence 't.i.c.'. Here it is fairly clear that the initiative is generally taken by the police.[38] Often the defendant signs a form before appearing in magistrates' court. So when the clerk notes that the defendant has asked that certain offences be taken into consideration it is hardly a spontaneous process.[39]

Instead of relying on plea negotiations to produce a high percentage of guilty pleas, the English prosecution generally relies more heavily on what may be characterized as 'defeat of the defendant'. The defendant who contests his case must be willing to risk remands which may cost him his job, the expense of contributing to the costs of his defence and a harsher sentence after trial. He must be willing to undergo the anxiety of awaiting trial, the strain on his family and the continued unpleasant relationship with the police. And in the average case the English defendant must battle forth on his own to the point of entering a plea of not guilty in magistrates' court before he is afforded legal aid. Often the result of such pressures is the 'get-it-over' syndrome. The defendant makes a statement to the police and pleads guilty to take the pressure off. This especially happens where the defendant is likely to receive a non-custodial sentence anyway. To defend his case the accused must be willing to undergo hard questioning for hours on end.[40] The extent to which the police violate the Judges Rules is problematical. For present purposes we will assume they do not. Still, the defendant is alone against sophisticated interrogators. He may be unaware that he is merely 'assisting the police with their inquires' and free to leave at any time. Even if he does request permission to ring a solicitor, often the police refuse.[41] From the moment the defendant arrives at the police station he is faced with the question whether or not to co-operate with the authorities. Many of the pressures on him are inherent in the process; others are subtly applied by his interrogators; but from the beginning the message is clear: 'Things will be better for you if you co-operate with us.'

Uppermost in the mind of the defendant is the urge to freedom, the desire to extricate himself from this uncomfortable situation. Few consider the long-term consequences of a decision to make a statement to the police. It is the hope or promise of release which causes defendants to co-operate. 'Co-operation' may mean either a statement by the defendant or a guilty plea. The police usually concentrate their efforts upon obtaining a statement, but for purposes of this section a statement and a guilty plea are treated as functional equivalents, since guilty pleas routinely follow the taking of a statement. To what extent do the police use their bail powers[42] to secure pleas of guilty? The Court of Appeal took judicial notice of the practice of 'bail bargaining' in R *v.* Northam.[43] An example is where an officer states to a defendant: 'If you tell me about this matter you can have bail.' The extent to which bail bargaining occurs has never been documented. However, two points are fairly clear. First, the police routinely ask for remands in custody in order to apply punitive pressure to defendants. About half of all defendants remanded in custody before trial do not return to custody after conviction.[44] Secondly, there is a correlation between remands in custody and guilty pleas. Keith Bottomley in *Prison Before Trial*, in an analysis of committals for trial, found that of the group committed in custody 61 per cent pleaded guilty, whereas of the group committed on bail only 36 per cent pleaded guilty.[45] The reason for this difference cannot be fully discussed here, but it is worth mentioning that the legal similarity of the two groups was indicated by the fact that of the defendants persisting in pleas of not guilty the acquittal rates were about the same (46 per cent and 43 per cent, respectively). The major detriment suffered by the defendant remanded in custody is that he often loses his job. He loses both the economic resources he may need to contest his case and the indicia of stability which would make him a better probation risk. If the defendant does attempt to prepare a defence from gaol, he is confronted with substantial difficulties. Among them are the inability to communicate freely with a solicitor and the inability to seek witnesses on his behalf. The end result of all these pressures, inducements and disabilities is that whether or not the defendant is guilty of the charge he feels he cannot fight back. He surrenders and enters a plea of guilty.

In the English system there is a considerable amalgamation of powers in the police. They interrogate suspects, gather evidence, make the decision on whether to charge and often conduct the prosecution before the court. Because of the relatively unchecked nature of their power there is a high risk that it may be used to defeat defendants rather than to convict them properly.[46] American police pressures and bail practices are concededly more abusive. But since virtually all defendants get minimal representation, the guilty plea process tends to rely more on plea bargaining than on defeat of the defendant as in England. One may rest assured that the vast majority of defendants in England and America who plead guilty are in fact guilty of something. Yet increasingly there is the feeling in Anglo-American legal communities that there should be more care in ensuring the accuracy of these convictions and that there should be a higher level of judicial control over the process of securing pleas of guilty.

Notes

1. Paul Thomas, 'An exploration of plea bargaining' (1969) *Crim. L. R.* pp. 69, 70; R. F. Purves, 'That plea bargaining business: some conclusions from research' (1971) *Crim. L. R.* p. 470.
2. *ibid.*, Thomas at p. 70.
3. *Bedwellty Justices, ex parte Munday* (1970) *Crim. L. R.* p. 601.
4. R *v.* Kennedy (1968) *Crim. L. R.* p. 566.
5. By the Criminal Justice Act 1972, s.17, the formal verdict of the jury need no longer be taken.
6. McCabe and Purves, *By-Passing The Jury* (Oxford Penal Research Unit, 1970) p. 32.
7. Graham Parker, 'Copping a plea', 135 J.P. 408.
8. Michael Zander, 'Legal advice and criminal appeals: a survey of prisoners, prisons and lawyers' (1972) *Crim. L.R.* p. 132.

9. Archibold, *Criminal Pleading Evidence and Practice* (37th edn. 1969), s.1377.
10. Criminal Justice Act 1967, s.11.
11. Harris, *The Criminal Jurisdiction of Magistrates* 2nd edn. (1972) p. 126; White, Newark and Samuels, 'Offences taken into consideration' (1970) *Crim. L.R.* p. 311.
12. R *v.* Marquis (1951) 115 J.P. 329.
13. R *v.* Northam (1968) 52 Cr. App. R. 97; R *v.* Jackson (1972) *Crim. L.R.* p. 325.
14. Harris, n. 11 Supra p. 28.
15. Criminal Statistics, 1971, 10.
16. Magistrates' Courts Act 1952, s.108.
17. Criminal Justice Act 1967, s.39(3); Criminal Justice Act 1972, s.14.
18. Pursuant to M.C.A. 1952, ss.28 and 29.
19. Criminal Statistics, 1971, 10–11 (11,544/282,060).
20. McCabe and Purves, n. 6 supra, p. 20.
21. Criminal Statistics, 1971, 10–11. Taking the composite male–female totals of Section (A), indictable offences tried in the magistrates' courts, and rounding all figures to the nearest thousand, we have the following. Of 350 proceeded against, 45 were committed for trial, 19 had charges withdrawn or dismissed and 282 were found guilty. This leaves 4 acquitted. If we assume a 90 per cent guilty plea rate, we have 29 pleas of not guilty (286 x 10 per cent = 29). Four acquittals in 29 summary trials yields a 14 per cent acquittal rate. If we change the assumption to a guilty plea rate of 80 per cent, we have twice the number of trials and a 7 per cent acquittal rate (4/58 = 7 per cent).
22. Magistrates' Courts Rules 1968, r.83. R *v.* Aylesbury Justices, ex parte Wisbey (1965) 1 All E.R. 602.
23. Case described in 'Plea bargaining', Dr E. Anthony, J.P., 135, *J. P. Newsp.*, p. 649.
24. ibid.
25. A. Keith Bottomley, *Prison Before Trial* (1970) p. 102, in an analysis of 148 defendants' cases before urban magistrates' courts, found that only 30 per cent were represented. Mrs Dell, *Silent in Court* (1971) p. 28, found that of 459 defendants tried in magistrates' courts only 93 were represented, a rate of 20 per cent (93/459 – excluding 68 'unknowns'). In 'Unrepresented defendants in the criminal courts' (1969) *Crim. L.R.* pp. 632, 633, Michael Zander, in an analysis of 1,141 cases in magistrates' courts, reports a representation rate of 27 per cent.
26. Dell, n. 25 supra p. 51.
27. In 'A study of bail/custody decisions in London magistrates' courts' (1971) *Crim. L.R.* pp. 191, 194, Michael Zander found that only 10 per cent of defendants were represented at their first appearance before the magistrates. Bottomley, n. 25 supra, pp. 102–03, found that 'in cases tried summarily, 11 per cent were represented as early as the remand hearing'.
28. Dell, n. 25 supra, p. 28, table 6, (53/368 – excluding 35 'unknowns').
29. ibid., p. 32.
30. ibid., pp. 52–3. A study conducted by Michael Zander confirms Mrs Dell's findings: 'Unrepresented defendants in the criminal courts' (1969) *Crim. L.R.*

pp. 632, 639. Of the 686 entering pleas before the magistrates' courts, Zander found that 80 per cent entered pleas of guilty (550/686), but only 55 per cent of the represented defendants as against 86 per cent of the unrepresented entered pleas of guilty.

31. For a more detailed presentation of the plight of the unrepresented defendant, see Dell, n. 25, supra, pp. 17–20.
32. M.C.A. 1952, s.38.
33. See, e.g., R *v*. Bennett, ex parte R (1960) 1 All E.R. 335; R *v*. Blandford Justices, ex parte G. (an infant) (1967) 1 Q.B. 82.
34. Cmnd. 1728, paras. 369 and 372, and Minutes of Evidence, pp. 1077 and 1221.
35. Dell, n. 25 supra, p. 31.
36. ibid., p. 33.
37. 'Granting bail in magistrates' courts – proposals for reform', Howard League (1972), p. 11.
38. White, Newark and Samuels, 'Offences taken into consideration (1970) *Crim. L.R.* p. 320.
39. See, e.g., R *v*. Nelson (1967) 1 All E.R. 358.
40. See, e.g., R *v*. Prager (1972) 1 All E.R. 1114.
41. Michael Zander, in 'Access to a solicitor in the police station' (1972) *Crim. L.R.* pp. 342, 343, reports that of defendants queried who requested permission to ring a solicitor 74 per cent were refused (42/57).
42. MCA 1952, s.38. In 'Bail: a re-appraisal' (1967) *Crim. L.R.* pp. 25, 100, Michael Zander found that police bailed an average of 42 per cent of the defendants in the study, and the magistrates the remaining 58 per cent.
43. (1968) 52 Cr. App. R. 97, 100.
44. Howard League, n. 37 supra, p. 1.
45. Bottomley, n. 25, supra, p. 33.
46. See generally, Justice, 'The prosecution process in England and Wales' (1970).

10. Inconsistent Pleaders

by SUSANNE DELL

Reprinted, with permission, from *Silent in Court* (Bell, 1971), pp. 30–7 (Ch. 4).

Of the 527 women tried at magistrates' courts, 106 when they were interviewed denied having committed any offence.[1] Of these 106 women fifty-six (53 per cent) pleaded guilty, forty-seven (44 per cent) pleaded not guilty, and for three the plea was not known. For convenience, the fifty-six women who pleaded guilty are referred to as 'inconsistent pleaders'.

That more than half of those who claimed to be innocent should plead guilty before the magistrates seemed a surprising finding. How much reliance could be placed on the women's accounts? The interviewers had no reason to believe that those who denied guilt but pleaded guilty were less reliable in their accounts than those who denied guilt and pleaded not guilty, but in neither case was there, as a rule, any way of checking the circumstances of the alleged offences. In spite of this, it seemed worth looking seriously at the fact that so many of those who maintained they were innocent, yet pleaded guilty, for what these women were saying was consistent with evidence from other sources,[2] and few people who have worked in courts or with offenders will be unfamiliar with cases of this sort.

Certain criticisms which some women made of the police are relevant to this subject, and it has not been easy to decide the best way to handle this material. As the prisoners had been guaranteed that the interviews would be confidential, it was impossible to approach the police for information in these cases without revealing what had been alleged. Without any means of checking the truth of what the women said, there were only two alternatives: one was to omit all material relating unfavourably to the police, the other was to report it, while pointing out that the information was derived from only one of the two interested parties. Despite the obvious objections, it was considered right to follow this second course; the subject seemed too important to omit, and weight was also given to the fact that similar allegations were made by a number of the women, and that other people have drawn attention to the same problem. Nevertheless, it should be emphasized that where quotations are given from the women's accounts of police conduct, it is only one side of the story which is available for quotation.

What makes people plead guilty to offences they deny? The fifty-six women who did this, or said that they were going to – nine were interviewed before they pleaded – gave various reasons: seventeen said they were pleading guilty in response to police advice or pressure; eight, including several charged with soliciting and drunkenness, said that there was no point in defending a case where it was only 'my word against the police'; five women said they had pleaded guilty to avoid remands, and another five had done so out of fear that a plea of not guilty meant a harsher sentence. The remaining women gave a variety of different reasons; one simply said she had not got the 'guts' to stand up in court and put her case.

In order to throw some more light on those who denied the offence, yet pleaded guilty, a comparison was made, over all the items of information collected, between the forty-seven consistent and fifty-six inconsistent pleaders who denied their guilt. The inconsistent group were somewhat younger, but apart from this there were no significant differences in social or medical background. There were, however, three main ways in which the two groups differed. The first related to the type of offence: the incidence of public disorder offences like soliciting and drunkenness was higher among the inconsistent, while property offences were more common among the consistent. Table 1 shows the position.

The second difference was that the consistent group, no doubt because of their plea, were remanded untried in custody much more often, thereby lending some justification to the inconsistent pleaders who said they would rather plead guilty and 'have done with it' than risk the remands that go with a defended case. Of the women who denied guilt sixty-two first came to prison after conviction, and forty-seven of them (76 per cent) had pleaded guilty; on the other hand, among the forty-one who denied guilt and first came to prison on untried remand, only a minority of nine (22 per cent) pleaded inconsistently. Thirdly, there was a marked difference in the representa-

TABLE 1. *Offences of 103 women, tried by magistrates, who on interview denied guilt.*

Offence	Plea	
	Not guilty (No.)	Guilty (No.)
Larceny and false pretences	22	10
Receiving	2	6
Soliciting	9	18
Brothel keeping	–	5
Drunkenness	2	8
Drugs	3	2
Other	9	7
Total	47	56

tion of the two groups. Seventy-eight of the women who denied guilt had no legal advice before pleading, and two-thirds of them (fifty two) pleaded guilty, but among the twenty-two women who were known to have had legal help before pleading, the proportion pleading inconsistently was 13 per cent – three women.[3] Does this mean that legal advice reduces inconsistent pleading? It can be argued that such a conclusion is not warranted, because in the lower courts those who are represented are likely to be those who are most determined to defend themselves: they do not plead not guilty because they are represented, rather, they are represented because they intend to plead not guilty. However, in the higher courts a different situation exists; virtually all who are sent for trial have legal assistance, irrespective of their wish to defend themselves, and the survey showed that in the high court trial cases inconsistent pleading was as rare as it was among the represented women in the lower courts: of thirty-three women tried in the higher courts who, when interviewed, maintained their innocence, five (15 per cent) pleaded guilty. Thus there does appear to be some evidence that in a group of defendants who have access to legal advice before pleading, few of those who believe themselves to be innocent will plead guilty.[4]

Perhaps the most disturbing feature about the inconsistent pleaders was the number of women among them who had no previous convictions. There were, among the cases tried by magistrates, twenty-four women without previous convictions who, when they were interviewed, denied having committed any offence: fourteen of them, nearly 60 per cent, pleaded guilty. Two said they had done so in order to avoid remands, and one . . . said her solicitor had told her to plead guilty. One girl who was remanded untried on a charge of possessing drugs said that the police had planted these on her; after much hesitation she decided not to say so in court, as she felt such an accusation would prejudice the bench against her.[5] The majority of the inconsistent first offenders, nine of the fourteen, gave police advice or pressure as their reason for pleading guilty. Some of them said that the police had threatened that they would be 'sent down' if they pleaded not guilty; others said that they had been told that they would 'get off' (with a fine or probation etc.) if they did not contest the case. Several girls said that they had been advised to plead guilty in a kindly, even fatherly spirit, the policemen telling them that this was the simplest way to get the case over, and to avoid the risk of publicity, or remands in custody. It was easy to see how those without experience of police stations or courts might gratefully accept such advice, and it was significant that, while only 9 per cent of inconsistent recidivists gave police advice as their reason for pleading guilty, 64 per cent of the inconsistent first offenders said they had done so in response to police persuasion.

Table 1 showed that certain kinds of offence were particularly associated with inconsistent pleas, soliciting being the outstanding case. Fifty-nine girls – all but one unrepresented – were charged with this offence; twenty-seven denied it but eighteen of them pleaded guilty. All but two of these eighteen girls admitted that they were prostitutes: what they denied was that they had at the time of arrest been plying their trade. Five of the nine women who pleaded not guilty also said the same. All these girls gave similar accounts: when arrested, they had been out in the areas where they were known, but not with 'business' in mind; some were walking with girl friends (often other prostitutes), others were talking to boy friends in the street, and one or two were arrested on getting out of cars. One professional – she pleaded not guilty – said she had been stopped on her way by a seaman who asked her to come aboard his ship to 'do business'. She refused and walked on, and was then arrested for soliciting.

The Street Offences Act 1959 undoubtedly puts these girls into a difficult position. If they have previous convictions or cautions,[6] they become by definition 'common prostitutes', and if a known prostitute is talking on a street corner to a man, the police may well arrest her for soliciting, although the man in fact may be a friend or a stranger asking the way. What is such a girl to do? She can attempt to defend the case but to do so effectively she needs as a witness the person she was talking to. A young girl of eighteen gave an account of the difficulties. She was arrested for soliciting, and remanded in custody when she pleaded not guilty. She did not ask for legal aid, nor did the court suggest it. When interviewed she said that she had been in Piccadilly when a man asked her the way to a club. She directed him, and was then arrested for soliciting. She said that she asked the arresting officer if he would go with her to the club to find the man, and so prove the contents of their conversation, but this was refused. In such circumstances it is not easy for a girl to try and contest the police evidence, and without legal advice and assistance it must be virtually impossible.

There may be little sympathy for the professional who is arrested when off duty, but the present legal position, which exposes persons with previous convictions or cautions for soliciting to the repeated risk of wrongful arrest, seems unsatisfactory. The women themselves generally accepted the situation as an inevitable hazard of their trade, and pleaded guilty in a more or less resigned kind of way: this, no doubt, explained the very low rate of representation. However, one might speculate what would be the outcome if an experiment similar to that described by Donald Goff[7] were tried with London prostitutes. Goff reported that in New York City, where public drunkenness is not an offence, alcoholics were habitually charged with 'disorderly conduct': they were never represented, cases were rarely defended and almost 100 per cent were sentenced to short stays in the workhouse. As an experiment, counsel was assigned to some 1,400 cases — to argue the legal point that drunkenness did not necessarily constitute disorderly conduct. Only seven of the 1,400 represented people were found guilty. It would be interesting to know what proportion of girls charged with soliciting would be found guilty, if they were represented on this scale.

Whilst sixteen of the eighteen inconsistent prostitutes admitted their trade, there were two girls aged eighteen and nineteen who pleaded guilty although they denied that they had ever solicited in their lives. Neither had a previous conviction of any kind. One said that the police told her that if she pleaded guilty she would have 'a better chance of getting off'. She added 'They say that to everyone but I didn't know that then.' The case of the other is outlined below.

Case 591   A nineteen year old girl with no previous convictions who was mixing with criminal friends. She had been cautioned for soliciting although she denied (to the probation officer, as well as to two different interviewers in the present enquiry) that she had ever done this. On the day of her arrest she was walking with a known prostitute and both were charged. She said that the police threatened her with a remand in custody if she did not plead guilty. 'I was frightened and wanted to get it over with.' She pleaded guilty and was then remanded in custody for medical enquiries. Until she reached Holloway she was ignorant of the nature of legal aid. 'I thought it was something needed for Quarter Sessions only.'

In two other types of offence particularly associated with inconsistent pleading — receiving and brothel keeping — the defendants' need for advice on the legal implications of the charge emerged very clearly. Six women who pleaded guilty to charges of receiving said when interviewed, that they had not known until the police told them, that the goods were stolen; none of them seemed to be aware that this could be a defence to the charge and none of them had legal advice. Similarly, the five women (all unrepresented) who denied that they had engaged in brothel keeping, yet pleaded guilty to the charge, did not appreciate the legal elements in the offence. It may seem quite unbelievable to the ordinary person that someone who believes herself to be innocent of brothel-keeping (or soliciting) can plead guilty to such an offence, yet the evidence was that a defendant may do so if she believes such a plea to be a lesser evil than the others she feels threatened with. A woman with no previous convictions, the mother of four young children, admitted when interviewed that she was promiscuous, but wholly denied any experience of prostitution or brothel keeping. On being charged with the latter, she said that she had been told at the police station that the quickest way to get the thing over and return to her children would be to plead guilty, and she did so. Once remanded to Holloway (for medical reports) she sought legal aid, and tried, without success, to change her plea. Another woman with no previous convictions pleaded guilty to brothel keeping although she denied it; she said that the police had told her it was unnecessary to contact a lawyer, since a contested case would only involve scandal and publicity, whilst a plea of guilty would enable her to be out of court within five minutes.

Whatever weight may be put on the women's accounts in these cases, the point which repeatedly emerged was the importance to the accused person of having legal advice before pleading. Although in open court the defendant is asked whether she understands the charge, and is given the opportunity to put her case, the findings suggest that this is not enough: the person who has become persuaded that she is 'legally' guilty, or that it is to her advantage to plead guilty to a charge she denies, has made her decisions before she appears in court.

Conclusions

It appeared that in the lower courts inconsistent pleading is a major problem, stemming in part from the lack of legal advice. Two-thirds of the unrepresented women who maintained that they were innocent nevertheless pleaded guilty, while among those who were represented, whether in the higher or lower courts, the percentage pleading inconsistently was not more than 15 per cent.

A contributory factor in inconsistent pleading appeared to be a tendency for the police to persuade defendants to plead guilty, although it should be emphasized that only a minority of prisoners mentioned this: of 139 women in the sample who said that they were innocent, 18 per cent (twenty-six) said that the police had tried to persuade them to plead guilty;[8] while of the fifty-six women who pleaded guilty in magistrates' courts although they said they were innocent, less than a third (seventeen) gave police persuasion as the reason. Nevertheless, among those who denied guilt and mentioned police persuasion, the majority – seventeen of twenty-six – pleaded guilty, the proportion being highest among first offenders.

The problem is not a new one; the Law Society, in their evidence to the 1962 Royal Commission on the Police, said that 'advice to plead guilty is too readily given by police officers' and suggested that the police should never discuss the plea with an accused person.[9] The evidence of the National Association of Probation Officers also drew attention to the problem:

A serious complaint commonly met by probation officers, and which we are convinced has substantial foundation, is that when questioning suspected offenders the police may offer to 'put in a good word' or indicate that a lenient treatment might be suggested in court if the offender will admit the offence . . . and plead guilty. This may happen when the offender is not clearly aware of the nature of the charge against him, and [may] . . . lead . . . to a conviction of an offence more serious than that on which a verdict would have been sought (or easy to obtain) in a contested case. We have no doubt from the strength of the evidence of our members that the practice . . . does take place, however subtly it may be employed.[10]

The Royal Commission accepted the evidence on this, and said that the practice should be 'firmly checked by Chief Constables'.

Since the problem still exists, what could be done? A number of suggestions have been made in the context of a similar abuse also discussed by the Royal Commission – the use by the police of undesirable methods of obtaining statements and confessions. One of these is that independent persons, such as magistrates or solicitors, should be present at the police interrogation.[11] Inconsistent pleading, whether in response to police persuasion or other causes, would certainly diminish if it could be ensured that every accused person had the chance of speaking to a legal adviser before the plea is entered. In effect, this is what happens in the cases tried before the higher courts where inconsistent pleading was not a significant problem. If the same happened in the lower courts, it would not only ensure that any person who had been influenced by police persuasion would have easy access to independent advice; it would also ensure that before a defendant entered the dock, he would have had expert advice as to the nature of the charge, and as to the need of legal assistance in facing it.

Notes

1. The 527 women included 43 tried by the lower courts and then committed for sentence. The 106 women were those who denied any kind of guilt; they do not include the 'technically guilty' nor do they include those who denied some offences while admitting to others.
2. See Royal Commission on the Police 1962, Cmnd. 1728, paras. 369 and 372; also Minutes of Evidence, pp. 1221 and 1077; and 'The prosecution process in England and Wales' by Justice (1970) pp. 5–8. See also Clive Davies' 'Innocents in jail', *New Society* (6 November 1969) p. 742.

3. Their cases were of some interest. One was a drug offence of the 'absolute' kind, the girl alleging that she did not know that the drugs were on her premises. Possibly in view of later interpretations of the law, such a case would today be defended. The second case was that of a prostitute, accused of assaulting and robbing a client. She denied the charge, and said she would plead not guilty. When visited by a solicitor in prison, it seems that she was told that the charge would be reduced to one of larceny if she pleaded guilty, and this is what she did, presumably in order to avoid months in custody awaiting trial at the Old Bailey.

   The last case was that of a middle-aged bookkeeper, a woman of good character: she was accused of falsifying accounts, and larceny thereby. She admitted that she had done the former in order to balance the books, but denied that she had ever profited from it. She said that her solicitor had nevertheless told her to plead guilty, on the grounds that it would shorten the proceedings.

   This last case — the only one of its kind in the sample — raised the question of how far lawyers may also persuade defendants to plead inconsistently. Justice in its 1970 report on 'Complaints against lawyers' says that such complaints are made, but it is clearly not easy to distinguish cases where the advice to plead guilty is given on legal grounds, in the client's best interest, from cases where it may be given for unworthy reasons.

4. If this is so, better legal aid arrangements in the lower courts may be expected to lead to an increase in the proportion of defendants who plead not guilty. This may well be the reason why the growth of legal aid in the higher courts has been accompanied by a rise in the proportion of defended cases. The Beeching Commission did not consider this possibility (Royal Commission on Assizes and Quarter Sessions, 1966—1969 Cmnd. 4153, paras. 410 and 411).

5. This point was put to the Royal Commission on the Police by the Society of Labour Lawyers, p. 1315 of the Evidence: 'An accused person who has reason to complain of the conduct of the police finds himself in a very difficult position. If he instructs his solicitor . . . to put forward his complaints, he does so at his peril since magistrates and judges are thought to be prejudiced against accused persons who . . . make complaints against the police. Moreover, there is seldom independent evidence to support complaints. . . .'

   The same point is made by Justice: 'If there are indications of police malpractice . . . the barrister has to consider very carefully whether or not to risk incurring the hostility of the trial judge.' (Complaints against Lawyers, Appendix B).

6. The Street Offences Act 1959 enables women who are cautioned to apply for the caution to be expunged by a magistrates' court; few girls seemed aware of the procedure and only one reported that she had tried to use it; she said that when she went to a police station for this purpose, she was told she needed to have the number of the officer who cautioned her, and she did not have it.

7. *The Drunkenness Offence,* ed. T. Cook, D. Gath and C. Hensman (Pergamon Press, 1969) pp. 89—95.

8. There was no evidence that complaints about police pressure to plead guilty came more frequently from those held in police custody, nor did such women plead guilty in response to the alleged pressure more often that did those who had been allowed police bail.

9. Royal Commission on the Police 1962. Minutes of Evidence p. 1077.
10. Royal Commission on the Police 1962. Minutes of Evidence p. 1221.
11. See R. M. Jackson, *Enforcing the Law* (1967), pp. 71–8. Also Justice, 'The Interrogation of suspects' (1967).

11. The Influence of the Sentencing Discount in Inducing Guilty Pleas

by JOHN BALDWIN and MICHAEL McCONVILLE
Original contribution, specially prepared for this volume.

That defendants ought customarily to be allowed some reduction in sentence if they plead guilty is an accepted principle of Anglo-American criminal justice. In this country (unlike the United States), no real debate has ever been generated by this principle[1] and it would probably be regarded, in legal circles at least, as fanciful to question it or even to suggest a reassessment of the premises upon which it is based. Yet there is no other single consideration that so pervades the workings of the whole administration of criminal justice or that so conditions and directs the nature of the choices open to a defendant. Indeed, it is probably the existence of the so-called sentencing discount principle that largely explains why only about 4 per cent of all those charged with indictable criminal offences, and therefore eligible to be tried by jury, actually are so tried. The vast majority of defendants decide, for reasons so far largely unexplored by researchers in this country, to forgo jury trial and plead guilty.

The voluminous American literature on the subject of plea negotiation suggests, at the very least, that more attention ought to be paid to the encounters that take place prior to the formal court hearing, either when the defendant is being interviewed by the police or when he is being advised by his lawyer. In a study we have ourselves recently conducted of cases heard in the Birmingham Crown Court, we interviewed a sample of 121 defendants who at a late stage had pleaded guilty, either to the whole indictment as it stood or else to a lesser count within it.[2] Our interest in this sample of defendants lay in the light it was able to shed on the practice of what has become loosely known as 'plea bargaining'. We found, within this sample, a surprisingly high proportion of individuals who said that they had 'negotiated' a settlement over plea. Many said that they had struck some bargain and accepted a promise (which, interestingly, was only very exceptionally broken) of a particular sentence in return for pleading guilty, or else that they had accepted the view of their barrister that it would be ill-advised to contest the matter in court and better to plead guilty and accept — as almost all defendants in the sample understood it — a considerable and automatic reduction in sentence as a result.

In the course of interviewing these defendants, we were struck by the decisive influence that this reduction in sentence, whether real or assumed, had had upon them. The legal position on this question is quite clear: the court may, in appropriate cases, be more lenient in dealing with a defendant who pleads guilty when this is indicative of his remorse, but that a more severe sentence is never justified simply because a defendant pleads not guilty.[3] Thus in *Harper*,[4] the Court of Appeal reduced sentences of five years for receiving to three years because of certain remarks by the trial judge who imposed them, and said:

> This court feels that it is very improper to use language which may convey that an accused is being sentenced because he has pleaded not guilty or because he has run his defence in a particular way. It is, however, proper to give an accused a lesser sentence if he has shown genuine remorse amongst other things by pleading guilty.

If an offender is genuinely contrite, it is natural that the judge will regard this as a reason for modifying the penalty. This can be defended on the basis, for instance, that such a defendant requires a lesser penalty to reform him because he has already reformed or that he will have already been partly punished by the feelings of remorse.[5] While it is true to say that evidence of contrition sometimes emerges in the social inquiry report or in counsel's speech in mitigation, there can be no doubt that courts do not ordinarily embark on any search for remorse and repentance. One indication of this is the fact that the defendant who pleads guilty in the Crown Court is almost never asked by the judge if he wishes to say anything before sentence is passed. The conclusion we draw from this is that the guilty plea itself is generally taken by the courts as strong, if not conclusive, evidence of remorse. There can be no doubt, however, that if the courts had engaged in a more searching inquiry in the cases that we examined, they would have been rarely satisfied that the defendant was genuinely contrite. The vast majority of defendants to whom we spoke assumed that they had received a reduced sentence by virtue of the fact that they had pleaded guilty, but very few of them made any pretence during the interviews that they were in any way contrite about their involvement in the offence charged. Indeed, over a half of them were protesting, with varying degrees of fervour and credibility, often weeks after their cases had been concluded, that they were actually innocent, wholly or in part, of the charges to which they had pleaded guilty. Of the remainder, perhaps half a dozen expressed some degree of remorse; the vast majority were instead bitter, cynical or angry about what they viewed as a mere charade in which they had participated.

The reasons defendants decide to plead guilty are many and complex[6] but the common thread that runs through them is in most cases the inducement provided by the reduction in sentence that is assumed to follow a guilty plea. This is one factor that heavily colours the advice that barristers give their clients about plea. Almost without exception, defendants within the sample said they had been told by counsel that they would be much more likely to receive a heavier sentence if they unsuccessfully contested the matter. The two following examples indicate the effect such advice can have:

Case 137   I took the barrister's advice and pleaded guilty, even though I wanted to go through with pleading not guilty. He told me that if the jury found me guilty, I'd get time for two or three years, you see. He said I'd get two years' suspended [sentence] if I pleaded guilty. He asked me if I was a big gambler or not. I told him I wasn't and he said, 'That's what you'd be taking — a gamble.' I had a good idea what he meant by a gamble — that I hadn't much chance, the way he was putting it. I didn't like pleading guilty at all but I did what he thought was best and pleaded guilty to something I hadn't done. I didn't think I had a lot of choice in it.

Case 147   The barrister said, 'If you plead not guilty and you're found guilty, you'll get three or four years [in prison]. If you plead guilty, you'll get about 18 months to two years.' [The defendant eventually received 21 months.] He more or less said what was going to happen in so many words. He said, 'It's up to yourself; we can do a deal of some kind with them [the prosecution] if you plead guilty to the assault.' He was more or less advising me to plead guilty. He said, 'You know yourself what this judge is like for violence: he's a domino player, it's all threes and fives.'

Since there has been virtually no discussion of the propriety of sentencing discounts in this country, despite their decisive influence on the nature of the advice that counsel gives to his client,[7] we attempted to assess the extent to which discounts are in practice awarded to defendants who plead guilty and thus to ascertain how far the main factor that caused defendants to plead guilty was more than a perceived reality. In our own conversations with members of the judiciary, we have come increasingly to recognize a spectrum of views on this question. Some judges regard a reduction of perhaps a quarter or a third of whatever sentence is to be imposed as a fair reward in most cases for a guilty plea; others view any reduction in sentence as being solely conditional upon evidence of contrition on the part of the defendant which is recognised as a fairly exceptional occurrence. No judge to whom we have ourselves spoken has suggested that any accretion in sentence is permissible following a not guilty plea and, as noted earlier, the Court of Appeal has repeatedly emphasised this point. However, it is easy to see why defendants often regard this sort of reasoning as meaningless. As far as we can tell, the sentencing differential is viewed by virtually all defendants as a penalty imposed on those who unsuccessfully contest their case.

Various tests have been used by American authors from time to time to assess the extent of any discount in sentence for a guilty plea.[8] The results to date are, however, inconclusive. Some studies have uncovered substantial reductions, others none whatsoever; but the crudeness of the measures used, together with the authors' failure even to take account of obvious complicating factors (such as the criminal records of the defendants concerned), probably renders the comparisons largely meaningless. The test we devised to assess the extent to which a reduction in sentence follows a guilty plea is, in essence, simple. We took the sample of 150 defendants who were late plea-changers (the same sample that formed the basis of *Negotiated Justice*, Baldwin and McConville, 1977) and matched them, on a group basis[9] according to several criteria relevant to sentencing, with two separate samples (both 150 in number) of defendants. One of the latter samples was made up of defendants who pleaded not guilty in the Birmingham Crown Court and were subsequently convicted; the other of what might be called straightforward guilty pleas, those individuals who pleaded guilty at trial, having determined to do so apparently at a date considerably in advance of trial. The criteria used to match these three samples were as follows:

(1) sex
(2) age
(3) category of offence
(4) the number of counts in the indictment
(5) the defendants' criminal record
(6) the length of time spent in prison.[10]

The three samples used thus included the same numbers of females, individuals of the same age, criminal experience and the like. In other words, we have attempted to control for those factors likely to affect markedly the severity of sentence imposed.[11] Having controlled for these factors, we postulated that any variation in sentencing patterns among the three groups could be attributed to the different pleas tendered by the defendants in question. The hypothesis we sought to test was that, of the three groups, those who were convicted after a not guilty plea would receive the most severe penalties since they would have forfeited, by virtue of their plea, the reduction of sentence which they might otherwise have obtained.[12] As between the group of late plea-changers and the straightforward guilty plea group, there were two possibilities. As indicated above, many of the former group claimed to have pleaded guilty only after they had struck a favourable sentence bargain or had otherwise (as by pleading guilty only to a reduced charge) extracted from the prosecution a concession which would have had the effect of a sentence reduction.[13] If these claims were untrue, we would have expected their sentences to be similar to those in the straightforward guilty plea cases. If, on the other hand, these claims that bargains had been made and concessions extracted were as the defendants described, then we anticipated that this would be reflected in sentences less severe than those meted out to the straightforward guilty plea group. Table 1 indicates that variations in sentence according to plea clearly support the latter hypothesis. It shows quite clearly that the defendants who unsuccessfully contested their cases were far less likely than either of the two other groups to receive non-custodial sentences. Of the three groups, the late plea-changers

TABLE 1. *Sentences imposed on defendants according to plea.*

	Late plea-changers (*n* = 150)		Guilty pleas (*n* = 150)		Convicted after not guilty plea (*n* = 150)	
	%		%		%	
Absolute or conditional discharge	10.0		5.3		4.0	
Fine	10.7	57.4%	9.3	50.0%	6.7	30.7%
Probation	12.0		11.4		2.7	
Suspended sentence	24.7		24.0		17.3	
Prison sentence	35.9	42.6%	44.7	50.0%	57.3	69.3%
Other custodial sentence (e.g. Borstal)	6.7		5.3		12.0	
	100.0%		100.0%		100.0%	

received the lightest sentences and were less likely than the two other groups to receive custodial sentences. The differences that emerge from the table are statistically highly significant ($p < .001$). The variations in sentence patterns support the hypothesis that a difference in plea significantly affects the sentence received, and provides further evidence that negotiated plea settlements did in fact take place in the way defendants in this group described.

Furthermore, when one examines the *length* of prison sentences imposed on each of the three groups, it is clear that more of those who pleaded not guilty and were convicted were sent to prison for a longer period.[14] This is set out in Table 2.

The results given in these two tables contradict any suggestion that there is a straightforward discount in sentence (of, say, a quarter of the

TABLE 2. *Length of custodial sentences according to plea.*

	Late plea-changers	Guilty pleas	Convicted after not guilty plea
	%	%	%
Not relevant — defendant given a non-custodial sentence	57.4	50.0	30.7
Custodial sentence:—			
less than 12 months	12.0	10.0	24.7
1 year less than 3 years	25.3	22.7	26.6
3 years or more	5.3	17.3	18.0
	100.0%	100.0%	100.0%

sentence) for a guilty plea. It is obvious that, for many individuals, the *form* of the sentence will be quite different if a case is unsuccessfully fought. The fact that many more of those who contested their cases received custodial sentences than was the case with either of the other groups cannot, if our analysis is correct, be explained other than in terms of the plea tendered.[15] It is not at all surprising, then, that such sentencing discounts represent an extremely powerful inducement to almost all defendants to plead guilty.

We have argued elsewhere that the sorts of reduction in sentence that many defendants anticipate if they plead guilty may be so strong an inducement that even the innocent may on occasions feel it prudent to plead guilty as a result.[16] As we see it, the principal argument against the so-called discount principle is that the inducements it offers operate on all defendants, the innocent as well as the guilty. Furthermore, the greater the discount, or, more accurately, the anticipated discount, for a guilty plea, the greater the risk that innocent defendants will plead guilty. In the course of the interviews we ourselves have conducted, we have been convinced that certain of the defendants in the sample pleaded guilty despite being innocent of the charges they faced. It would be wrong to suggest that this is a frequent occurrence in this country, but the fact that it happens at all should cause us to reflect upon the justification for awarding some considerable reduction in sentence to those who plead guilty.

We would contend that, except in relatively rare cases in which defendants demonstrate genuine contrition, there is no legal justification for wide differences in sentence according to the plea tendered. It was noted above that, at least as far as the late plea-changers were concerned, manifestations of remorse or contrition were, in our judgment, extremely rare. As one writer has aptly put it, 'A judge who recognises contrition so frequently as to give rise to a de facto policy of differential sentencing probably has an overly generous view of contrition.'[17]

Other justifications have been put forward by several commentators, though none of these seems to us sufficient reason to warrant more than minimal reductions of sentence.[18] The arguments encountered in favour of differential sentencing (in addition to the question of remorse) take two main forms: first, a belief that those who have pleaded not guilty and been convicted will have caused unnecessary distress to witnesses and as a rule perjured themselves,[19] and second, an administrative consideration, that defendants who fight lost causes in court ought to be punished for wasting the time of the court at enormous public expense.[20] Neither of these arguments is easily defended, however. As to the first, the inevitable lack of precision of trial by jury makes such a proposition dangerous. Preliminary analysis of the results of our own research on the outcome of jury trials in the Birmingham Crown Court suggests that wrongful conviction of innocent defendants is a more frequent occurrence than has hitherto been indicated by researchers or other commentators. The second argument is of even less legal validity, based as it is on the adminstrative requirements of the court bureaucracy with little relevance to the question of justice. It is customary to speak of the right to trial by jury and the right to require the prosecution to prove its case beyond reasonable doubt. Either these are rights or they are not, and if they are rights, it is indefensible in principle that any defendant be subjected to what amounts to an additional penalty merely because the prosecution is able to prove its case. Now it may well be that the resources of the courts are such as to require some major disincentive to defendants who wish to be tried by jury. As Professor Cross puts it:

> The English system of criminal trials would break down if everyone charged with an offence in a superior Court were to plead not guilty. It is extremely improbable that the prospect of a reduced sentence would cause an innocent accused to plead guilty and, provided it is understood to refer only to those accused who are guilty, moderate encouragement to plead is, as the Court puts it, in *R. v. de Hahn*, 'clearly in the public interest'.[21]

However, a system of justice that is crudely based upon rewards and disincentives cannot accurately distinguish between the guilty and the innocent and we do not see how a sentence discount can be, as Cross says, 'understood to refer only to those accused who are guilty'. The truth is that discussions by lawyers on this question tend to be disingenuous. What in one situation is deemed to be wholly improper is held in other situations to be laudable. Consider the following illustrations:

Case A: A defendant interviewed at a police station
           Detective: You haven't a chance when your case gets to court. It will save everybody's time if you make a statement admitting the offence.

Defendant: Will you give me bail if I do?
Detective: Yes.
Defendant: All right then — will you write it out for me?

Case B: A defendant interviewed before trial at the Crown Court
Defence counsel: The evidence against you is overwhelming. My advice to you is to plead guilty, then you'll get a shorter sentence for saving the court's time.
Defendant: All right then if you'll get me off more lightly.

Case A: At the Crown Court trial
Defence counsel: My client was induced to make a confession by being promised bail.
Judge: The confession is inadmissible in evidence. The behaviour of the police officer in making such a promise was reprehensible and his conduct should be brought to the notice of the authorities so that disciplinary action can be taken.

Case B: At the Crown Court trial
Defence counsel: By way of mitigation, I must draw your Honour's attention to the fact that my client has pleaded guilty and thus avoided a protracted trial.
Judge: In passing sentence, I take into account that the defendant, no doubt after receiving advice, has very properly altered his plea to one of guilty.

It may be the case that lawyers would have no difficulty in justifying the above comments of the judges, though others might find the logic of the distinction unconvincing. Layman may be forgiven for thinking that the detective in question had done a greater public service by saving even more time than the defence counsel. If a reduction in sentence for a guilty plea is administratively necessary, it should, in our view, be so stated and not disguised in the legal play on words which may be convincing to lawyers but would be viewed by anyone else as mere cant and hypocrisy.

Notes

1. There is a sizeable American literature on the subject: see particularly, Note, *Yale Law Journal* (1956); Whitman (1967); Folberg (1968); Gentile (1969); LaFave (1970); Newman and NeMoyer (1970); Parker (1972); Alschuler (1975) and Rosett and Cressey (1976).
2. This research, which is part of a larger study concerned with the outcome of jury trials, has been funded since 1974 by the Home Office and is reported in Baldwin and McConville (1977). The views expressed in this paper are those of the authors alone and are not to be taken as those of the Home Office. We are particularly grateful for the helpful comments made to an early draft of this paper by Mr A. F. Wilcox, Dr J. P. Wilson and Dr A. K. Bottomley.
3. On this, see particularly Thomas (1970) pp 52–4. The Court of Appeal in *Cain Criminal Law Review* [1976] p. 464 has stated the position in unusually blunt terms:

   > it was trite to say that a plea of guilty would generally attract a somewhat lighter sentence than a plea of not guilty after a full dress-contest on the issue. Everybody knew that it was so, and there was no doubt about it. Any accused person who did not know about it should know it. The sooner he knew the better.

4. [1967] 3 All E.R. 618n. And see *de Hahn* [1967] 3 All E.R. 618.
5. See Cross (1971) p. 152.
6. These reasons are dealt with at some length in Baldwin and McConville (1977), Chs. 2–4. See also McCabe and Purves (1972) and Bottoms and McClean (1976) Ch. 5.
7. As McCabe and Purves (1972) put it:

   > it seems fair to say that in most, if not all, cases, [a change of plea to guilty] followed after the defendant received 'certain good advice' from his legal representatives [who], drawing on their general court experience and their knowledge of the supposed idiosyncracies of the local judiciary, play a crucial role in the plea-changing process.[p. 9]

8. See particularly Note, *University of Chicago Law Review* (1964); Mileski (1971); Shin (1973). We are not aware of any attempt in this country to measure the extent of the discount.
9. On this matching procedure, see Hood and Sparks (1970) pp 146–51.
10. Categories (2) to (6) were broken down into various subgroups. Thus age was divided into eight subgroups; category of offence into twenty; number of counts into nine; criminal record into five and time spent in prison into seven.

11. In addition, we examined the extent to which the three samples differed in terms of the identity and status of the sentencing judge; the occupation of the defendant and whether there was a remand in custody before trial. In each of these respects, however, the three samples were virtually identical.

12. Several barristers have made the point to us that an effective speech in mitigation becomes almost impossible if the defendant refuses to plead guilty.

13. A detailed description of the nature and extent of such plea bargaining is given in Baldwin and McConville (1977) Chs 2 and 3.

14. For the purposes of this comparison, detention centre and borstal sentences are treated as equivalent to custodial sentences of less than twelve months.

15. There were in each sample a number of defendants already subject to suspended sentences, probation orders, conditional discharges and the like. Rather more of the late plea-changers (39) were subject to such orders than was the case with either of the two other groups (34 in each). In relation to numbers of defendants already subject to suspended sentences when they appeared in court, there were virtually no differences among the three groups: 20 defendants within the late plea change category, 17 within the straightforward guilty pleas and 21 within the not guilty plea group had, because of their conviction on the current offence, breached such orders.

16. See Baldwin and McConville (1977) Ch. 4. The matter is well-expressed in the following extract from the *Annual Survey of American Law* (1966):

> Courts [in America] have said that a plea is involuntary when the defendant is deprived of the ability to make a reasoned choice. . . . This does not seem to state the problem accurately. A defendant faced with either a long prison term if convicted or a suspended sentence if he pleads guilty, does not lack the capacity to make a reasoned choice — his choice is clear. The problem is not that his ability to decide has been impaired, it is rather that he is being compelled to decide between improper alternatives. [p. 544]

17. See Note, *University of Chicago Law Review* (1964) at p. 186.

18. There seems to us no justification whatever for giving greater rewards to those who change plea at the last moment than to those who acknowledge their guilt from the outset. The latter group can claim that they should receive the same, or even greater, benefits because they have saved more time and expense for all concerned. One possibility is that those who initially enter a plea of not guilty gain an advantage by being in a position to bargain with the prosecution for a reduced charge — if so, it appears that cunning pays better than honesty.

19. See Note, *Yale Law Journal*, (1956); Fay (1968); Cross (1971) and Note, *University of Richmond Law Review* (1972).

20. See Note, *Yale Law Journal* (1956); *Annual Survey of American Law* (1966); Folberg (1968), and Parker (1972). A succinct summary of this 'bureaucratic' argument is given by Glanville Williams in a letter to *The Times* (25 February 1976). He writes:

> offenders who have no defence must be persuaded not to waste the time of the court and public money; pleas of guilty often save the distress of

witnesses in having to give evidence as well as inconvenience and loss of time; and in present conditions such pleas are essential to prevent serious congestion in the courts.
21. R. Cross (1971) at pp 153–4. Cross had previously pointed out that it is difficult to see why professional criminals would ever plead guilty if there were no sentencing discount available: Cross (1965) at p. 220.

References

Alschuler, A. W. (1975) 'The defence attorney's role in plea bargaining' *Yale Law Journal* 84, pp. 1179–1314.
Annual Survey of American Law (1966) 'Plea bargaining' pp. 537–52.
Baldwin, J. and McConville, M. J. (1977) *Negotiated Justice* (Martin Robertson).
Bottoms, A. E. and McClean, J. D. (1976) *Defendants in the Criminal Process* (Routledge & Kegan Paul).
Cross, R. (1965) 'Paradoxes in prison sentences' *Law Quarterly Review* 81, pp. 205–22.
(1971) *The English Sentencing System* (Butterworths).
Fay, E. D. (1968). 'The "bargained-for" guilty plea' *Criminal Law Bulletin* 4, pp. 265–72.
Folberg, H. J. (1968) 'The "bargained for" guilty plea – an evaluation' *Criminal Law Bulletin* 4, pp. 201–12.
Gentile, C. L. (1969) 'Fair bargains and accurate pleas' *Boston University Law Review* 49, pp. 514–51.
Hood, R. and Sparks, R. (1970) *Key Issues in Criminology* (World University Library).
LaFave, W. R. (1970) 'The prosecutor's discretion in the United States' *American Journal of Comparative Law* 18, pp. 532–48.
Mileski, M. (1971) 'Courtroom encounters: an observation study of a lower criminal court' *Law and Society Review* 5, pp. 473–538.
McCabe, S. and Purves, R. (1972) *By-Passing the Jury* (Blackwell).
Newman, D. J. and NeMoyer, E. C. (1970) 'Issues of propriety in negotiated justice' *Denver Law Journal* 47, pp. 367–407.
Parker, J. F. (1972) 'Plea bargaining' *American Journal of Criminal Law* 2, pp. 187–209.
Rosett, A. and Cressey, D. R. (1976) *Justice By Consent* (Lippincott).
Shin, H. J. (1973) 'Do lesser pleas pay? Accommodations in the sentencing and parole processes' *Journal of Criminal Justice* 1, pp. 27–42.
Thomas, D. A. (1970) *Principles of Sentencing* (Heinemann).
University of Chicago Law Review (1964) Note: 'Official inducements to plead guilty: suggested morals for a market place' *University of Chicago Law Review* 32, pp. 167–87.
University of Richmond Law Review (1972) Note: 'Plea bargaining: the case for reform' *University of Richmond Law Review* 6, pp. 325–46.

Whitman, P. A. (1967) 'Judicial plea bargaining' *Stanford Law Review* 19, pp. 1082–92.

Yale Law Journal (1956) Note: 'The influence of the defendant's plea on judicial determination of sentence' *Yale Law Journal* 66, pp. 204–22.

PART IV

Trial and Conviction

Introduction

Many of the assumptions commonly made by lawyers, police officers and indeed the general public about the English trial system have been deflated by researchers in the past two decades. The boast that the English system is the fairest in the world is usually made only by those whose acquaintance with other jurisdictions is minimal. For not only is it the case that such comparisons are meaningless given the uniqueness of our system – and indeed of most other systems – but any observer who cares to pay even a casual visit to, say, a busy magistrates' court on a Monday morning is likely to see a system almost visibly creaking under the work load. The legal commonplace that the dice in this situation are loaded in favour of the defence is scarcely defensible. Anyone who has seen an inarticulate and frightened defendant struggling to engage in the complex and technically difficult business of cross-examination in even a straightforward or minor court case will have felt the same sense of frustration and humiliation that the defendant himself must have experienced. It cannot be squared with justice. As Winifred Cavenagh succinctly puts it:

> The court situation, its size, formality, and publicity, the conspicuousness and isolation of [the defendant's] position, and the feeling of being required to perform according to the rules, the details of which are unknown to him but appear familiar to the other side, all tend to handicap him. [*Juvenile Courts, the Child and the Law* Penguin, 1967 at p. 31]

The extent to which the English system relies on laymen would be viewed as unthinkable in most other jurisdictions. It is often assumed that lay magistrates deal only with minor and routine cases, but it must be remembered that a half of all defendants receiving terms of imprisonment are sentenced by lay magistrates. Yet these magistrates may be inadequately equipped to make decisions of this nature. The limited research that has been conducted in magistrates' courts has on the whole uncovered a disturbing state of affairs: magistrates are often poorly trained for the job; they spring from a narrow social base; they tend very often to be inexpertly guided by inexperienced junior court clerks, and the decisions they take (for instance with regard to sentence, awarding of costs, or the granting of bail) vary enormously, even for apparently similar cases and defendants, from one area of the country to another. The system falters partly because of inadequate funds, and it is not surprising that researchers have concluded that justice has too often been subordinated to bureaucratic and administrative considerations.

Given the savage criticisms made of lay magistrates both by researchers and by the media, it is strange that the other main body of laymen within the English system − jurymen − not only have largely escaped such criticism, but have traditionally been defended with a vigour otherwise reserved perhaps only for the monarchy. The jury system is very much the sacred cow of the English legal system, and researchers have been able to examine the way it operates in only a very limited way. Ely Devons's searing comment that 'if the jury is to remain part of the English legal system, it is just as well that its proceedings should remain secret' is probably much closer to reality than the exaggerated notion of juries as representing the last bastion of freedom.

It is clear that the operation of justice diverges from the principle: the 'law in action' and the 'law in books' are not by any means concordant. Yet it is naive to think that even the kind of critical research of the courts conducted in recent years is likely to change the way that justice is administered. This is not merely a question of bureaucratic inertia or resistance. Nor is it simply that prevailing views are too firmly held to be much affected by limited research enterprises conducted by those who are seen as inexperienced in the practical business of judicial administration or as 'academic' in the most pejorative sense of that word. The truth is that research raises more fundamental questions concerning the definition of justice itself; whether, for instance, it be justice according to some abstract set of legal rules or else according to some unarticulated assumptions made by the researcher himself as to what constitutes fair play.

Further Reading

Baldwin, J., 'The compulsory training of the magistracy' *Criminal Law Review* (1975) p. 634.

Baldwin, J., 'The social composition of the magistracy' *British Journal of Criminology*, 16 (1976) p. 171.

Baldwin, J. and McConville M. J., 'The acquittal rate of professional criminals: A critical note' *Modern Law Review*, 37 (1974) p. 439.

Brandon, R. and Davies, C., *Wrongful Imprisonment: Mistaken Convictions and their Consequences* (Allen & Unwin, 1973).

Cornish, W. R., *The Jury* (Penguin, 1968).

Criminal Law Revision Committee, Eleventh Report: *Evidence (General)* Cmnd 4991 (HMSO, 1972).

Departmental Committee, *Evidence of Identification in Criminal Cases* (Chairman Lord Devlin) (HMSO, 1976).

Erlanger, H. S., 'Jury research in America: its past and future', *Law and Society Review*, 4 (1970) p. 345.

Hain, P., *Mistaken Identity* (Quartet Books, 1976).

JUSTICE, *The Unrepresented Defendant in Magistrates' Courts* (Stevens, 1971).

Kalven, H. and Zeisel, H., *The American Jury* (University of Chicago Press, 1966).

Lewis, D. and Hughman, P., *Just How Just?* (Secker & Warburg, 1975).

Mark, Sir Robert, *Minority Verdict* The 1973 Dimbleby Lecture (BBC Publications, 1973).

Marshall, J., 'Trial, testimony and truth' pp. 237–56 in S. S. Nagel, (ed.) *The Rights of the Accused* (Sage, 1970).

McCabe, S. and Purves, R., *The Jury at Work* (Basil Blackwell, 1972).

McCabe, S. and Purves, R., *The Shadow Jury at Work* (Basil Blackwell, 1974).

Royal Commission on Justices of the Peace 1946–1948 Cmd 7463 (HMSO, 1948).

Sheehan, A. V., *Criminal Procedure in Scotland and France* (HMSO, 1975).

Simon, R. J. (ed.), *The Jury System in America* (Sage, 1975).

Walker, N. (ed.), *The British Jury System* (Cropwood Conference, Institute of Criminology, University of Cambridge, 1974).

Zander, M., 'Unrepresented defendants in the criminal courts' *Criminal Law Review* (1969) p. 632.

Zander, M., 'Acquittal rates and not guilty pleas: What do the statistics mean?' *Criminal Law Review* (1974) p. 401.

Zander, M., 'Are too many professional criminals avoiding conviction?' *Modern Law Review*, 37 (1974) p. 28.

12. The Defendant's Perspective

by A. E. BOTTOMS and J. D. McCLEAN

Reprinted, with permission, in abridged form from *Defendants* in the Criminal Process (Routledge & Kegan Paul, 1976), pp. 55–7, 83–4.

To the court administrator, to the judge or magistrate, to the professional lawyer, the court is a familiar place. Familiar rituals are re-enacted daily, often many times a day. These men know with almost unfailing precision what will happen next — a prosecutor's speech, or the introduction of evidence, or whatever. They share also a common stock of experience which, despite their different roles in the courtroom drama, pulls them together, and enables them to communicate with each other in ways which are incomprehensible to an uninformed outsider.

There is nothing sinister about this. No overt collusion to manipulate justice exists; what does exist are the shared understandings of habitués. These understandings may become so routine and commonplace that the habitué forgets that the outsider finds them strange, and often alienative. Some time ago, for example, one of us spent some time with a group of experienced but disbelieving magistrates, explaining not only that this sort of verbal shorthand exists, but, specifically, that the defendant may be alienated by the routine and wholly innocent pieces of verbal shorthand at the beginning of a summary trial. It is true that his rights are in no way being eroded in these exchanges, but the point is that only the habitué can be sure of that. The defendant, unsure as to what exactly is going on, can be excused if he is suspicious that exchanges which he does not understand might in some way be affecting his interests adversely.

For the defendant is usually not an habitué. First-time defendants in particular expressed to us their sense of confusion and exclusion in the court process:

134

I felt awful: I was in a daze most of the time.

The police statement of the facts [after defendant's guilty plea] gave completely the wrong impression. But I wasn't given a proper chance to explain — I was so amazed at what the police said that I couldn't say anything.

When I was in the dock I felt very nervous — I tried hard to be subservient, and not to smile nervously.

I've never been in court before, and I found it all very interesting — but considering what I was up for [a minor shoplifting charge], I felt so scared.

It was all unexpected — I've never been through it before — it was very nerve-racking.

The second and third of these quotations are perhaps of special interest. In the second case, the defendant had, formally speaking been given his chance to explain the incident to the court: but to him, he hadn't had a proper chance, because of his astonishment and confusion in the court situation. The third defendant, a skilled technician, expressed his uncertainty of role in the dock, a feeling of a need to be subservient rather than assertive in the courtroom situation. . . .

Other respondents isolated other factors which help to produce confusion and lack of articulation in the typical defendant. One factor was the agony of uncertainty, the need to have the matter settled one way or the other: one defendant of the 'passive inadequate deviant' type (see West, 1963) had been given 4 years' imprisonment for a series of relatively minor burglaries, but refused to re-open the issue on an appeal, because 'while you are waiting, you don't know what you'll get'. To the defendant in this state of worry and uncertainty, the possibility of effective personal intervention in the court scene is remote. Second, some defendants perceive themselves to be placed in a subordinate and confusing position even before they reach the dock — before the case they have had to surrender to their bail, and for administrative convenience all defendants are then grouped together in a special part of the court, waiting until their case is called. One defendant, a technical representative, strongly disliked being thus 'herded around like a gang of labourers'; another saw it as simply the first stage in a cumulative process of humiliation: 'It is unfair from the moment you go into court — the police say "sit there" and so on — it's a very small-minded attitude.'

Nor was the contrast between their own position and that of the court staff and lawyers lost on defendants. As one first-offender eloquently put it: 'To them, it's everyday life. It's just like a hospital: to relations, sickness is a worry, but to staff it's an everyday thing.'

The defendant in court, then, is typically confused, worried and relatively inarticulate, and the court processes themselves often do little to alleviate this position. . . .

[The] choice of venue is always made in open court, and the procedure is regulated by s.19 of the Magistrates' Courts Act, 1952, so far as the most common case, involving an indictable offence triable summarily, is concerned. This section (as amended) provides, in part:

> (3) . . . [T]he court . . . shall tell [the defendant] that he may, if he consents, be tried summarily instead of being tried by a jury and, if the court thinks it desirable for his information, shall explain what is meant by being tried summarily.
>
> (4) The court shall also explain to him that if he consents to be tried summarily and is convicted by the court he may be committed to the Crown Court [for sentence] . . . if the court, on obtaining information of his character and antecedents, is of opinion that they are such that greater punishment should be inflicted than the court has power to inflict.
>
> (5) After informing the accused as provided by the last two preceding sub-sections, the court shall ask him whether he wishes to be tried by a jury or consents to be tried summarily. . . .

This procedure will be gone through perhaps as often as a dozen times in a morning's sitting; anyone spending any time in a magistrates' court becomes quite familiar with it. We have seen that the great majority of all defendants have spent time in a magistrates' court before their current case, and they may well have sat through several other cases on the day they had to make the choice as to venue. So it might be expected that few defendants would be unaware of the choice before them.

On the other hand, it may be that this bit of court procedure makes little impact on the observer. It forms part of a larger set-piece at the beginning of each case in which the prosecuting solicitor or officer and the chairman also have speaking parts; it is delivered at some speed by a clerk who has done it a thousand times before; it may simply not 'register'. Certainly there are occasions on which the defendant who is being addressed has to be woken from his trance-like state, and the question repeated. It has something of the quality of a television washing powder commercial: slick, rapid, familiar — and yet the viewer may pay so little attention that he could not tell you the name of the product at all. As one defendant put it:

> I found this very confusing — so quick that I didn't really know what was going on. I didn't really choose — I thought, go to prison or Assize or something — I just said 'tried here' to get it done there and then.

And several other interviewed defendants also (though less articulately) indicated this sense of bewilderment at the whole venue set-piece. . . .

Reference

West, D. J. (1963) *The Habitual Prisoner* (Macmillan).

13. The Staging of Magistrates' Justice

by PAT CARLEN

Reprinted, with permission, in abridged form from *Magistrates' Justice* (Martin Robertson, 1976), pp. 21–31.

A magistrates' court is a very formal and ritualistic social setting; in it social space is preformed and distributed by the fixtures and fittings which comprise its definitive physical dimensions. The conditional essence of formality is the maintenance of existing social forms; the *raison d'être* of the criminal law is an assumption of the vulnerability of existing social forms. It is not surprising, therefore, to find that, in the courts, not even the usually implicit rules of spacing and placing are left to chance interpretation. Instead, judicial violation of the mundane expectations which usually enable fully adult people to cope with unfamiliar situations, judicial tolerance of flawed communication systems, and a judicial perversion of the accepted modes of conversational practice, realise a structure of tacit coercion which makes nonsense of recent claims that judicial proceedings are loaded in favour of the defendant (Criminal Law Revision Committee, 1972; Mark, 1973).

In the courtroom spatial dominance is achieved by structural elevation, and the magistrate sits raised up from the rest of the court. The defendant is also raised up to public view but the dock is set lower than the magisterial seat, whilst the rails surrounding it are symbolic of the defendant's captive state. Of all the main protagonists the defendant is the one who is placed farthest away from the magistrate. Between the defendant and the magistrate sit clerk, solicitors, probation officers, social workers, press reporters, police, and any others deemed to be assisting the court in the discharge of its duties. Spatial arrangements, however, which might signify to the onlooker a guarantee of an orderly display of justice, are too often experienced by participants as being generative of a theatrical autism with all the actors talking past each other.

138

Difficulties of hearing are endemic to magistrates' courts. At one court where microphones are used they distort voices so badly that most people in the courtroom laughingly wince when they are turned on and visibly sympathise with the lady magistrate who always has them turned off because 'they make us sound like Donald Duck'. At other courts they have microphones but do not use them. Magistrates and clerks can go to elaborate lengths to explain the meaning of legal phraseology to defendants who either do not hear them and say 'Pardon, Sir?' or who nod in the 'dazed' or 'blank' way noted by so many policemen and probation officers. The Chief Clerk at Metropolitan Court was concerned that he so often had to shout at defendants. 'It's the acoustics. The defendants are close to us but as you speak you can feel it coming back at you – you really have to shout.' And nearly all the probation officers mentioned poor acoustics when they tried to assess defendants' understanding of court procedures: 'I'm frequently amazed. I say, "What did the magistrate say to you?" They don't know. They haven't heard.' (Miss W; probation officer) 'Sometimes the probation officer can't hear the policeman and certainly the magistrate can't hear the chap in the dock.' (Mr W, probation officer). . . .

Acoustics, however, cannot bear total responsibility for the chronic breakdown of communication in magistrates' courts. The placing and spacing of people within the courtroom is a further cause of the series of 'pardons' and 'blank stares' which characterise and punctuate judicial proceedings.

It has already been stressed that defendants and magistrates are set well apart from each other. Distances between bench and dock vary from court to court but in all courts such distances are certainly greater than those usually, and voluntarily, chosen for the disclosure of intimate details of sexual habits, personal relationships and financial affairs. Certain communications are conventionally presented as intimate communications, and both their timing and situating are delicately arranged. Indeed, 'there are certain things which are difficult to talk about unless one is within the proper conversational zone' (Hall, 1959).

In magistrates' courts, where the vast majority of defendants do not have a solicitor as a 'mouthpiece', defendants are set up in a guarded dock and then, at a distance artificially stretched beyond the familiar boundaries of face-to-face communication, asked to describe or comment on intimate details of their lives; details which do not in themselves constitute infractions of any law but which are open to public investigation once a person has been *accused* of breaking the law. This ceremonial 'stripping of a man of his dignity' as a prelude to judicial punishment has been thoroughly explicated and analysed by Harold Garfinkel (1956); degradation or humiliation of the man in the dock was spontaneously mentioned by several solicitors and probation officers at Metropolitan Court. 'People laugh about something he says which may sound funny, or some aspect of his private life which comes out in court, you know? People *laugh*. It's treated without any respect at all.' (Mrs W, probation officer).

Further, during such sequences of interrogation, defendants' embarrassed stuttering is often aggravated by judicial violation of another taken-for-granted conversational practice. For in conventional social practice the chain-rule of question-answer sequence (Sacks, 1967; Schegloff, 1972) is also accompanied by the assumption that it is the *interrogator* who demands an answer. In magistrates' courts, however, defendants often find that they are continually rebuked, either for not addressing their answers to the magistrate or for directing their answers to their interrogators in such a way that the magistrate cannot hear them. As a result, defendants are often in the position of having to synchronise their answers and stances in a way quite divorced from the conventions of everyday life outside the courtroom.

For defendants who often do not immediately distinguish between magistrate and clerk, for defendants who do not comprehend the separate symbolic functions of dock and witness box, for defendants who may have already spent up to three hours waiting around in the squalid environs of the courtroom, the surreal dimensions of meaning, emanating from judicial exploitation of courtroom placing and spacing, can have a paralysing effect. A senior probation officer summed up the present situation in the Metropolitan Magistrates' Courts very well when she commented: 'Many of them don't even go in to the witness box because they can't face walking round there. They're too nervous.' A policeman once told me that magistrates do not like to see a man in the dock in handcuffs. Magistrates' sensibilities seldom have to be offended by the paraphernalia pertaining to physical control. The tacit dimensions of control, emanating from the judicial manipulation of place, time and space ensure that:

> The court *will* proceed, as you've seen. Everybody acts their certain role. It's like a play in a way. You've got your clerk, your magistrate, your usher. Everbody performs at the right time, on cue, and I think

that, at times perhaps, the tendency is to forget that the other actor in the play hasn't had so many rehearsals. [Miss G, probation officer]

Though it is unlikely that absolute control of the situation can be obtained in a cramped courtroom which may have thirty to forty people in its main area, and over that number in its public gallery, officials, as I have already argued, appear to be well aware of how to facilitate control through exploitation of the courtroom's physical dimensions. Courtroom ceremony is maintained partly to facilitate physical control of defendants and any others who may step out of place and partly to refurbish the historically sacred meanings attached to law. Yet, because of the volume of criminal business dealt with by magistrates' courts, control of the proceedings is often precarious. Continuous inroads on the putative sanctity of the courtroom are made by the daily wear and tear of judicial proceedings which may involve the consecutive appearances of twenty or thirty defendants at one court session. A series of brief but complex scenes have to be welded into a fast-moving but judicially satisfying documentary. Lines of spatial demarcation provide the base-lines for the overall performance; once the action starts the movement of documents and persons from the various regions of the court has to be synchronised by the mainly backstage activities of the police.

In the management of social occasions, time, like place, always belongs to somebody or some group. During formal social occasions certain persons are appointed to oversee the timing of events, to ensure both the continuity and punctuation of performances. During judicial proceedings in magistrates' courts the timing of events is monopolised by the police. They are the ones who set up the proceedings; it is their responsibility to see that all defendants arrive at court; it is their job to ensure that all relevant documents are in the hands of the clerk of court. And policemen are very jealous of their competence in programming the criminal business.

> Court inspector: We get remands over first. It stands to reason — when you've just got to read the charge and ask for a remand — it's quicker — to get it over.
> Pat Carlen: Do you keep contested cases until last?
> Court inspector: Oh no, not always. And when we do it's not as a punishment. Think of it from your own point of view — if you'd

pleaded guilty you wouldn't want to hang around all the afternoon for something that was going to take two minutes.

Pat Carlen: Do you ask them if they're going to plead 'guilty'?

Court inspector: Yes. But only as a matter of convenience. It doesn't matter to us. We have to be here all day anyhow. [Court A]

Like other occupational groups doing a complex job publicly and under constant criticism, the police have developed plausible accounts to demonstrate the rationality of the ways in which they arrange the cases (Moore, 1912). The Court Inspector appealed to a tacit assumption of the 'reciprocity of perspectives' (Schutz, 1955): 'Think of it from your own point of view,' he said to me, and, situationally, it was difficult to think of grounds for rejecting such an appeal. The appeal was to *common*sense and 'Common-sense has its own necessity; it exacts its due with the weapon appropriate to it, namely an appeal to the "self evident" nature of its claims and considerations.' (Heidegger, 1949) Certainly the police always maintain that they have no vested interest in whether a defendant pleads guilty or not. Plainly, as they themselves point out, police get no monetary bonus if a defendant goes down. But time is also valued. When a court has a morning and an afternoon session, prolongation of the morning session curtails the lunch hour. Conversely, a shortened session can provide a leisure bonus. 'Older policeman sit there thinking whether they'll be out by twelve, in time to have a round of golf, or an hour on their allotments.' (warrant officer, Inner London) Given the volume of business dealt with by the magistrates' courts, such bonuses would be unheard of if the majority of defendants did *not* plead guilty.

Policemen are well aware that concern with time-saving can influence their decision concerning the nature of the charge in the first place: 'Most of them you just charge with being drunk, because if you say "drunk and disorderly" they won't plead guilty. It's a waste of time.' (policeman, Court A) And at the hearing both solicitors and defendants experience police pressure to save time. At one court, a detective, telling a solicitor that he would not accept a surety who lived in Birmingham, said: 'It's not worth raising. *You* don't want to hang around while he's contacted and I'm sure *I* don't.' Similar dependence on an assumption of a consensual evaluation of time gives the police a lever in their pre-trial negotiations with defendants. A policeman at Metropolitan Court with whom I had been discussing this topic turned to me after he had been speaking with a defendant in the gaoler's office, saying: 'He didn't have to give me *that*,' pointing to some written information he had just elicited from the defendant, 'so when he got a bit stroppy I said, "We could always put it over." ' In courts where there are two or more stipendiary magistrates presiding over different courtrooms, the warrant officer will draw on his knowledge of their relative performing times when he does the court lists. . . .

Time-saving is an organisation value, yet, for the majority of the *defendants*, the court experience is characterised by long periods of waiting, unpunctuated by any official explanations about the cause of the delays. "Witnesses, defendants come at ten and their case may not be heard until twelve-thirty.' (Miss B, probation officer) This uncertainty is not diminished by the dearth of information available to them:

> At present some of them turn up at court at ten o'clock, don't appear until half-past twelve. Two and half hours could be agony. They could tell them why their case might be called last — guilty pleas to be dealt with, the police officer detained in another case. All these things are very practical, simple information which an official at the court *can* find out and convey to the client. [Mr G, senior probation officer]

Worse, because cases can be arbitrarily switched from courtroom to courtroom, a defendant can have his case heard in one courtroom while his friends (among them potential witnesses) sit unsuspectingly in the public gallery of an adjacent courtroom. During the long hours of waiting, many defendants become more and more nervous, harbouring fears (usually unfounded) that they will be sent to prison and, in the majority of courts, unable to get either refreshments or privacy in which to talk to their solicitors or probation officers.

So defendants, told to arrive at court at 10 am may wait one, two or even three hours before their cases are 'called on', but the police do the court lists according to a rationality which is rooted in two strands of situational logic. First, they calculate the time a case will take from the experience of the past performing times of the presiding magistrate and clerk. Second, they treat as an organisational norm their assumption that quicker business should take precedence over longer business. What the policemen successfully present as commonsense, however, also has a symbolic pay-off. If, early on in the proceedings, it is established that the court dispenses a swift and sure justice, untarnished by the ambiguity which characterises the later contested cases, then the contested case can structurally be presented as the deviant case, the one which needs special justification and management. Successful assertion by the police of their claim to present these cases in their 'own time' displays a basic feature of their control over the courtroom situation.

Agencies which routinely handle large numbers of people usually develop strategies for promoting their disciplined movement between and within regions. Conventionally, organisational traffic is facilitated by signposting, information-desks, printed rubrics and organisational maps. In magistrates' courts, however, such information is almost non-existent. Arrows indicate courtroom, gaoler's office and various other offices, but inquiring or first-time defendants are predominantly dependent upon the oral and tactile directions of the police.

During the hours when the court is in session, court officials work at speed and under considerable pressure. Not only do they have to hold the prisoners in custody, they have to preserve the law as it is invested in their formally prescribed offices and in their situated personal appearances. Policemen, who know that loss of a prisoner can result in a monetary penalty, have most to lose from any breach of security. As a result, people are differentially monitored and scheduled through the court at different times. The in-built technology of the court's fixtures and fittings are strategic props in the police management of ritual and security.

Locks and keys, doors with spyholes and grilles, inquiry windows opened from the inside, all ensure that only well-screened and officially approved persons move into and between the different regions of the court. As Peter Manning has pointed out: 'Keys imply key-holders and non key-holders; those with access, and those denied it; the important and the excluded; the powerful and the less powerful.' (Manning, 1972)....

All defendants are escorted into the courtroom by the policeman calling the cases. Once the defendant is in the dock the escort acts as a kind of personal choreographer to him. He tells him when to stand up and when to sit down (often in contradiction to the magistrate's directions!), when to speak and when to be quiet, when to leave the dock at the end of the hearing. During the hearing the policeman can tell the defendant to take his hands out of his pockets, chewing-gum out of his mouth, his hat off his head and the smile off his face. Thus even at the outset a series of physical checks, aligned with a battery of commands and counter-commands, inhibits the defendant's presentational style. Once he is in the distraught state of mind where he just 'wants to get it over', judicial fears that he might slow down the proceedings by being 'awkward' are diminished.

With human agents working so watchfully to maintain control, technical appurtenances are not allowed to be remiss in making security doubly secure. . . .

The rules of place are not only binding on defendants. The higher the status of an official in court, the greater the symbolic investment he has in the place. Magistrates, clerks and warrant officers all used the possessive 'my' court when speaking to me, the implication often being that the physical arrangements of 'their' courts were important aids to the realisation of the law's symbolic and instrumental mandate. I asked one of the magistrates at Metropolitan Court: 'Don't you think many people are scared when they come to court?' He replied: 'It's a good thing they are. It makes them tell the truth.'

Some fittings in the courtroom have their own legal and presentational significance. In the witness box people are speaking voluntarily under oath; in the dock they are involuntarily under guard. People who take the oath in a careless or derisory manner are asked to repeat it and enjoined to take it seriously, and at all times the importance of the symbolism of law as an absolutely sacred arbiter of justice is in the minds of most people who work in the courts. . . .

Most courtworkers are concerned with maintaining credibility with the magistrate, but magistrates themselves argue that their own authority is invested in the *place* rather than in their trans-situational statuses as magistrates. They none the less see the degrees of respect shown for the court as reflections of, and on, the image of the bench, and many of the organisational and ceremonial strategies of stage management centre round the presentation of the magistrate. His entrance to the courtroom is both staged and heralded. The opening of the court is signalled by usher calling 'All stand' and 'Silence in court'. When everybody in the courtroom is standing in silence the magistrate enters, his appearance being staged via the door of which he has the exclusive use and which appears to seal off those innermost areas of the court to which the public never has access. Throughout the court hearing, usher ensures that the magistrate is granted deference, interposing himself between those who, without further intermediary, would try to hand documents or letters directly into the magistrate's hands. Each magisterial entrance and exit is marked by the same ceremony.

Interprofessionally and collusively a concerted portrayal of authority and wisdom is maintained by the ceremonial courtesies of complimentary address and reference. Frozen in the rhetoric of their own self-justificatory vocabulary the magistrate becomes 'Your Worship' and 'Your Honour'; the clerk of the court becomes the 'learned clerk'; policemen become 'public servants'; probation officers and social workers become 'these experts who can help you'. What in vulgar parlance might be called the 'scratch-my-back' syndrome becomes in court the rhetorical embroidery on the judicial backcloth. By contrast, the defendant too often becomes just 'this man', unentitled, 'Smith'.

References

Criminal Law Revision Committee (1972) Eleventh Report, *Evidence* (HMSO).

Garfinkel, H. (1956) 'Conditions of successful degradation ceremonies' *American Journal of Sociology* 61 pp. 420–4.

Hall, E. T. (1959) *The Silent Language* (Doubleday).

Heidegger, M. (1949) *Existence and Being* (Vision Press).

Manning, P. (1972) in Henslin, J. *Down to Earth Sociology* (Free Press).

Mark, R. (1973) *Minority Verdict* Richard Dimbleby Memorial Lecture (BBC Publications).

Moore, G. E. (1912) *Principia Ethica* (Cambridge University Press).

Sacks, H. (1967) Transcribed lectures, unpublished.

Schegloff, E. A. (1972) 'Notes on a conversational practice formulating place' in Sudnow, D. *Studies in Social Interaction* (Free Press).

Schutz, A. (1955) 'Symbol, reality and society' in Brysen, L., *et al.* (eds) *Symbols and Society* (Harper).

14. Discussions in the Jury Room: Are They Like This?

by SARAH McCABE

Reprinted, with permission, from *The British Jury System*
(University of Cambridge Institute of Criminology, 1975)
pp. 22–7, being a paper presented to the Cropwood Round
Table Conference, December 1974.

The long-standing debate among lawyers about the justice and propriety of trial by jury has been joined by social scientists who have injected into the argument demands for empirical data that have given rise to surveys and experiments on both sides of the Atlantic. While most of the presuppositions and assertions of judges and legal historians are being put to the test, the most notable concerns the criminal record of the accused, the knowledge of which has been consistently withheld from the jury (save in certain clearly defined circumstances) on the ground that such knowledge would be prejudicial to the accused. The London School of Economics study vindicated this belief only partially, and, in doing so, showed how complex were jurors' collective reactions.

The source of certain other beliefs about jury behaviour — particularly those which ascribed to some jurors irresponsibility, a disregard for the evidence and a considerable urge to punish the defendant — was the publication of accounts of their experience by articulate jurors who seem to have found the discussion in the jury room irrelevant or trivial.[1]

Until the last few years, however, no independent evidence was available to justify or to correct our jury myths. To the Chicago study and the LSE jury experiment we are indebted for the first systematic attempts to present reliable evidence of how twelve men and women in

147

what might be called the 'jury situation' react to the mock trials in which specific issues of evidence were being tested.

I have already referred to one of the conclusions of the LSE study. Of equal interest is Rita James Simon's attempt[2] to see whether there was any difference in an experimental jury's reaction to a plea of insanity when they were instructed in accordance with the M'Naghten or the Durham rules or were left without any instruction whatever. One chapter is devoted to an analysis of the mock juries' discussions, which clearly reflect an attention to the evidence and a responsibility that had not generally been thought to exist in jury deliberations. Indeed their concentration upon the issues before them and their evident involvement in the case led them, at times, to impatient outbursts about the need for more information upon which to base their verdicts. Moreover the vindictiveness that theoretical writers had suggested would be present was replaced by a degree of consideration for the defendant and careful thought about his proper treatment.

There is considerable agreement between these general findings and the evidence of the experiment conducted by the Oxford University Penal Research Unit.[3] Since these shadow juries, however, were recruited to observe a series of actual trials, the evidence that they may provide about jury behaviour is diffuse rather than specific. Nevertheless there could be little doubt that the principal concern of each shadow jury was the evaluation of the evidence presented in court. Of the 'urge to punish' there was little sign; shadow jury members, referring constantly to their own experience, indicated a belief that distinctions between right and wrong are difficult to make in the first place, and certainly almost impossible to discern in the expressed or implied intention of the individual defendants before them. These differing perceptions of right and wrong were ascribed by one shadow juror to the variety of circumstances in which people live:

> You have said you've never known anything to be sold cheap in a pub, or you've never been offered it. Well you see, we've all lived different lives in different circumstances. What I would do, or what I would think or what I would say would not necessarily have to be the same to you or to the woman in question.

On the whole such clearly expressed recognition of the variety of human experience that must be accommodated in a unanimous verdict[4] was infrequent. In their concentration on the evidence, however, 'shadow' jurors gave a great deal of weight to this consideration by looking at the character and background of the accused and assessing his explanation of the offence with this in mind. Throughout the recorded discussions there are references to what kind of character the accused might be, a notion that might derive from his appearance or from his account of himself in the witness box. Thus, a young man accused of carrying an offensive weapon (an open knife) and possessing drugs was variously assessed at different times in a long discussion:

> By his manners in court I gathered him to be the type that would carry an open knife in his pocket and to me I thought he was guilty on this particular count;

or otherwise:

> I don't think he is a vicious type of chap. I think he is more brash than anything else and he carried a knife more for showing off. I don't think he really intended to use it.

Later, near the end of a long debate, the first speaker, who had initiated the evaluation of the defendant's character, returned to this issue and introduced another powerful notion — that of dishonesty.

> Once again I am going back to the character of the lad himself, I am afraid it would appear that lies roll off his tongue for any particular occasion.

The whole series of discussions in this experiment show a subtle and intricate pattern of moral evaluations in which the defendant and his accusers are given different ratings. This is of particular importance since, as we have indicated in an earlier paper,[5] the majority of defendants admit their involvement in an incident which, on the face of it, seems to be criminal. They plead in defence that what seemed to be criminal was not really so, because their intention was not criminal, or they had no guilty knowledge or that the act itself could, in the circumstances, not be called a crime. The defendant, simply by being in the dock (so our shadow jurors seemed to argue), had a guilt potential and therefore a lying potential which had to be counterbalanced by a credible account of his behaviour and a convincing appearance in court. Prosecution witnesses, on the other hand, suffered from no such handicap. For, although their motives, their background, and their character might be subjected to keen scrutiny, their actual honesty was rarely questioned. This notion of deliberate dishonesty as a grave wrong-doing tilted the balance in favour of the prosecution, as this extract may indicate. The accused was charged with the possession of a prohibited drug[6] — he had been chased by the police, caught and taken to the station but no drug was found. Later the police returned to the scene of the arrest and picked up a packet of tablets which they alleged that he had thrown away. The majority of the shadow jury had left the court room convinced of the defendant's guilt. But a long discussion, under a foreman who was pressing for a conviction, failed to bring agreement. Three men held out, and the other members of the shadow jury combined to convince them. On the facts of the case it was argued that *someone* was responsible for putting the drugs where they had been found and the most likely person was either the accused or one or other of the police witnesses. In other words the evidence might have been 'planted'. The foreman took this up

I think this 'plant' thing should be got rid of straight away. Can I go round?

He turns to the most obstinate of the dissenters:

Do you believe in fact that this could have been planted by the police?

The dissentient evaded the question — but was pressed hard by the foreman to make an open admission of his belief in police dishonesty. This no one in the whole course of the discussion could bring himself to do. The most that dissenters would say was that they were dissatisfied with the police evidence (police witnesses were vague in their descriptions of the location), that they had showed ineptitude in not finding the drugs immediately, and so on. In the end the foreman managed to persuade all his fellow shadow jury members that the police were more credible witnesses than the defendant.

In another case where the prosecution's evidence was provided by police witnesses, one shadow jury member expressed a general feeling:

Quite honestly, I don't think we'll get very far if we don't take the evidence of the police. You know they are paid to look after our interests, and that sort of thing.

Explicit references to inaccuracies in the evidence of non-police prosecution witnesses did occur: but on most occasions an understandable explanation was put forward and accepted. Thus, there were several references to the incredibility of the accounts of some store detectives when they sought to obtain convictions against shop-lifters. For example:

Foreman: I don't think the store detective was telling *lies;* she did seem a bit vague about some things.

Another speaker then suggested that the store detective was hired from an agency, and probably had to justify her existence by catching shoplifters and having them convicted.

This view of the prosecution witnesses as being mistaken rather than perjurous shows an understanding of the distortion in all our observations and judgements that comes from our own prejudices. 'We all know that we can become subconsciously biased in which way we want to' (a shadow juror sympathetic to a prosecution witness whom he doesn't quite believe).

In the face of the shadow juror's determination to give all possible credence to the prosecution case, and their acceptance as a fact that defendants were unreliable by definition, how do we explain their high rate of acquittal?

The answer must be in the express requirement that the members of the jury must be 'sure'. When a defendant, however suspect he might appear to be, produced an explanation that seemed to be credible, our shadow jurors would accept it in the absence of any prosecution attempt to disprove it. Indeed the animus against the police and other prosecution witnesses was manifestly not because they were disbelieved but because they did not provide sufficient evidence to support the shadow jurors' insatiable appetite for evidence that they might believe. This requirement of a high standard of proof was interpreted variously by different shadow jurors, but the majority of opinion was that the defendant had a clear right to acquittal if his account of himself was not adequately rebutted by the prosecution. Of course in all cases the defendant's own behaviour was scrutinised to see if it was consistent with his or her story. One woman shoplifter was convicted by a shadow jury because two women jurors convinced their fellows that the defendant's words and behaviour after she was caught did not accord with her plea of forgetfulness. Similarly, a charge of handling was rejected by another shadow jury because the defendant's behaviour after he had received what were later shown to be stolen goods was wholly consistent with his story that he had no suspicion that the goods

were stolen. The prosecution could not cast doubt on this circum-
stantial evidence of the defendant's innocence.

These general observations, about the different degrees of credence
given to prosecution and accused, about the exasperation felt by
shadow jury members at what they conceived to be prosecution
inadequacies and about the understanding of the defendant and his
circumstances that was communicated during the discussion of each
case, cannot be assumed to be applicable to the deliberations of the real
jury: but there is sufficient agreement between the verdicts of real and
shadow juries to indicate that the course of discussion may also have
been similar.

A previous paper[7] has shown that in roughly 75 per cent of cases
there is agreement in the final verdict. This seems reasonable enough
when we remember that the majority of defences are based on the
explanation of his actions that the accused produces in court. Such
explanation may commend itself to one jury and not to another. In the
Oxford experiment there were six cases where the real and shadow
juries were totally at odds. It was possible to see from the evidence how
the verdict could have gone either way. In none of these cases did the
defendant deny that there was some connection between him and the
incident that was the basis of the criminal charge. Three defendants
were charged with handling. Two were acquitted by the real jury and
convicted by the shadow jury. In each of these cases the defendant had
no previous convictions and this was brought forward in their defence.
Our shadow jurors took this into account but could not accept their
story. One woman shoplifter, acquitted in court, was convicted by the
shadow jury on the strong persuasion of two women members who
pointed to the actions of the accused after she had lifted up the goods
she was alleged to have stolen, and suggested that they were
inconsistent with innocent behaviour.

One assaulter was convicted by the shadow jury against the angry
protest of a single member who insisted that the occasion for the fight
was just a 'bundle' where everyone was involved and the accused should
not have been singled out for a criminal charge. Did the majority of the
real jury take this view?

The last case of disagreement may have been partly due to the urgent
representations, in the shadow jury room, of some members who
disliked the production of a police notebook to refresh the memory of
one of the prosecution witnesses.

The conclusions to be drawn from the hours of discussion on which our evidence is based are far from firm, and many more experiments are needed. The reasonable level of discussion, however, the attention to the evidence, the absence of bias, the concern for an idea of justice that was not always based on the case presented in court, are strong impressions that would seem to deny the popular image of a body of men and women behaving in the jury room in an unacceptably irrational, irrelevant and unjust way.

Notes

1. See, for example, the article by Ely Devons in *Modern Law Review, 28* (1965) pp. 561ff.
2. Rita James Simon, *The Jury and the Defence of Insanity* (1967) Little Brown and Co., Boston.
3. This was part of the study of contested trials which has already been reported. Members of the public who were, at that time (1968—70), eligible for jury service were recruited to form 30 shadow juries. They were present at a series of 30 actual trials. Afterwards they were taken into a private room and asked to consider the evidence and bring in a verdict. The deliberations were recorded on tape and form the basis of the present report.
4. Our shadow jurors had listened to the judges' direction, which in all cases stressed the need for unanimous verdict if that were possible. They were not told when or if a majority verdict could be returned, although some of them with jury experience knew that after two hours the jury was usually recalled and instructed to bring in a majority verdict.
5. *The Shadow Jury at Work* Oxford University Penal Research Unit Occasional Paper No. 8 (1974) Basil Blackwell, Oxford.
6. He was also charged with being in possession of an offensive weapon.
7. *The Shadow Jury at Work*. Oxford University Penal Research Unit Occasional Paper No. 8. (1974) Basil Blackwell, Oxford.

15. Serving as a Juryman in Britain

by ELY DEVONS

Reprinted, with permission, in abridged form from *Modern Law Review* 28 (1965), pp. 561–70.

Although a great deal has been written, mostly by lawyers, about the role of the jury in the legal system, none of it, in England at least, is based on information about what goes on in the jury room.

Let me make it clear at the outset that what I have to say is based entirely on two periods of jury service which I was called for in Manchester a few years ago; the first period for the quarter sessions and the second for the assizes, each period for about a week. On each of these two occasions, I served myself on juries for two cases, neither of which lasted more than a single day. The rest of the time I spent sitting around in court, listening to other cases, waiting to be called. But in some of these cases, which I merely listened to, I had none the less an opportunity of discussing, perhaps unlawfully, with the jurymen concerned after the case was over, what had gone on in the jury room and what had influenced the jury in arriving at its conclusion.

It is this question which is the central theme of my lecture – what evidence influences a jury in its findings. But I must repeat, at the risk of boring you, that in answering this question I am merely giving a view of my personal experience which is confined to a small number of cases, and for all I know may be quite unrepresentative. . . .

I tried to find out how people were picked to serve on a jury panel. But the law books that I consulted in England are silent on this. The process of selection seemed to have worked in a peculiar way in my own case; for my legal friends were certainly surprised that I should have been called twice within a period of two years. On the second occasion too those who were called were heavily concentrated in my local area of suburban Manchester, for most of the panel came from three or four adjoining streets.

I was also curious to discover how the jury was picked for a particular case in the courts from the assembled panel. The textbooks suggest that this is a random process, with the method of securing this randomness varying from court to court. It certainly was not random in my case. I was called to attend on Monday morning; all day Monday and Tuesday morning I sat at the back of the court hoping that I would be called for a case, but I was not. To put it mildly, by mid-day on Tuesday I was bored, angry and frustrated. I approached the police sergeant who seemed to be in charge of affairs, and engaged him in general conversation, flattered him not very subtly by saying 'How difficult his job must be', explained that I was getting bored just hanging around not being called. He commented in a strong Lancashire accent which I will not try to reproduce – that sometimes some of those called for the panel did not serve at all. I hoped that that was not going to happen to me. 'Leave it to me,' he said, 'the next case should be quite interesting.' Sure enough, the clerk called my name for the next case. A lesson no doubt in the application of the theory of personal relations.

Before getting to the central theme of the lecture – what influenced the jury in arriving at their decisions in particular cases, I would like to say a little about the general atmosphere in which the jury operated.

First, what struck me was the great contrast between the way the officials – the clerks and the police – treated us, and the attitude of the judges. The clerks and officials treated us so to speak as 'jury fodder', conscripted by legal process: therefore without rights or deserving of consideration. We were herded into rooms, kept waiting without any indication as to when we would be called, or how long our service was likely to run; roughly dismissed with a rude grunt, if we dared to ask 'Is it safe to go off for an hour or two?' Indeed, we began to feel that we were the criminals, awaiting trial.

But once in the court room, the atmosphere changed. We were no longer 'jury fodder', but part of the English legal system; twelve citizens good and true. The judge particularly treated us with great respect and almost ostentatious kindness, making us feel that we were his equals; that indeed we and he were the only sane, normal people, in the whole place. We were the guardians of reason, common sense and everyday language – the fictional 'reasonable men' beloved of the law – in a tangle of doubtful evidence, police jargon and far-fetched legalistic arguments. . . .

When I sat in the jury box on my first case, I was impressed with the following. First, that Englishmen must have been of much smaller bulk when the jury box was first designed, for we were miserably cramped and had to sit bolt upright for long periods; perhaps it was an astute move to make us so uncomfortable that when we did retire to the jury room we would be so weary that we would make our decision quickly. Secondly, how difficult it was to keep track of the evidence without taking notes. But no paper and pencil were provided. Perhaps I ought to have spoken up and asked the judge if I could have some. The fact that I wanted to take notes may just be an occupational failing; but as I shall show later, this implicit reliance on the memory of the jury, especially when the case was a complicated mass of evidence depending on an intricate web of times and locations, had important consequences for the way in which the jury arrived at its conclusions.

Nobody really told the jury what it was supposed to do. True the judge in his summing-up talked to us at some length about the evidence and kept on emphasising 'matters of law are for me; matters of fact are for you'. But I do not think that most of the jurymen understood what this meant — or if they did, they took little notice of it. At no stage did any judge state clearly and boldly 'This court is concerned with (a) whether the man is guilty, (b) what the punishment should be; (b) is not your concern *at all*, but is for me to decide within the limits of the law; (a) you and I have to decide together — for I have to make clear to you what the law is, and you must then decide in the light of the evidence whether you think this man did what he is accused of.' No doubt plain language of this kind is out of place in a court of law, because my phraseology would be ambiguous and uncertain in its meaning to lawyers. Legal language may be certain, but it is over the heads of the jury, and tends therefore to be very largely ignored. Similarly I think that expressions such as 'reasonable doubt', 'reasonable man', 'reasonable case', terminology beloved of the legal theorist, have little meaning for the juror when he meets them for the first time. Perhaps when one has done a week or two's jury service one begins to learn, but by then although one has learned from experience one can no longer benefit by it.

No one told us how we should proceed when we went into the jury room to consider our verdict. For example, that we should elect a foreman. On my first case when we went into the jury room, we stood around, looking at each other rather sheepishly, not knowing where to start. One amongst us then volunteered: 'I know all about this, I have been on a jury before. We have to elect a foreman. Since I know all about it, perhaps you would like me to be foreman.' We all murmured our assent.

You will gather from all this that we all felt in very strange circumstances, not knowing quite what was expected of us or how to proceed. All this could have been avoided if the panel that had been called had been addressed at the outset by, say, the clerk of the court, for a quarter of an hour, explaining to us the procedure of the court, our role in it, and the way in which we were required to fill that role. But a little instruction of this kind would no doubt be thought by the lawyers to be tampering with the open-mindedness of the jury.

All this is preliminary, for the substance of my lecture is concerned with how we arrived at our verdict in the cases we dealt with. My main conclusion, which I can state at the outset, is that you could never tell what bit of evidence would influence the jury, and that frequently they were influenced in arriving at their verdict, not merely by whether they thought the accused was guilty but also whether he should be punished. If they thought there were special circumstances, even if they thought the accused guilty, they were likely to find him not guilty to make sure he was not punished. As the police sergeant, with whom, as I indicated earlier, I had struck up a talking relationship, said to me,

> I have been serving in this court for nigh on twenty-five years. I have listened to hundreds of cases. At first I used to try to assess in advance in each case whether the jury would bring in a verdict of guilty or not guilty. But having experienced some of the craziest decisions imaginable, I have given it up. It is a complete waste of time to try and guess what the jury will do. You might as well toss a coin.

The first case I would like to deal with, which I call 'The Case of the Officious Bureaucrat', concerned a man who was being prosecuted for re-selling used national insurance stamps. The accusation was that the man had got hold of some national insurance cards, steamed off the stamps, rubbed off the cancelling dates, and had used them again, thus avoiding paying the national insurance contribution and defrauding the Insurance Fund. The main evidence came from a Ministry of National Insurance expert, who told us of tests he had done on the gum which had been used to stick on the stamps, and the small bits of fibre that were still attached to the stamps. The first demonstrated that two kinds of gum had been used, one of which was not the kind used on the reverse side of the stamps as issued; the second that there were some bits of fibre adhering to the stamps, different in texture from those of the current card, and clearly giving evidence of some previous adhesion.

Then came evidence from a Ministry of National Insurance official, about how the cards were handled in the Ministry of National Insurance. This was to get clear a small technical point on other evidence which was brought to show the stage at which the employer had the opportunity to purloin old cards. The official, who seemed to me to be quite a junior one, gave his evidence clearly, but somewhat disdainfully, cryptically and officiously − or so it seemed to me − in answer to questions by prosecuting counsel. He was almost the prototype of the petty bureaucrat. Defence counsel was apparently quick to realise this. He started his cross-examination in a slow, drooling manner, purposely I think, wanting the official to think that he, counsel, was a fool, and just did not have the least glimmering of understanding of how an efficient office organisation − like that of the Ministry of National Insurance − was run. As these rather admittedly stupid questions went on, you could almost sense that the civil servant was losing his temper, and at one stage he replied to one of counsel's questions 'that is irrelevant'. Counsel now changed his mien completely; from an apparently silly, rather sleepy, inefficient cross-examiner, he became alive and as sharp as a hawk. He riled the witness who, getting angrier and angrier, got to the point of making the fatal reply, 'That is a silly question'. You can imagine what happened then; the judge intervened, admonished the witness and told him to answer and not to comment on the questions, which the witness did from then on, but in an obviously sulky and surly manner.

In his summing up the judge concentrated on the evidence of the technical expert, pointing out that it had not been seriously challenged, and that the defence had no explanation for it. He hardly mentioned the officious clerk's evidence since this was on quite a minor point. And he pointed out to us that the onus was on the prosecution to prove guilt.

The point of all this is its influence on the jury. When we retired to the jury room − the jurymen turned to each other saying: 'Did you hear that little pipsqueak of a civil servant'; 'These petty bureaucrats, they need to be taught a lesson'; 'I would not like to have to work for him'. When the self-appointed foreman asked for our views on the case, I said that the technical evidence seemed to me to show conclusively that the stamps had been re-used, that this was not rebutted by the defence, and that the accused had given no explanation whatsoever except just flatly to deny having used old stamps. This seemed to me conclusively to point towards his guilt. The others disregarded this altogether and just said one after another: 'But look at that tinpot dictator'; 'these officials'; 'it might happen to us any day'; 'I'm not going to find him guilty'; 'let's teach these civil servants a lesson'. So they all argued for 'Not guilty'. I argued with them for about twenty minutes that they were not directing themselves to the evidence; I called attention to the judge's summing-up and argued that the officiousness of the civil servant was really quite irrelevant. But it was no use; this was what impressed them, and they were determined to do the official world one in the eye. I gave way and we returned a verdict of 'Not Guilty'.

The second case, which I call 'The Case of the Unidentified Intruder', was concerned with a man accused of 'breaking and entering' a domestic household. The evidence can be summarised briefly. First, a married woman, who explained that she went out to work daily during the week coming home at around 5.30. She usually locked the doors and thought she had done so on the particular day in question. When she came home she found the back door open, she heard a noise upstairs, and then a man rushed down the stairs passed her out of the back door. She was so upset and the man dashed by so quickly that she did not see his face and could not identify him. The next witness was a fingerprint expert, who explained that he had examined various fingerprints in the house and that they were identical with those of the accused. He explained that to be sure of a fingerprint identity one had to be able to point, I think it was, to eight characteristics, and that in this case he could identify fourteen, so that he had no doubt whatsoever that the fingerprints were those of the accused.

The accused just flatly denied being in the house, and it was his counsel, in cross-examining the housewife, who had elicited the information that she had not really seen the intruder's face. In summing up the judge drew special attention to the evidence of the fingerprint expert, pointing out the significance of the certainty given by the number of identical characteristics he had found, and indicating that in view of this the fact that the woman was not able to identify the intruder did not really matter.

At this stage the jury withdrew. I ought to point out that this was not a case where I was a member of the jury, but I discussed it at some length with the foreman of the jury afterwards. After about half an hour the foreman of the jury reported that they were in disagreement and unable to reach a verdict. The judge, it seemed to me, was rather surprised by this, told them to go back again and try a little harder. Another three-quarters of an hour passed and the jury reported again inability to agree on a verdict. On this occasion the judge asked counsel for the prosecution what he had to say. As I understand it, he could have asked for a retrial with another jury. His reply was to throw his papers on his desk and his hands up in the air in desperation, indicating that the Crown would not wish to pursue the matter further. And so the accused was released.

When I asked the foreman why the jury could not agree when the fingerprint evidence was so conclusive, he said that about half the jury were sceptical of so-called 'scientific' evidence, and were not prepared to find the man guilty since he had not been seen and identified by the housewife. 'But' I exclaimed, 'fingerprint evidence is in any case more conclusive than someone's memory of a face, which can often be so misleading.' He then told me that he was one of those who were suspicious of fingerprint evidence. I argued with him, but after a few moments it became clear to me that we were really not in communication with each other and I gave up.

The attitude of juries to the evidence of expert witnesses called by the Crown was in general one of suspicion. As many of them said to me, 'That's what they are paid for; they are sure to give evidence against the accused.' It was on this kind of view that they tended on the whole to dismiss the evidence of the police surgeon, in cases of people prosecuted for being in charge of a motor-vehicle while under the influence of alcohol. They persisted in the view that since the police surgeon was a Crown, or as they put it, a police witness, and was paid, he was bound to say that the accused was drunk, and, therefore, no reliance could be placed on his evidence. While I had to admit that the police surgeon always gave evidence that the accused was drunk — if he had not found him drunk the case would not have been brought — I had no success in persuading fellow jurors that it did not follow from this that his evidence should be dismissed.

The third case, which I call 'The Case of the Aged Opera Lover', was concerned with a man prosecuted for being drunk in charge of a car. The police gave evidence that late at night they observed him driving in a swerving manner, and that when they stopped him and opened the car-door, he sat there singing at the top of his voice. They asked him to get out of the car which he did, but could then hardly stand upright. At the police station, where they took him, he was examined by the police surgeon, who gave evidence that in his view the man was quite unfit to drive. The man's own doctor then gave evidence that when he examined the accused (true, about an hour later), in his view he was quite fit to drive. The accused himself gave evidence that he was a great lover of light opera, and that he frequently sang; on the particular occasion in question he was singing something from Gilbert and Sullivan. He admitted that it might seem odd to be singing in his car so loudly, but that the reason was simply that he was bursting with joy of life. He seemed to be quite an elderly man; his defending counsel gave his age as seventy-two. One of the most significant things in this case was the way in which defending counsel managed to get the witness to slip out two points in his evidence, although they were quite irrelevant to the charge, and as I understand it ought not to have been mentioned (and so the judge said in his summing-up). First, that in his business the man depended on being able to drive a car, and that if his driving licence were taken away from him he would be ruined; secondly, that he had been driving for thirty years and had never been in trouble before.

The case was absolutely clear, and after a short time the jury brought in a verdict of guilty. The judge then said 'I now have no option under the law but to suspend your driving licence for twelve months [I think it was twelve], but you may apply after a certain time for it to be restored.' I noticed that one of the lady members of the jury tried to rise as if she wished to say something, and she was pulled down to her seat by the man whom I later discovered was the foreman. You see this was another case on which I was not a juryman but observed the proceedings at the back of the court, and discussed the case with some of the jurymen afterwards. When I did so in this case I asked what was the explanation of the smothered incident in the jury box. The juryman I spoke to explained that when the jury discussed the case they were all agreed that the man had obviously been drunk. But the two women members of the jury had said 'It's a pity for the poor old man; it is the first time he has been in trouble, and he will be ruined if he cannot use his car in his business; let us be merciful and find him not guilty.' The others protested, saying that it was for the jury merely to decide whether the accused was guilty or not. If they were clear on that they must bring in a verdict accordingly. The punishment was for the judge who would no doubt be sympathetic and probably only impose a small fine. 'All right,' said the two women jurors, 'on the clear understanding that the judge will only fine him and not take away his licence we will agree to a verdict of guilty.' But none of the jurors apparently knew that for an offence of that kind the judge had no option, as indeed he explained, but to suspend the man's licence. When he was delivering sentence to that effect, one of the women jurors apparently wanted to protest that she had been misled and wished no longer to find the accused guilty. She had to be restrained by the foreman; this accounts for the smothered incident which I referred to earlier.

My last case — here I did serve on the jury myself — I call 'The Case of the Unrepresented Defendant' was a man who was accused of stealing a portable second-hand wireless set from a pawnbroker's shop that had been broken into. One of the important features of this case was that the defendant, notwithstanding advice from the judge, refused to be legally represented and insisted on conducting his own defence. The details of the case were very complicated, for they involved evidence about the time at which the shop had probably been broken into; identification of the wireless set by the man who had pawned it to the shop, as the same as the one found in the defendant's possession. There was argument by the Crown, notwithstanding evidence brought by the defendant from friends as to where he had been at various times on that day, that he could have been in the neighbourhood of the pawn-broker's shop at the crucial time. The defendant pleaded that he had bought the wireless set in a pub for three pounds from a stranger whom he did not know and whom he could not now get hold of to bring forward as a witness. I must admit that I do not now remember in detail all the evidence; but I do recall that it was long and complicated, involving a whole series of arguments about times. I also recall that when the judge came to sum up I found it impossible to follow or remember the crucial points because, as I mentioned right at the beginning, we were not in a position to take notes. Towards the end of the evidence the judge said to the defendant. 'Are you quite sure that you have asked all the witnesses all the questions that you wish to, and that you have called all the witnesses you wish to call?' At this late stage the accused murmered 'there are two witnesses who could conclusively support my evidence that I was not at the shop at the relevant time, but it is no use trying to call them'. The judge persisted in explaining to the defendant that if he wanted to call witnesses they would be called. The defendant then made what seemed to me to be the mistake of saying 'It is no use because they are in Strangeways Gaol.' But the case was adjourned and the witnesses were called. Out of the questions that he asked there emerged incidentally the fact that the defendant and these witnesses had been in jail together several times, and from that moment onwards he was clearly regarded as a criminal type by the jury.

The judge summed up the complicated evidence about times and places and told us to ignore the fact that had emerged in the evidence that the defendant had already been in jail for previous offences. When it came to the jury room discussion we were pretty well at sea; for not having taken any notes, none of us could reliably remember the detailed evidence about times and places. We concentrated on two issues; the plausibility of the accused's evidence that he had bought the wireless set for £3 in a pub, and his criminal record. On the first we asked each other 'Do people really buy and sell wireless sets in a pub?' None of us went to working-class pubs – here the class composition of the jury was important – and we just did not know whether transactions of this kind were likely to take place there. But we *thought*, and I repeat *thought*, that it was most unlikely. Secondly, most of the jurymen were influenced by the criminal record of the accused's friends and of the accused himself. And so, I repeat with practically no consideration of the evidence, we found the man guilty. Perhaps no injustice was done. Certainly when the list of his previous convictions was read out before the judge pronounced sentence, it took quite a long time to get through.

This completes my cases, and the story I have to tell of serving as a juryman in Britain. Do I draw any conclusions? Perhaps I ought not to; except one which I will venture with some assurance. That if the jury is to remain part of the English legal system, it is just as well that its proceedings should remain secret, and that it should only be on very rare and special occasions like this that jurymen should discuss their experience.

16. Anything but the Truth? The Reliability of Testimony in Criminal Trials

by D. S. GREER

Reprinted, with permission, in abridged form from *British Journal of Criminology*, 11 (1971), pp. 131–54.

One of the virtues traditionally claimed for the common law trial is its emphasis on the need for first-hand evidence delivered orally and in person by direct eye-witnesses of facts relevant to the issue being tried. A second characteristic feature is that the accused is not to be convicted unless it has been proved beyond a reasonable doubt that he committed the crime with which he is charged. Although many lawyers concede that the oral evidence of individual witnesses is often open to reasonable doubt, they usually deny that criminal trials in general fail to discover the 'true' facts in most cases, on the ground that various procedures have been devised to eliminate erroneous testimony either substantially or altogether. It is therefore fairly generally assumed that the evidence provided by witnesses is sufficiently reliable to justify conviction or acquittal. The purpose of this article is to examine some of the evidence which tends to show that such an assumption may well be unfounded.

To say that the common law relies heavily or primarily on the oral evidence of witnesses rather over-simplifies the position in a number of ways. Thus, in several cases where evidence is contained in a document, the court will give precedence to that document over the oral testimony of the party or parties who drew it up (Cross, 1968, p. 494). Similarly, many rules have developed to determine which witnesses may give what evidence, and when and how they may give it. The most notorious of these rules is, of course, the one which generally excludes hearsay evidence. These rules are supposedly designed to aid the court in its search for the true facts. But it is a curious paradox that those very rules are themselves based on no evidence which would be admissible in any court applying those rules. Take for instance one exception to the hearsay rule. A declaration of a deceased person is admissible in certain cases if, at the time it was made, that person was under a 'settled hopeless expectation of death'.[1] No one has ever produced any evidence which tended to show that persons in such circumstances actually do tell the truth. That such is the case is indeed more of a judicial 'hunch' than a proven fact. . . . This applies to many other rules of evidence and of procedure and it would seem to be a fair comment that those rules have largely been constructed from what is claimed to be reason backed by experience and intuition, but what more realistically could be described as 'conjecture about human behaviour' (Cleary, 1952, p. 289).

If no evidence were in fact available or discoverable to verify or refute such conjectures there could be no cause for criticism of or concern with this approach. But there is already in existence a considerable body of scientifically obtained evidence which may well provide data on the basis of which more accurate rules of evidence and of procedure could be constructed. The reference is, of course, to the findings of psychologists, and in particular to the findings of applied psychologists, who have for a long time been working in this area.

Unreliability of witness evidence has at least three aspects: (1) witnesses may testify dishonestly; (2) witnesses may testify honestly but incorrectly; and (3) witnesses may disappear, recant or die before the case comes on for trial. This article is limited to a consideration of the second source of unreliability mentioned — the testimony of honest witnesses — and the ways in which this may be compounded by the adversary system, by rules of evidence and procedure and by the law's methods of determining 'facts'.

The psychology of such testimony was, in fact, one of the earliest concerns of applied psychology (Anastasi, 1964, p. 548). Although this concern probably originated in France (Binet, 1895), the best known of the earliest experiments — and probably also the most interesting from a legal point of view — were those conducted in Germany at the turn of this century by William Stern (1939). The methods used by him, though since revised and considerably refined, are still the basic methods of this type of psychological research. In these experiments, the subjects (who are the experimental equivalents of witnesses) are shown a picture, a series of pictures or a moving film for a certain length of time; either immediately after this exposure or some time later, they are asked to describe the various details of what they saw. These descriptions are obtained either by asking each subject to narrate or write down as much of the details as he can recall, or by asking each of them to answer a number of questions about these details. This method of investigation has come to be known as an 'Aussage' or 'Remembrance' test.

By way of example, in one of Stern's earliest experiments he presented to his students certain pictures, the content of which was to be reported on after study for forty-five seconds. The students knew while they were viewing the pictures that they would be required to report on their content. This report was called for immediately after the presentation; and the students were asked to include only those items which they still remembered *with certainty*. In the result, the reports contained a considerable number of incorrect statements, and as Stern comments, 'these errors did not always pertain to non-essentials'. Some weeks later, the students were again asked to describe the picture from memory: the result this time was that the amount of error had doubled (Stern, 1939, pp. 7—8).

This method of experiment however does not, at least on first sight, seem very appropriate for investigating the reliability of witnesses who have actually observed the events about which they are asked to testify. It would seem clear, on a common-sense basis at least, that there is a considerable distinction between seeing and reporting on an actual event and being shown and reporting on details of a picture or series of pictures. Perhaps for this reason, psychologists have developed a refinement of the Aussage test and this has become known as a 'reality experiment'. In this the sort of events and actions experienced by and testified to by witnesses are actually simulated by actors.

Thus it was on Stern's suggestion that Professor von Liszt, a professor of law, conducted the following experiment in 1901. During a seminar with law students, a 'controversy' developed between two of the students. A quarrel arose and increased in vehemence until one of the participants actually drew a revolver. At this point von Liszt intervened and asked for written and oral reports from those who had witnessed the incident. The results of this experiment, according to Stern, were that (i) none of the reports was faultless; (ii) the number of errors varied from four to twelve per report; (iii) the erroneous statements accumulated to the second half of the occurrence — that is towards the more exciting events — tending to show that increasing interest not only did not augment but was in fact detrimental to the exactness of the testimony (Stern, 1939, pp. 16—17; Munsterburg, 1908, pp. 49—51).

Seven years later, *On the Witness Stand*, the first book on what has come to be known as 'legal psychology', was published by another German psychologist, Hugo Munsterburg. In 1892 Munsterburg had been appointed professor of psychology at Harvard. He was very interested in applying psychology to practical problems and his attention soon turned to legal procedure. He conducted classroom demonstrations and experiments to show that trained observers (i.e. psychology students) with generous advance warnings could not agree on such matters as the number of squares on a board, the amount of time between two clicks, the pitch of a sound and the shape of an ink blot. The testimony of such observers, even though taken immediately after their exposure to an object, tended to range widely. Thus in an experiment to test perception of time the students were asked to give the number of seconds between two clicks. The actual number was ten; but the answers ranged from ½ to 60, most being about 45. On this Munsterburg commented that:

> these large fluctuations showed themselves in spite of the fact that the students knew beforehand that they were to estimate the time interval. The variations would probably have been still greater if the question had been put to them without previous information; and yet a District Attorney hopes for a reliable reply when he enquires of a witness. . . how much time passed by between a cry and the shooting in the cab. . . . [Munsterburg, 1908, p. 22]

The first common lawyer to take an interest in these developments appears to have been Wigmore (1931, pp. 536—40). In 1905 he had conducted at Northwestern University Law School in Chicago a series of 'Testimonial and Verdict Experiments' which carried the 'reality experiment' a couple of stages further in legal relevance. The details of the dramatic incident — a quarrel between four of the students in his class — were agreed on beforehand and written down. The 'row' was then enacted during a lecture. An immediate adjournment took place to the law school courtroom. There, a jury of law students who had not witnessed the row was empanelled. Thirteen witnesses of the incident were arbitrarily selected and each was asked a series of nine questions about what had happened. The jurors then retired to consider the evidence and returned with their verdict — i.e. their version of the row. This version was then compared with the pre-arranged version and the following are some of the differences discovered:

(1) The person found by the 'jury' to have made the first move did not in fact make it.

(2) Several relevant 'facts' were not mentioned in the jury's version — e.g. that one of the participants had shouted 'That is an insult and I shall here resent it.'

(3) The jury's version of another statement uttered during the incident differed from that actually made.

Little notice appears to have been taken in the British Isles of these developments for some time. The first article of legal interest would seem to have been that by a Cambridge psychologist in 1916 (Muscio, 1916). This accepted the basic proposition that the answer to a question is, under certain conditions, partly determined by the form of the question, and attempted to compare two particular question forms by looking at the information yielded by each as compared with the 'objective' facts. From a lawyer's point of view, this is a very relevant area for research. The legal definition of a leading question is 'one which either (a) suggests the answer desired, or (b) assumes the existence of disputed facts' (Cross, 1968, p. 192). Whether or not a question suggests the answer desired is usually assumed to be axiomatic or self-explanatory and reference is seldom made to the possibility that some questions may be more suggestive than others. Muscio attempted to determine the relative suggestiveness of two forms of question — a 'subjective-direction' question (such as 'Did you see a pistol on the table?') and an 'objective-direction' question ('Was there a pistol on the table?'). His conclusions were that:

(1) Witnesses are more cautious in answering subjective-direction questions than objective-direction ones. In other words, a witness is more likely to answer 'I do not know' if asked '*Did you see* such and such?' than if asked '*Was there* such and such?'

(2) But if the witness is prepared to answer either 'yes' or 'no', he is more likely to answer 'yes' if asked '*Did your see* etc.?' than if asked '*Was there* etc.?'

Finally, one of the first instances of actually using a psychologist in court to evaluate testimony appears to have occurred in Belgium in 1910. A psychologist was asked to evaluate evidence obtained from two little girls by questioning at a preliminary hearing. In an attempt to discover to what extent their evidence could have been the result of suggestion stimulated by the questions they were asked, a series of experiments incorporating similar questions was devised These questions were then put to a number of children of similar age and background to the two witnesses. Their answers clearly showed that the original testimony could well have resulted from the suggestiveness of the questions. The results of the experiments were presented in evidence and the jury brought in a verdict of acquittal of the accused (Rouke, 1957, p. 55).

By 1910, then, there had already been quite a lot of interest shown in the application of psychological findings to the evaluation of the reliability of testimonial evidence. In some instances, these findings had actually been applied in real or in simulated criminal trials. Important claims were being made for the development of a legal-psychological approach to problems of evidence. . . .

Before dealing with some of the more recent psychological evidence, it would be useful to consider why, after such a promising beginning, the findings, claims and exhortations of the early psychologists have had so little apparent effect on the law of evidence. It seems reasonable to attribute this inactivity partly to psychologists, partly to lawyers and partly to the fact that, although the banns were read on different occasions, the proclaimed impending marriage between the two disciplines was never consummated.

Although a number of psychologists carried out various experiments concerned with aspects of legal testimony (e.g. Slesinger and Pilpel, 1929; McCarty, 1929; Burtt, 1931) the initial burst of enthusiasm for this field of applied psychology was not sustained and had all but disappeared by 1930. Psychologists came to be more concerned with animal and child psychology. . . . This changing concern may have been influenced by a general lack of interest and encouragement from the legal profession and from academic lawyers and the poor reception (often unfortunately justified) which psychologists were given when allowed to give evidence in court. In the United Kingdom, for instance, the first reported 'reality experiment' appears to have been as late as 1952. . . . And the first general reference to the findings of psychology in a discussion of the law of evidence is G. Williams's *The Proof of Guilt*, published in 1955 (Williams, 1955, Chapter 5). But **whatever** may be the reason for the changed emphasis of the psychologists' concern, the timing would at first sight seem to be unfortunate for the development of legal psychology in that the decline of psychological interest in the reliability of testimony coincided fairly closely with the rise of legal interest in 'realism' and in particular with the development of what came to be known as 'fact-scepticism' (Frank's *Law and the Modern Mind* was published in 1930 (Frank, 1930)).

It was perhaps natural for the legal profession to distrust 'new' disciplines. Consider for example the reluctance of lawyers and courts to accept modification of the McNaghten Rules to take account of contemporary developments in psychiatry. Psychology was evidently viewed with a similar distrust. This was apparent from the first beginnings of 'legal' psychology.

It seems [however] that there is nothing inherent in the nature of the psychologist's approach to problems of evidence which compels its rejection out of hand. The proper approach is to look at particular experiments and the conclusions based on them and consider their validity for legal purposes on a pragmatic basis. . . .

It *was* [nevertheless] the case that 'testimonial experts' had failed to produce data which were sufficiently precise and accurate and conclusive to justify a specific new rule of evidence or amendment of a particular existing rule. There can be little doubt that this lack of precise data and the concomitant crudeness from the legal point of view of most of the experiments were primarily due to the fact that most of this work was done by the psychologists on their own. As a result they apparently failed not only to appreciate the intricacies and complexities of legal procedures for eliciting testimony but also to grasp the important point that 'the truth' is not the only objective of the criminal trial. . . .

Many of the psychologists, therefore, tended to over-sell the legal implications of their work and seemed to expect their findings to be regarded as virtual saviours of the integrity of the legal system. In fact these findings tended to be too vague and inconclusive to have any practical legal value. Nevertheless, they did present a *prima facie* case worthy of further investigation by lawyers. This was never done because lawyers have tended to take the attitude that it is up to the psychologists to prove their case beyond a reasonable doubt or even beyond all doubt. Failure to do so was taken to indicate defects in the psychologists or in their methods rather than a need for expert legal assistance.

Whether or not this is an adequate analysis of the failure to cooperate, it seems clear that the failure to produce precise and relevant data is attributable not to inherent and necessary weaknesses in the experimental methods, but to almost complete absence of real co-operation between experts in the two disciplines. This is reflected in the literature on legal psychology. Much of this is concerned either with a general review by a lawyer of what are considered legally relevant psychological findings, or with a report by a psychologist of an experiment on what is considered a legally relevant topic. There are few published reports of co-operative investigation of specific legal rules. The remainder of this article will therefore attempt to present experimental findings which relate to a small number of specific rules.[2]

Reconstructing the Scene of the Crime

In certain cases a trial judge may direct a 'view' in which the witnesses return to the scene of the crime and point out to the jury where they stood when observing the acts on which the defendant's guilt is alleged.[3] This may be an unjustified reliance on the perception of the witnesses.

On the whole, it seems, psychological theory in the field of perception is fairly well advanced. It is now generally recognised that there is an important distinction between 'actual' and 'perceived' characteristics of the environment. . . . What a witness cognises perceptually is not necessarily an exact reproduction of the data presented and for legal purposes at any rate the most important finding in this area is that there can be a very considerable discrepancy between the two.

Many of the causes of this discrepancy are already well known e.g. the adverse effect on accuracy of testimony of poor lighting, long distance, short duration of exposure, etc. (Vernon, 1966). Less well-known factors influencing perception include emotion, interest, bias, prejudice, or expectancy, on the part of the perceiver. Take for instance, the effect of 'expectancy' or 'set'. It is a well-documented fact that we frequently perceive what we expect to perceive (Vernon, 1966, Ch. 5). If we expect to see an individual performing a particular action we are more likely than not to interpret a stimulus which is in fact ambiguous as evidence that the person is performing the expected action.

One example of this is provided by Haward (1963), a psychologist who was called in by the defence in an English case where two men were charged with having committed an act of gross indecency in a public convenience. Complaints had been made to the police that the convenience was being used for indecent purposes and the accused were apprehended by two policemen who were keeping the convenience under secret observation. The defendants denied that any criminal acts had taken place. The psychologist reproduced the defence version of the facts (i.e. no criminal act) in a series of photographs and he showed these to twelve adults under different conditions of light, for varying lengths of time, and with reference to three different questions: In A they were merely asked to say what they saw in the pictures; in B they were asked if they could see any crime being committed in any of the pictures; in C they were told that some of the pictures actually portrayed criminal acts being committed and they were asked to identify the pictures concerned.

The result was that the number of errors increased considerably from A to B to C. In other words, the witnesses most frequently erred in asserting that a crime was being committed when they were led to expect to see this criminal behaviour. The police, therefore, expecting to see an indecent act being committed might well have put an erroneous interpretation on innocent facts. In the event, the accused were acquitted.

'Spontaneous' Exclamations as Exceptions to the Hearsay Rule

One exception to the hearsay rule in some common law jurisdictions (though not conclusively established by the authorities as far as English law is concerned (Cross, 1968, pp. 464—7)) is statements made contemporaneously with a relevant event and which directly concern it. . . . On this reasoning, spontaneity excludes the possibility of fabrication by allowing no time for conscious thought. This may well be justified although experiments have shown that the difference in time between an ordinary 'spontaneous' reaction and a deceptive reaction to significant words is so minute that it can only be measured with the aid of instruments (Marston, 1920). As far as the honest witness is concerned, it has been shown that the emotion due to the agony of the moment causes physical and psychological changes which distort intellectual activity and make perception very unreliable (Gorphe, 1927, p. 213). Thus in one experiment a pre-arranged fight took place in a classroom. Afterwards the students who took part were asked to write an account of the incident. It was found that the testimony of the most upset students was practically worthless. This and other experiments have prompted the suggestion that the rule referred to above should preferably read — Hearsay is inadmissible, especially if it be a spontaneous exclamation! (Hutchins and Slesinger, 1928a).

Effect of Pre-trial Publicity

Apart from the laws of contempt and defamation, there are no restrictions on publication by the Press and other news media of material relating to the commission of a crime until criminal proceedings are 'pending or imminent'. News media are therefore quite free to publish all sorts of stories about a crime which may subsequently turn out to be wholly erroneous. Paradoxically, the latest attempt to reduce the possibility of prejudicial publicity may have had the opposite effect — 'where the press could formerly report factual evidence given on oath at committal proceedings, they may now feel constrained to rely increasingly on rumour' (Napley, 1967, p. 25). The usual fear in this context is that jurors at the subsequent trial will be prejudicially affected by the pre-trial publicity; but it may well be that we should be at least equally concerned about the effect of such publicity on the accuracy of a witness's recall of what he perceived.

According to many, the classic text on memory is still Bartlett's *Remembering* published in 1932. The thesis laid down there as a conclusion warranted by his experiments was that the processes of memory are dynamic ones which are susceptible to influence from the same factors as perception. Memory is not a simple storage and reproductive system; we organise, synthesise and distort our memories according to psychological and physiological demands. In other words, a person's temperament, interests and attitudes determine the content of what is recalled. The result of this is that a person's memory is often inaccurate or inadequate, and that completely accurate recall is exceptional (Hunter, 1964, pp. 172–5). There is a tendency, however, usually unconscious, to fill in gaps in one's memory with plausible details which are consistent with one's general perception and memory of the event (Bartlett, 1932, pp. 204–05). A witness can often be quite certain that he actually perceived a certain detail although in fact it is the product of unconscious suggestion.

As a result, lawyers may tend to under-estimate the importance to a witness's memory at a trial of events occurring before the trial. In one experiment a lecturer made a number of statements about the results of a series of experiments. A reporter for the student newspaper printed an entirely erroneous account of these statements. At the end of the week the students were examined on the lecture. Those who had not read the article reported the lecture with just their customary inaccuracy. But those who had read the press report were even more inaccurate in their recall of what the lecturer had actually said (Bird, 1927).

This time factor is also relevant with regard to the rule restricting counsel from asking his own witness leading questions during the trial. This is intended presumably to prevent counsel from 'leading' a witness to give evidence favourable to his side. But that witness will probably have been questioned before the trial either by that counsel or his solicitor, and during this interview leading questions may well have been used which suggest to the witness details of evidence which he later gives in reply to proper questions on direct examination. In other words, coaching of a witness may take place unconsciously (Frank, 1949, p. 86).

The Efficacy of the Oath

In his *Rationale of Judicial Evidence*, Bentham [1843] considers which 'instruments' tend to secure trustworthiness in evidence, and which are false securities for trustworthiness. It is into the latter category that he puts the oath. . . . His main reason for rejecting . . . [it] . . . (apart from saving the Almighty a lot of overtime and some difficult questions of interpretation) was that mendacity, if called for by an exciting motive, takes place unrestricted by the fact of an oath having been taken. . . .

Most writers on this topic have been concerned with the efficacy of the oath to restrict deliberately false evidence. There is, however, a possibility that taking an oath encourages an honest witness to be *more* careful and therefore to give more reliable evidence.

For example, Stern found that the effect of asking subjects to underline passages in reports upon which the writer would take an oath was that some subjects narrowed down the report markedly and by omitting erroneous passages improved the quality of the testimony. But *most did not* — they were still willing to confirm nearly all details. The result of this was that each report contained on average one or two false statements (Stern, 1939, p. 9).

In a more detailed study students were asked to scrutinise a picture and answer sixty questions about it at various time intervals after observation. They were also asked to indicate on how many answers they would be prepared to take an oath as to accuracy. The results showed that the effect of asking the subjects to take an oath reduced slightly the number of wrong answers. A similar effect has been found in other experiments (Burtt, 1931, pp. 153–5; Hutchins and Slesinger, 1928b).

Methods of Eliciting Facts in Court

The third stage in the process of giving evidence is the method by which testimony is elicited. The common law approach is almost exclusively that of the question-answer method, the questions sometimes being of a leading character (Cross, 1968, Ch. X). In a few instances, however, the method of elicitation can be regarded as roughly equivalent to free narration of his story or part of it by the witness. This occurs in those few circumstances where the witness is allowed to refer to a document in order to refresh his memory, or where a written statement made by a witness is allowed to be read out in court. Apart from the work done on the suggestiveness of leading questions, to which some reference has already been made, psychologists have been interested in at least two problems of legal significance in this area — which form of eliciting testimony is most likely to produce reliable evidence and the extent to which the persuasiveness of evidence is influenced by the order of its presentation.

The first question was the basis for a well-known experiment in 1924 (Marston, 1924). The usual sort of dramatic incident was staged during a lecture on legal psychology. The persons attending the lecture were all qualified lawyers and the incident contained a large number of details (over 100) of possible legal significance. None of those present had any intimation that an experiment was to be performed, and none was

TABLE 1. *Comparison of methods of eliciting testimony.* *

	Free narration	Direct examination	Cross-examination
	%	%	%
Completeness	23.2	31.2	28.7
Accuracy	94.05	83.2	75.7
Caution	–	40.1	51.8

*Average *percentage* score of witnesses reporting an unexpected incident.

aware that a test was in progress until the incident had been concluded and the lecturer began to issue instructions for recording of testimony.

Table 1 shows the results of this experiment. 'Completeness' refers to the number of details given *correctly* in the reports. For example, the 'witnesses' testified correctly to an average of a little over 34 details in the 'free narration' part of their evidence. This was out of a possible total of 147, and represents a score of 23.2 per cent. Accuracy refers to the number of correct details given as compared with the total number of details included in the report. Thus the witnesses on free narration gave an average of 36 details in their reports, and on average 34 of these were correct (94.05 per cent). 'Caution' compares the number of times the witnesses answered 'Don't Know' or failed to answer with the number of erroneous answers. The conclusions drawn by Marston from Table 1 were that

(1) Free narration is less complete but more accurate than the other two methods: i.e. on free narration a witness will not give as many details, but those he does give are most likely to be correct.

(2) Direct examination is both more complete and more accurate than cross-examination: i.e. on direct examination a witness will give more details than on cross-examination and these are also more likely to be correct.

(3) Cross-examination shows greater caution than direct examination without any corresponding gain in either completeness or accuracy. It would appear to follow that added caution does an important, though hidden, work in redeeming cross-examination from a degree of inaccuracy which would render it almost wholly worthless; i.e when a witness does not know the answer on

cross-examination, he is as likely to answer erroneously as 'I don't know', but on direct examination he is more likely to answer erroneously than 'I don't know'.

These conclusions again are confirmed by later experiments (e.g. Anastasi, 1964, p. 548). On the whole, then, cross-examination is alleged to be the most unreliable method of eliciting testimony. These, remember, were the answers of lawyers. When given these figures many of them complained that the poor results were due to the fact that the details of the staged incident were all very usual, and they argued that, if the details were less usual or they were forewarned that something to be especially observed was about to occur, then the results would show considerable improvement. Consequently this same incident (with slightly different details) was again staged some time later. In this way, it was claimed, as nearly as actual conditions usually obtained in observations of actions especially attracting a witness's attention, and on which he knew, while making the observation, that he would be called on to report later, could be and were reproduced experimentally. The reports of those who were witnessing the incident for a second time are compared with their scores on the first test in Table 2. It will be seen that, although completeness has generally increased, the accuracy of the reports has generally *decreased* and the witnesses have become much less cautious. In other words, the gain which might have been expected to result from repetition of identical perceptions and report of almost identical observations in the second experiment was largely counteracted, and during a considerable part of the testimony was completely reversed, by the over-confidence or self-assurance of the subjects witnessing the same incident for a second time.

TABLE 2. *Average percentage superiority of witnesses reporting incident for a second time.* *

	Free narration	Direct examination	Cross-examination
Completeness	+22	−3.1	+7.2
Accuracy	−11.2	−16	−27
Caution	−	−23.1	−33

*Comparison is with score on first report (Marston (1924) p. 15).

The Effect of Order of Presentation on Persuasiveness of Evidence

One method of experiment has been designed to investigate the hypothesis that the persuasiveness of a witness's evidence is not a constant, but may depend on the order in which it is produced during the trial. The method is to take the transcript of an actual trial and present the testimony to a simulated 'jury' (Weld and Roff, 1938; Miller and Campbell, 1959). The testimony given in the real trial is divided into instalments and at the end of each instalment, each 'juror' is asked to record his opinion, at that point, as to the relative guilt or innocence of the defendant on a points basis ranging from certainty of innocence to certainty of guilt. Thus in Weld and Roff, 1938, p. 619, a trial was divided into thirteen instalments and a nine-point scale of guilt/innocence was used. The lines in the table represent the median value of all the jurors' judgments for each instalment in two different experiments. The dotted line represents evidence for the prosecution, the unbroken line evidence for the defence. In Experiment 1 the evidence was presented in the usual order – prosecution, then defence. But in some exceptional cases the prosecution is allowed to call a witness after the close of the defence (Walker and Walker, 1967, p. 371). This order is simulated in Experiment 2. In both experiments exactly the same evidence was adduced, only the order was changed. Yet the final verdict in Experiment 1 was 2.3 (a strong belief in innocence) whereas in Experiment 2 it was 5.4 (somewhere between doubtful and slight belief in guilt). The conclusion does seem warranted that the final result was influenced by the order in which the testimony was given. It can also be shown by this method that the effectiveness of

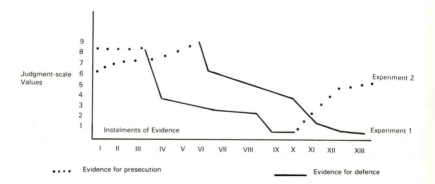

the same testimony depends in part on its ordinal place. However, the particular experiment referred to here loses a lot of its validity because summing-up by counsel and the trial judge has not been included among the thirteen instalments. Nor was the evidence presented orally by witnesses subject to cross-examination. The experiment would therefore be vulnerable to many of Wigmore's criticisms; but these weaknesses do not rob the experiment of all its validity – and many of those weaknesses are curable. A more damning criticism is that some later writers have argued that the effects of primacy in a courtroom situation have been considerably exaggerated (Hovland, 1959).

Conclusions

These, then, are some of the experiments by which psychologists and others have sought to test the reliability of witnesses' testimony and the validity of some legal rules of evidence and procedure. Although by no means conclusive, they do seem to justify the following conclusions:

(1) The testimony of honest witnesses is less reliable than is generally supposed.

(2) This is due partly to factors already recognised but not fully understood and partly to factors not yet recognised.

(3) Psychologists have established a *prima facie* case at least for recognition by lawyers that they can contribute to the study of evidentiary and procedural problems.

(4) By proper development and use of the experimental methods of psychology we may well be able to construct a law of evidence more closely related to known facts of human behaviour.

There is therefore a strong case for immediate interdisciplinary study in depth of these problems. Fortunately interest in such study appears to have revived, especially in connection with the various jury projects in the United States and in England (Simon, 1967; Marshall, 1966; Cornish, 1968). And on at least one recent occasion the decision whether or not to recommend the introduction of a new rule of evidence has been deferred pending further experimental investigation (JUSTICE, 1968). It is to be hoped that this revived interest in 'legal psychology' will now rapidly develop and assist in the creation of a more rational law of evidence.

Notes

1. E.g. R. *v.* Perry [1909] 2 K.B. 697 (C.C.A.).
2. It will be noted that the examples chosen all concern what may be called 'actuarial' rules of evidence; no attempt is being made here to consider experiments designed to evaluate the reliability of an individual witness.
3. Eg. R. *v.* Martin (1872) L.R. 1 C.C.R. 378, Karmat *v.* R. [1956] 1 All E.R. 415.

References

Anastasi, A. (1964) *Fields of Applied Psychology* (New York: McGraw-Hill Book Co.).

Bartlett, F. C. (1932). *Remembering* (Cambridge: University Press).

Bentham, J. (1843). *Rationale of Judicial Evidence* (in *The Works of Jeremy Bentham* (Bowring, ed.), Vol. VI (Edinburgh: Tait).

Binet, A. (1895). *La Suggestibilité.* (Paris: Reinwald).

Bird, C. (1927). 'The influence of the press on the accuracy of report', *J. Abnorm. and Soc. Psychol,* 22, pp. 123–9.

Burtt, H. E. (1931). *Legal Psychology* (New York: Prentice-Hall).

Cleary, E. W. (1952). 'Evidence as a problem in communicating', *Vanderbilt Law Review,* 5, pp. 277–93.

Cornish, W. R. (1968). *The Jury* (London: Allen Lane).

Cross, A. R. N. (1968). *Evidence* (3rd edn) (London: Butterworths).

Frank, J. (1930). *Law and the Modern Mind* (Magnolia, Mass.: Peter Smith Co).

—— (1949). *Courts on Trial* (Princeton: University Press).

Gorphe, F. (1927). *La Science du Témoignage.* (Paris).

Haward, L. R. C. (1963). 'The reliability of corroborated police evidence in a case flagrante delicto', *J. Forensic Science Soc.,* 3, pp. 71–81.

Hovland, C. I. (1959). 'Reconciling conflicting results from experimental and survey studies of attitude change', *Amer. Psychol.,* 14, pp. 8–23.

Hunter, I. M. L. (1964). *Memory* (Harmondsworth: Penguin).

Hutchins, R. M. and Slesinger, D. (1928a). 'Some observations on the law of evidence – spontaneous explanations', *Columbia Law Review,* 28, pp. 432–40.

—— (1928b). 'Some observations on the law of evidence – competency of witnesses', *Yale Law Journal,* 37, pp. 1017–28.

JUSTICE (1968). 'Report of Committee on Admission of Accused's Record' London: mimeo.

McCarty, D. G. (1929). *Psychology for the Lawyer* (Englewood Cliffs NJ: Prentice-Hall).

Marshall, J. (1966). *Law and Psychology in Conflict* (Indianapolis: Bobbs-Merrill Co.).

Marston, W. H. (1920). 'Reaction-time symptoms of deception', *J. Experimental Psychol.,* 3, pp. 72–87.

—— (1924). 'Studies in testimony', *J. Criminal Law and Criminology,* 15, pp. 5–32.

Miller, N. and Campbell, D. T. (1959). 'Recency and primacy in persuasion as a function of the timing of speeches and measurements', *J. Abnorm. and Soc. Psychol.,* **59**, pp. 1−9.

Munsterburg, H. (1908). *On the Witness Stand* (New York: Clark Boardman Co).

Muscio, B. (1916). 'The influence of the form of a question', *Brit. J. Psychol.,* **8**, pp. 351−70.

Napley, D. (1967). *A Guide to Law and Practice under the Criminal Justice Act 1967.* (London: Sweet & Maxwell).

Rouke, F. L. (1957). 'Psychological research on problems of testimony', *J. Social Issues,* **13**, pp. 50−65.

Simon, R. J. (1967). *The Jury and the Defense of Insanity* (Boston: Little Brown & Co.).

Slesinger, D. and Pilpel, E. M. (1929). 'Legal psychology − A bibliography and a suggestion', *Psychological Bulletin,* **26**, pp. 677−92.

Stern, W. (1939). 'The psychology of testimony', *J. Abnorm. and Soc. Psychol.,* **34**, pp. 3−20.

Vernon, M. D. (ed.) (1966). *Experiments in Visual Perception.* (Harmondsworth: Penguin).

Walker, R. J. and Walker, M. G. (1967). *The English Legal System.* (London: Butterworths).

Weld, H. P. and Roff, M. (1938). 'A study in the formation of opinion based upon legal evidence', *Amer. J. of Psychol.,* **51**, pp. 609−28.

Wigmore, J. H. (1931). *Principles of Judicial Proof* (2nd edn) (Boston, Mass.: Little Brown & Co).

Williams, G. (1955). *The Proof of Guilt.* (London: Stevens & Sons).

17. Innocents in Jail

by RUTH BRANDON

Reprinted, with permission, from *New Society* (23 October 1969), pp. 633–4.

Nobody knows how many people are sent to prison every year for a crime which they did not commit. Justice, the organisation which is most likely to deal with such cases, receives three or four letters a week from people in prison, complaining that they shouldn't be there. Naturally, one can't take everything at its face value; but Tom Sargant, Justice's secretary, says he tends to believe most of them. He may be exceptionally soft-hearted, but even if only a fraction of them are telling the truth, that's still quite a lot of people. One estimate is that about 350 cases a year are involved. Again, it's a small fraction of cases tried — but a lot of individual misery.

To be wrongfully imprisoned is galling, and that's putting it mildly, but cases differ. They fall into two main categories. The first, of which there are fewest, perhaps 50 a year, are people who are completely innocent, with a clean record, or at worst one or two petty offences, and who are through some unlikely circumstance accused of the crime. And then there are the real villains, who have always managed to get away with what they *have* done, and finally get had for what they *haven't*. Once inside, it is highly unlikely that any will get out again before their sentence is completed.

All, of course, suffer loss of liberty; those in the first category also suffer the loss of their reputation in the community of which they have hitherto been a pillar. People tend to believe that there's no smoke without fire, even in the rare cases where innocence is proved. I spoke to a man wrongly convicted of attacking a girl; the real attacker had since come forward. He said:

I think that people, at bottom of them, they're still not forward, and don't speak to me as a friend normal. In fact some of them say, 'Now did you really do that job, Harry? We believe you did, you know. We believe so.' I say, how can I have done it when the young lad confessed to it? 'Aye, he could have been bribed to say so'.

This man had been forced, because of social ostracism, to move away from the part of town where he had previously lived, to another district altogether. The case may be extreme; I doubt whether it is unique.

There's no doubt that the commonest cause of wrongful conviction is misidentification. In English law — though not in Scottish — you can be convicted on the uncorroborated evidence of a single identification, either in an identification parade, or even when you're actually in court. There are various things wrong with this, the most obvious one being that most people's memory for faces is anyway unreliable, and doubly so when, as is usually the case, the face has been seen hurriedly, in a moment of stress. Another curious but often-proved psychological fact is that, the more uncertain a person is whether he's picked the right man at the parade, the more dogmatic he becomes as he goes on.

Another important contributory cause of wrong conviction is that the police do not always check thoroughly on alibis. This may often, of course, be the saving of someone who's putting up a false alibi; but it may be the thing that sends the person falsely accused, to prison. If a man is accused of a crime he didn't commit, it stands to reason he must have been somewhere else at the time. It ought, of course, to be easy to prove this; but it isn't. Try and remember exactly where you were, and who you were with, a month, two months, three months ago, and you'll see how difficult it can be. If you're lucky, you'll have kept an engagement diary.

Many people don't, and especially not the kind of people who tend to get caught up in this sort of mistake. The only case on record where a man has been released after conviction on the evidence of his alibi, is one where he suddenly remembered that at the exact time in question, he was in a police station reporting an assault upon himself — and that really could not be gainsaid. Where alibis have gone unchecked, it isn't that they aren't available for checking. Under the Criminal Justice Act, 1967, if you're going to plead an alibi defence, the defence solicitor must notify the prosecution of the details of the alibi. If he fails to do this, the alibi defence is not admissible in court.

Take the case, now a *cause célèbre*, of ex-PC Fred Luckhurst, who was imprisoned and dismissed the force for taking some money — a charge which he strenuously denies. He had what might seem a near-perfect alibi — a fellow-PC who had been with him on the beat during the time the crime was being committed, and who gave evidence to the effect. Luckhurst is convinced that

> 'If I'd told them nothing, and simply been picked out on an identification parade, and said nothing till the trial, it would simply be a case of going into the trial and a person would have said 'I identify this man' and then the police would have had no idea where I'd been that day. I would simply have given my true story of where I had been, which may have surprised everybody — when I say surprised, I mean they would have had no previous knowledge of it — and then, of course, they had no way of shooting down my story of where I'd been.

Once you are actually in prison, the likelihood of your getting out before the end of your sentence is, as I've said, small. You can, of course, appeal. In 1967, the last year for which figures are available, 5,789 people appealed, either against conviction or sentence or both. Of these appeals, 3,710 were abandoned, and 1,535 refused; 553 were granted leave to appeal. Of these, 72 had their convictions quashed; 29 had their sentences quashed; and 7 retrials were ordered. Your chances of achieving anything by way of the appeal court are therefore roughly 54–1 against; long odds, if not as long as many people think. From the inside, they seem very long indeed. 'The petitions sent in to the Home Secretary are very, very poorly looked into,' opined one (innocent) ex-con. 'Possibly one in ten thousand has any luck.'

Even if you *are* innocent, it won't do you much good saying so; everyone does that. The same man commented: 'When you're in prison, everyone's guilty. I might have told one or two, perhaps three people altogether, all the time I was there, but I just never wasted my time telling people I was innocent.' The commonest reason for refusing appeals is the failure to bring new evidence; evidence that has already been heard in court cannot be accepted.

Opinions as to what constitutes new evidence differ. Fred Luckhurst spent five weeks with his solicitor and friends collecting new evidence before his appeal came up.

> When we arrived at the appeal, the Lord Chief Justice refused to hear the evidence which we'd secured, on various grounds, mainly because he thought that it had been heard at the trial or there had been opportunity for it to have been heard at the trial, and of course the appeal failed.

In order to get your case reopened, then, you generally need some stroke of luck. You may find out who actually committed the crime you are in for, and he may, perhaps, come forward and confess, either because his conscience pricks him, or because he's got nothing to lose any more, like the man who confessed to something he'd done two years earlier because he was inside now anyway, serving 15 years for something else. Or your case may attract enough publicity for the authorities not to be able to ignore it any longer.

This is what has happened in the case of the Townsend brothers, which hit the headlines a few weeks ago. This is the case where one of the brothers, Leathlan, is serving a life sentence for a murder which he says his brother Castin committed. Castin was sentenced to four years at the same trial, for inciting his brother to wound a man; he is now out, and although he has, at various times, confessed to the murder, he refuses to sign a statement to this effect. Two brothers of the murdered man state that, when they visited him in hospital before he died, he told them that the tall, dark one stabbed him. (Castin is tall and dark; Leathlan has ginger hair.)

The law of hearsay evidence, however, rules that reports of what someone else said which are not supported by first-hand evidence cannot be admitted (unless the man is dying, when, in a more superstitious age, he was commonly believed to tell only the truth, and in which case the evidence is referred to as a 'dying declaration'). The man in this case was dying, but the doctor had not told him so, and so the evidence was disallowed. It therefore looked as though Leathlan was irremediably inside when the press happened to pick up the story at a relatively obscure meeting of the British Academy of Forensic Sciences. The case made lead stories that day and for several days following, and Callaghan immediately ordered his officials to re-examine the trial papers.

How can such miscarriages of justice be prevented? First, there are one or two relatively simple points of procedure which could be cleared up. Take the question of identification. Under Scottish law, no corroborating evidence is needed if you are identified by two separate people, but if it's only a single identification, then evidence must be produced. Why not adopt such a system here? A move to change this law was rejected by the Home Secretary only this January. He said a jury always needs to weigh the strength of identification evidence against the evidence brought by the defence. Quite; but it frequently fails to do so.

Another instance where, as the law stands, no corroborating evidence is needed, is where the suspect makes and signs a confession. In general, this seems fair enough; but there are people, particularly the feeble-minded, who need protection here. The view of Justice is that, where the confession is to be used in evidence, or where the suspect wants it, a magistrate should be present when it is taken and signed. Some people may think this would make the hard job of the police even harder. But the vulnerable position of the feeble-minded was amply illustrated by the case of Ron Avard, recently released from Rampton where he had spent four years on a charge of rape. He was found unfit to plead at his trial, and was imprisoned solely on the strength of a confession. He was not guilty; after a lot of time and effort, his MP managed to convince the Home Secretary of the fact; and when he came out, after four years, Ron still didn't know what he was supposed to have done.

There's no doubt that people like him ought to have some special protection of the sort recommended by Justice. Then the grounds on which appeals are granted should perhaps be widened. Evidence may have been heard at a trial, but nobody can guarantee that the jury will give it full weight. Then there's the *time* taken before an appeal comes up. At the moment, the average wait is four and a half months. The main reason it takes so long is that the shorthand-writers who transcribe the trials are so overworked that they don't have enough time to translate their shorthand records so that the appeal judges may examine them, since they're in demand for trials presently under way. The answer to this one is to train up more shorthand writers.

But basically, it seems to me that the whole system needs re-examining; and within it, two specifics: the role of the police, and the validity of the present, accusatorial system of justice as operated in this country.

Take first the role of the police. At the moment, they gather the evidence. In ninety-nine per cent of cases, they also decide whether the case shall be brought, *and* are the prosecutors. The police, after all, are only human. How can they always be expected to resist the temptation to try for a conviction at all costs when they have gathered the evidence which has brought the man into the dock? An example of what may happen is shown in the Townsend case. Norris Edwards, the murdered man, was interviewed in hospital by Detective Sergeant Babb, who had just previously arrested and charged Leathlan with the stabbing. Babb's account of the conversation in his original deposition was as follows:

Q: Who stabbed you?

A: Budsey or Boosey [nicknames of Leathlan]. He cut me. The tall one was there as well.

Q: What does he look like?

A: He's a tall dark man.

This account was supported by Detective Constable Hill. On the other hand, the hospital nurse who was present at the interview made a statement to the effect that only one police officer had interviewed him, that he had told the officer how the fight started, and where he had got his injury, and when asked who had caused the injury had replied: 'The tall man, you know, brown suit' (ie, Castin). The nurse had then asked the officer to leave and Edwards died shortly afterwards. But little weight was given in court to the nurse's statement.

It must also be remembered that, when the police prosecute, the whole weight of the state's resources is on their side.

Above all, should it be left to the police to decide whether or not the case stands up and should be brought? This is generally decided by the superintendent in charge of each station; a highly-placed and responsible officer. But is his first responsibility towards his own men, or towards the public? How can he expect his men to retain any enthusiasm for their work, if he keeps rejecting potential prosecutions? (And, whether or not promotion goes by convictions in the police force — and this is always indignantly denied — nobody can tell me that a good record of convictions ever did a policeman any *harm*.)

Who, then, should make the decision as to whether or not the case should be brought? This brings us to the second point, the desirability of the inquisitorial, as opposed to our accusatorial, system of justice. In the accusatorial system, the whole trial becomes a sort of monstrous wrestling-match, where each counsel attempts to win over the jury to his client's side; while the judge does a more or less successful balancing trick in the middle. In the end, one or the other will hit the jackpot, and everyone, except possibly the prisoner, if convicted, will be happy.

It works both ways, of course; it is as likely that a villain will be acquitted as that an innocent man will be convicted. There's not much doubt that the strict truth can, in this system, be obscured by the dramatic abilities of counsel, or other outside factors. Take the Townsend case again. I quote from the Justice memorandum on it:

From the beginning, the police and the prosecution appear to have directed their fire more towards Leathlan than towards Castin, but with the exclusion of the dying declaration, the admission of the hearsay evidence of Sergeant Babb, and the withdrawal by Leathlan of his letters accusing Castin, the prosecution turned all its guns on Leathlan. The judge supported this line towards the end of his summing-up:

Ask yourselves these questions on the first count: first of all, are we quite satisfied that somebody deliberately stabbed Norris Edwards? . . . The next question is this: Are we all satisfied that the person who stabbed Norris Edwards was Leathlan Townsend? If yes, then Leathlan Townsend is guilty of murder or manslaughter, as the case may be. If no, you ask yourselves: Are we satisfied Castin Townsend is guilty of murder or manslaughter as the case may be, though you remember, as I have already said to you, Mr Morton, I think, suggested that you should not come to that conclusion'.

What jury could stand up to that? The question is, should the jury have to make this kind of choice in the first place? They are not lawyers; cases of this sort are often very intricate; who can blame them if they are easily swayed by rhetoric? In the inquisitorial system, on the other hand, as practised in many continental countries, this burden is to some extent taken from their shoulders, as the burden of deciding whether or not to bring the case to trial is taken from the shoulders of the police. The police put the evidence before the examining magistrate, who goes through it, interviewing all parties concerned. It is then up to him to decide whether or not the case shall be brought.

The system has its disadvantages. It is unwieldy; there may be delays of years before a case is finally brought to trial; and, since someone must prosecute, the judge takes the prosecutor's role. In Scotland, the procurator fiscal has some of the same powers, though the accusatorial system still holds. But it seems to me there is little doubt that, under the inquisitorial system, many cases of wrong conviction, of the sort discussed here, would not occur. They would simply not be brought to trial.

PART V

Sentencing and the Evaluation of Penal Measures

Introduction

Empirical investigations into sentencing disparities in magistrates' courts and the evaluation of penal measures have played a major part in the postwar development of academic criminology and penology in Britain. In retrospect, it is easy to see how the characteristic features of much of this research directly influenced the nature of the radical critiques of established criminology in the late 1960s: by and large, the empiricism lacked historical and theoretical awareness, and was often constrained by practical and political straitjackets, whether in terms of research funding or in securing the necessary co-operation of the agencies and personnel involved. We would not wish to detract entirely from the achievements and significance of this traditional research; indeed, possible new directions for the future would not be as clear today were it not for the lessons that can be drawn from the experience and cumulative findings of that earlier research.

The research concerned with disparities in magistrates' sentencing has uncovered a somewhat confused picture. Such disparities have been explained by a great variety of factors, including magistrates' personalities and perceptions, their social background, the attitude of the local community and the type of information available to the court before sentencing. There has not been enough consistency or agreement between different studies to enable firm conclusions to be reached. Roger Hood's analysis of magistrates' sentencing of motoring offenders, based on a carefully controlled experimental study of decisions from detailed transcripts of actual cases, is important as much for the negative as for the positive findings that emerged (see Chapter 21 below): a great number of personal background factors and differences between the types of local communities seemed unimportant in explaining the disparities. On the other hand, the influence of the specific bench to which a magistrate belonged did seem to have a significant influence upon the decisions. We ourselves support Hood's conclusions that more attention needs to be paid to 'the way in which magistrates learn their sentencing trade and local benches develop their policies'. In other ways, too, the focus of sentencing research needs broadening, moving away from a narrow concentration upon magistrates' individual attitudes or court interaction and procedure, into wider sociological and political analyses of the role of magistrates, judges and other lawyers in the criminal process (for preliminary studies of this kind, see Cain, 1976; Paterson, 1974; Wilson, 1973). In Britain, lay magistrates, with their relative accessibility, have for too long borne the brunt of researchers' investigations, higher court judges and the upper echelons of the legal profession largely escaping systematic study from a sociological or criminological perspective. Research into the decision-making of the judiciary, complemented by studies of their socio-political role, could make a valuable contribution to the wider public debate and judicial accountability we look for in the future.

Finally, in considering the achievements and current status of research in the evaluation of penal measures, we must take stock of the situation not only in the context of the relatively recent spate of published British studies, (of which a selection of the main ones is indicated in the suggestions for further reading), but in the light of the more advanced stage reached in the United States, both in research terms and the wider discussion of possible implications for policy. There is an urgent need for the study of sentencing to go back to 'first principles' and for all parties involved in the penal process to clarify their underlying assumptions and objectives. In relation to evaluative research, the priorities and objectives need to be clarified. These objectives should not be conceived in the traditional 'treatment of offenders' mould but in terms of an approach to penal policy and criminal justice which comprehends a wider range of penal objectives.

Further Reading

Bailey, W. C., 'Correctional outcome: an evaluation of 100 reports' *Journal of Criminal Law, Criminology and Police Science* **57** (1966) p. 153.

Bottoms, A. E. and McClintock, F. H., *Criminals Coming of Age* (Heinemann, 1973).

Brody, S. R., *The Effectiveness of Sentencing* (Home Office Research Study No. 35) (HMSO, 1976).

Cain, M. E., 'Necessarily out of touch: thoughts on the organisation of the English bar' in P. Carlen (ed.) *The Sociology of Law*, Sociological Review Monograph 23 (Keele, 1976).

Carlen, P., *Magistrates' Justice* (Martin Robertson, 1976).

Clarke, R. V. G. and Sinclair, I., *The Controlled Trial in Institutional Research* (Home Office Research Study No. 15) (HMSO, 1972).

Cornish, D. B. and Clarke, R. V. G., *Residential Treatment and its Effects on Delinquency* (Home Office Research Study No. 32) (HMSO, 1975).

Dunlop, A. B., *The Approved School Experience* (Home Office Research Study No. 25) (HMSO, 1975).

Folkard, M. S. *et al.*, *IMPACT Vol. 2: The Results of the Experiment* (Home Office Research Study No. 36) (HMSO, 1976).

Hogarth, J., *Sentencing as a Human Process* (University of Toronto Press, 1971).

Hood, R. G., *Sentencing in Magistrates Courts* (Stevens, 1962).

—— and Sparks, R. F., *Key Issues in Criminology* (Weidenfeld & Nicholson, 1970).

Lemon, N., 'Training, personality and attitudes as determinants of magistrates' sentencing' *British Journal of Criminology* 14 (1974) p. 34.

Lipton, D. *et al.*, *Effectiveness of Correctional Treatment — A Survey of Treatment Evaluation Studies* (Praeger, 1975).

Logan, C. H., 'Evaluation research in crime and delinquency: A reappraisal' *Journal of Criminal Law, Criminology and Police Science* 63, (1972) p. 378.

Martinson, R., 'What works? – questions and answers about prison reform' *Public Interest* (Spring 1974) p. 23.

—— *et al.*, *Rehabilitation, Recidivism and Research* (National Council on Crime and Delinquency, 1976).

Millham, S. *et al.*, *After Grace — Teeth* (Human Context, 1975).

Paterson, A. A., 'Judges: a political elite?' *British Journal of Law and Society* (1974) p. 118.

Shaw, M. J., *Social Work in Prison* (Home Office Research Study No. 22) (HMSO, 1974).

Sinclair, I., *Hostels for Probationers* (Home Office Research Study No. 6) (HMSO, 1971).

Thomas, D. A., *Principles of Sentencing* (Heinemann, 1970).

Walker, N., *Sentencing in a Rational Society* (Penguin Books, 1972).

White, S., 'The effect of social enquiry reports on sentencing decisions'. *British Journal of Criminology* 12 (1972) p. 230.

Wilkins, L. T., *Evaluation of Penal Measures* (Random House, 1969).

Wilson, R. J., 'British judges as political actors' *International Journal of Criminology and Penology* 1 (1973) p. 797.

18. Aims and Information in Sentencing

STREATFEILD COMMITTEE

Reprinted with permission from *Report of the Inter-departmental Committee on the Business of the Criminal Courts* Cmnd. 1289 (HMSO, 1961), pp. 76–85.

The Aims of Sentencers

257. Sentencing used to be a comparatively simple matter. The primary objective was to fix a sentence proportionate to the offender's culpability, and the system has been loosely described as the 'tariff system'. The facts of the offence and the offender's record were the main pieces of information needed by the court, and the defence could bring to notice any mitigating circumstances. The information was about past events which could normally be reliably described; and it was readily available.

258. In addition, the courts have always had in mind the need to protect society from the persistent offender, to deter potential offenders and to deter or reform the individual offender. But in general it was thought that the 'tariff system' took these other objectives in its stride. Giving an offender the punishment he deserved was thought to be the best way of deterring him and others and of protecting society.

259. Over the last few decades, these other objectives have received increased attention. The development has been most obvious in the increased weight which the courts give to the needs of the offender as a person. It is realised that whatever punishment is imposed, he will eventually return to society, and sentences are increasingly passed with the deterrence or reform of the offender as the principal objective; and in assessing the offender's culpability his social and domestic background is more closely examined. In addition, sentencers give special

attention to the need to protect society from persistent offenders and increases in crime have emphasised the need to deter potential offenders.

260. As this side of sentencing has developed, it has been found that in individual cases these other objectives sometimes suggest a different sentence from the one which would have been imposed under the 'tariff system' and also that one objective may suggest a different sentence from another. Sentencers have to resolve these competing claims and decide which considerations should be dominant in a particular case. . . .

262. In short, sentencing is becoming a more complex task. In many cases, particularly those appearing at the superior courts, the court can do little more than punish the offender for what he has done, and in every sentence the offender's culpability has to be taken into account. But in a considerable, and growing, number of cases the 'tariff system' can no longer be relied on to fit all the considerations in the court's mind. The need to deter or reform the offender, the need to protect society and the need to deter potential offenders may in a particular case be conflicting considerations. These objectives have an importance of their own and have a separate effect on the decision of the court.

263. This wider range of objectives naturally calls for different information. The information which enabled the court to assess culpability is not necessarily the information which indicates how the offender should be reformed, much less how potential offenders should be deterred. . . .

Information Relevant to Sentences Which Seek to Control Future Events

267. Where the court is considering culpability there is little room for doubt about the sort of information which is relevant. The facts of the offence indicate its seriousness, and it is reasonably clear what additional information will count in mitigation. But where the court is seeking, for instance, to deter or reform the individual offender it is less clear what constitutes relevant information. The court obviously wants to know what sort of person he is, but what are the specific items of information which are required. Does it, for example, help the court to know how many jobs the offender has had? and if so, in what detail? Furthermore, where a court, a probation officer or a prison governor forms an opinion about the likely effect on an offender of a particular

sentence, it is desirable that the opinion should be as reliable as possible. Is the reliability of these opinions taken for granted? or can some check be devised? can their reliability be improved in any way?

268. These are difficult questions, and in the present state of knowledge it is not possible to give wholly satisfactory answers. There are many gaps in our knowledge, and it must be frankly recognised that some of the objectives which sentencers have in view require information which is not at present available. . . .

269. In our view the key to advance in this field is to recognise the fundamental difference between assessing culpability and pursuing the other objectives of sentencing; namely, that where the court is seeking to reform, to deter or to protect, it is seeking to control future events rather than simply to pass judgement on past events. The court can never know for certain that the sentence will in fact control events in the way desired, but if such an objective is to be based on more than a hunch, the court must, in logic and justice, have reasonable grounds for believing that the sentence is likely to have the desired effect. For example, where a court passes a sentence of corrective training rather than imprisonment, it is implicit that it has reason to believe that corrective training has a better chance of reforming the offender; or where a court passes an exemplary sentence for a particular crime of violence, it is implicit that it has reason to believe that the exemplary sentence will make a significant contribution to deterring potential offenders.

270. The most satisfactory ground for such beliefs is that similar sentences previously imposed in similar circumstances have had the desired result; for although these objectives are concerned with future events, the events are — in theory at any rate — capable of being subsequently observed. Unless the results of this observation are properly marshalled and systematically made available to the courts, sentences aimed at controlling future events are largely speculative, and the courts cannot even know whether such objectives are practicable.

Current Developments

271. Sentencers seek to control future events in three ways: they seek —

    (a)   to stop the offender offending again;
    (b)   to deter potential offenders;
    (c)   to protect society from the persistent offender.

(a) *Stopping the Offender from Offending Again*

272. The most obvious way in which a sentencer seeks to control future events is by imposing a sentence with the aim of stopping the offender from offending again. Whether the sentence is said to aim at deterring the offender or reforming him, the real objective is to check his criminal career.

273. Relevant experience of the effect of sentences on offenders' criminal careers is at present available to the courts mainly in the form of reports from prison governors and probation officers, who have seen how sentences have turned out in the past and can use this experience to form an opinion on the likely effect on the offender before the court. The mere fact that a probation officer, for example, has supervised probationers for many years does not of itself enable him to predict how a particular offender might respond to probation. Every effort should be made, by individual reporting officers and by the various services, to consider exactly what their experience shows to be the results of sentences and what facts about individual offenders are relevant to the effect on them of particular forms of sentence.

274. The sentencer, too, can profitably reflect on the lessons to be drawn from his own experience, but his experience is necessarily restricted. In the course of time he sees a good many offenders who have previous convictions and have therefore not been deterred or reformed by previous sentences. But this is only a narrow picture. Every day he passes sentences without knowing whether they achieve what they aim at. For all he knows, every offender whom he seeks to reform or deter may commit another offence within a few days of finishing the sentence imposed to prevent this happening. But unless he has information of this kind, he can never make an informed re-appraisal of his practice; and each case continues to be treated as a self-contained exercise.

General research

275. A sentence can be followed up not only by the person concerned with imposing or administering it but also as part of a general, objective study of the effect of different sentences on a cross-section of offenders who undergo them. In this way individual experience becomes generalised.

276. Considerable research has now been carried out on these lines, and some useful results are available. . . .

277. It is of obvious importance that these research results should be communicated to sentencers. They provide in systematic form information about the effect of sentences on criminal careers (as measured by re-convictions) and they indicate what kind of information about offenders is a predictor of the success or failure of penal treatment and therefore what information is relevant where the court is seeking to stop the offender from offending again. They are also useful as background information for those who report to the courts on the offenders.

278. Ultimately, it is hoped, these research studies will advance to a point where it is useful to apply the results directly to offenders before the court. By analysing a multiplicity of known characteristics of offenders who have undergone a particular sentence, it has been found possible to use certain of these characteristics to construct a formula which will give for a particular offender the statistical probability of his being re-convicted within a stated period. It may be hoped that it will eventually be possible, by bringing together the formulae for all forms of sentence, to discover to what extent the chances of an offender not being re-convicted depend on the form of sentence imposed, and then to indicate, in respect of individual offenders, whether one form of sentence which the court has in mind is likely to have a different effect from another. These results would be of great importance to sentencers. Comparison with other possible sentences is implied in any decision to impose a particular sentence with a view to checking the offender's criminal career.. . . .

(b) Deterring Potential Offenders

280. To some extent it is one of the objectives of practically every sentence to fix a penalty which will deter others from committing a like offence or will at any rate not have an anti-deterrent effect. In general, the courts proceed on the assumption that this will be achieved by fixing a sentence proportionate to the offender's culpability, but occasionally the need to deter others is regarded as so pressing that it becomes the dominant consideration and the court passes a sentence which is specially designed to be exemplary. . . .

281. The justification for exemplary sentences lies in the supposi-

tion that they deter, and it is important that the courts should have reliable information on this supposition. With crime at its present high level, the need to deter potential offenders is obvious, and the courts would be greatly helped by information showing, for example, that particular offences have been found to be more amenable to this treatment than others. It is also desirable, in fairness to the offenders who are made an example of, that the courts should have reasonable grounds for the supposition that the example will have the result intended.

282. This sentencing objective has not been studied to the same extent as others, partly because it is not easy to obtain reliable and relevant information and genuine trends in crime are difficult to discern and interpret. At first sight it might be thought that the statistics of crime known to the police give such information, but, besides the unavoidable deficiencies of these figures, they are not really suited to the purpose. As they are statistics of crimes known rather than of offenders convicted, they cannot distinguish between the ages of the offenders involved; they can give the number of offences, but not the number of offenders; and most of the offence classifications contain offences of widely differing character. Moreover, it is difficult to distinguish between real trends and the natural fluctuations which always occur in crime figures from period to period; and even a distinct trend may be due to causes other than exemplary sentences.

283. Nevertheless, we hope that it will be found possible to study objectively the deterrent effect of sentences. It seems to us that a start could usefully be made by gathering systematic information on the deterrent effect of sentences generally from representative samples of relevant opinion, possibly through the Government Social Survey. Such a study might throw up material and hypotheses which could then be used in a survey of the reactions to particular sentences; and eventually, with the participation of the courts, of the reactions to individual sentences which were specifically intended by the courts to be exemplary. At the same time individual courts can seek out their own information. Provided that the difficulties of interpretation are recognised, there is some information which can be used: the national crime statistics, local police statistics, the content of the court's own calendar. . . . None of these items may in itself confirm the efficacy of exemplary sentences, but they constitute relevant information which should be considered when the court forms its own judgment.

(c) Protecting Society from Individual Offenders

284. Where a court imposes a sentence in order to protect society from an individual offender, it is still concerned with future events, but in a somewhat different way. It is not so much seeking to control future events as determining the course of future events in order to prevent them taking another course. Its decision involves not a prognosis of the effect of the sentence, but a prognosis of the effect of not giving the sentence. For example, a sentence of preventive detention will assuredly prevent the offender from committing crime for a substantial period, but the justification for passing such a sentence depends on the court's estimate of the crime the offender is likely to commit if he is not sent to preventive detention. The immediate object in the court's mind is certain of achievement, and although the decision is based on a prognosis, the accuracy of the prognosis cannot be observed.

285. At present sentencers proceed on the basis of their own experience of offenders appearing before them and of seeing criminal careers at various stages of development. The material on which their judgment is formed consists of the offender's criminal record and information about his mode of life when at liberty. . . .

287. There is nevertheless a need for further general information about recidivism. Not all offenders with substantial records continue in crime indefinitely. Those who stop are not normally seen by the courts, who cannot therefore know whether the features which distinguish them from those who continue are present in a new case before them. If these distinguishing features can be observed at a sufficiently early stage, they will be valuable information for a court considering whether to impose a sentence for the protection of society. We hope therefore that the studies in this field will be developed. It may eventually be possible to construct a formula which gives, so far as recidivism is concerned, the degree of risk for any given offender. Such information would then provide a basis on which the court could judge the need to protect the public, for it would give an indication, in objective terms, of what the public would be protected from. . . .

The Responsibility of the Court

290. We recognise that no amount of information, however relevant, reliable and comprehensive it may be, will determine the relative weight

to be given to the different considerations in the court's mind. The court will still have to decide whether preventive detention would be too harsh for the petty thief and whether the first offender convicted of a serious offence can be placed on probation without detriment to the public interest; and in every case it will have to have regard to the facts of the offence as well as to the possibility of controlling future events. But these competing considerations cannot be properly examined without adequate assessment of what each amounts to by itself in the particular case; and this requires the relevant, reliable and comprehensive information which our recommendations are designed to secure, so far as it is available. We are not concerned with the relative weight to be given to the different objectives of sentencing but with the information which is the essential basis of an informed judgment on where the right balance lies. . . .

Information Should be Relevant, Reliable and Comprehensive

292. In making our detailed recommendations our cardinal principle throughout is that sentences should be based on reliable, comprehensive information relevant to what the court is seeking to do. We have already shown how the increased attention now given by sentencers to the effect of sentences on future events makes it necessary to emphasise the need for relevant and reliable information; and we consider that this emphasis will also serve to promote public confidence in the administration of justice. In view of the controversy which the sentencing of offenders can excite, it is important that the sentences imposed by the courts should have a sound factual basis and should not appear to be in any way speculative or based on vague impressions.

293. But information should not be proliferated for information's sake. It is not simply a matter of providing the courts with the fullest possible information about offenders. A mass of background information can be collected with comparative ease, but irrelevant information is not only useless but possibly harmful. There is a risk that it may cloud the issue before the court and induce a cosy feeling in which the absence of really useful information passes unnoticed. The test to be applied is whether information can help the court to reach a better decision; and actual experience and the results of research (as it develops) should be used to check the relevance of particular facts about offenders as indicators of the likely effect of penal treatment.

19. Social Inquiry for the Courts

by MARTIN DAVIES

Reprinted, with permission, in abridged form from *British Journal of Criminology* 14 (1974), pp. 18–33.

Social Inquiry Reports and the Sentencing Process

[At the start of this paper] let me clear the ground with three negative assertions:

(a) There is no evidence that the growth in the use of social inquiry reports has occurred simultaneously with any significant improvement in the 'effectiveness' of sentencing as measured by its success in reducing the level of crime.

(b) As the number of social inquiry reports has risen, there has been no directly related reduction in the number of men received into prison.

(c) Nor does it appear that the growth in the use of social inquiry reports has occurred simultaneously with any lessening in the range of sentencing disparities, the evidence for which 'among the judiciary at all levels is over-whelming'.[1]

But, it is now clear, the increase in the preparation of social inquiry reports has occurred in step with the 'growing recognition by the courts of the principle of individualisation of sentence'.[2] D. A. Thomas claims that, in the period from 1932 (when 'the Departmental Committee on Persistent Offenders could describe sentencing behaviour almost entirely in terms of a tariff system') to the present time, a major change has come over the decision-making process of the courts:

By 1961, the Streatfeild Committee (paras. 257–262 . . . [suggested that] the courts had increasingly come to consider the offender as an individual, whose needs, rather than whose guilt, would form the basis of the sentence passed. . . . The acceptance of individualism . . . did not mean, however, the disappearance of the tariff: the older order, based primarily on the concepts of retribution and general deterrence, continued to exist parallel to the newer (and still far from comprehensive) pattern of individualised measures. The result is a dual system of sentencing.

Thomas (p.3) describes how the task of the sentencer is first to decide whether in any particular case the tariff is to apply or whether one of the individualised measures is to be used. 'Once the primary decision has been made, the secondary decision follows — where on the tariff is the sentence to be located, or precisely what individualised measure is relevant.' Of course, he recognises (pp. 6–7) that such a crude breakdown inevitably over-simplifies a complex pattern of decision-making processes (especially in borderline cases); we shall see in the course of this paper that some offenders apparently warranting a tariff sentence might receive individualised treatment because of mitigating factors or even sometimes because of social or personal circumstances, and that an individualised case might nevertheless receive a prison sentence if it was held to be appropriate to his 'need'.

Social Inquiry and Tariff Sentencing

The primary decision of whether or not an offender is to be sentenced on the basis of the tariff should not in theory be influenced by the social inquiry report. But even here the pattern has been changing, especially since 1963. Following the publication of the Streatfeild Report, the Home Office issued a series of circulars[3] which, while not compelling courts to obtain social inquiry reports, have nevertheless greatly influenced them in their practice. . . . The groups for whom it is now recommended that reports should be prepared were listed in Home Office Circular, 59/1971, and they cover a wide range of defendants including, for example, all those under 31, all others who have not received a custodial sentence since the age of 17 and all women. Hence it is by no means uncommon for reports to be available in many cases where the court would previously have had no hesitation in imposing a tariff sentence. If they are available, they are more likely to be read; and, if they are read, it is at least conceivable that they might influence the primary decision of the court.[4] . . . What is apparently happening in such instances is that the social inquiry report is being used as an additional plea of mitigation; this was certainly the case in the *Oz* obscenity trial, where the judge obviously made a primary decision in favour of a tariff sentence, but felt obliged by the recommendations of the Home Office to remand the defendants in custody for reports; the probation officer's report referred to the defendants' pride in their work, to their idealistic hopes that the journal might be a vehicle for social change, to the fact that they were all highly intelligent and had no interest in material gain — all factors which were, of course, quite irrelevant so long as the judge stood his ground on the primary decision. But it is easy to see that it is a short step from social inquiry as a means of isolating mitigating factors once the primary decision has been made to social inquiry as a means of helping to determine the primary decision; indeed, in practice, it would be very difficult to distinguish between the two processes.

Social Inquiry and Marginal Cases

Thomas identifies a number of offender-groups 'where the primary decision tends to favour individualisation' because of the characteristics of the offender rather than the nature of his offence: young offenders, intermediate and inadequate recidivists, mentally disordered offenders and, to a lesser extent, adult first offenders and women.[5] In respect of the first four groups, he claims (p. 29) that 'a tariff sentence will normally be upheld [by the Court of Appeal] only after a careful consideration of the claims of an individualised measure'. The implications of this seem far-reaching. It does not need a social inquiry report for any of these groups to be identified: all except the mentally disordered can be diagnosed on sight and with access to their record of previous convictions. But if it is accepted in principle by the Court that, even in instances where their behaviour would normally lead to a tariff sentence, the personal and social circumstances that they display render an individualised sentence necessary or at least worthy of consideration, then surely the convention whereby the primary decision is based on offence behaviour alone is undermined. If that is so, it becomes even more important to consider, both theoretically and empirically, the basis on which individualised sentencing decisions are made, and the developing role of the probation officer in the decision-making process.

Social Inquiry Reports and the Individualised Sentence

The social inquiry report, along with other pre-sentence information (from the police, the prison governor, medical personnel, etc.), is intended, according to the Home Office, to enable courts 'to select the most appropriate form of treatment for offenders' (Home Office Circular 59/1971, para. 2). Thomas talks of the court seeking the individualised measure 'most suited to the particular offender'. And again: 'The choice of individualised measure is made empirically in each case on the basis of an assessment of the individual offender's needs.'[6] Now, there are at least two interpretations of the twin concepts of 'need' and 'appropriateness of (suitability for) treatment'; and it is because of the confusion which exists between these two interpretations that the notion of individualised sentencing seems to have been inadequately considered and that the social worker's (probation officer's) role within the penal system remains uneasily ambiguous.

Put in its simplest form, the confusion is between individualised sentencing with a reductivist or reformist aim and individualised sentencing with a rehabilitative and helping aim. Is it the task of the social inquiry report to indicate aspects of the offender's personality and circumstances which, in the officer's judgment, cause him to break the law? And is it then the task of the court to deal with the offender in such a way that the pattern of law-breaking will most probably be reduced? Or, alternatively, does the probation officer in his report draw attention to personal and social problems which appear to indicate a need for support, casework, advice, guidance or what you will, so that the court, in its individualised sentence, can then allocate the offender to that form of treatment most suited to the aim of combating elements of personal and social stress?

It is probably safe to assert that most courts would deny that their primary aim was to provide a social service for offenders no matter what their identified needs, although many sentencers might say that they believed that, by helping his clients, the probation officer was in fact contributing to a reduction in the level of crime; it is almost certain that implicitly the courts hope that individualisation is not only a humane method of dealing with offenders, but that it is also efficient in the sense that it allocates them to those sentences most calculated to reduce the likelihood of their committing further offences. In other words, the courts are attempting to practise a form of social engineering in which their decisions determine, not only the fate, but the future behaviour of individual subjects. If this is so, however, it is in fact no more than a charade of social engineering, for, on present evidence, an individualised sentencing decision can be appropriate to the needs of the offender only in the sense that it should be in some way relevant to the probation officer's description of his background and present circumstances. There are three factors which have to be taken into account in reaching this conclusion.

(1) The first can be dealt with briefly. Probation officers are trained as social workers and not as correctional agents; in so far as there is a body of knowledge and theory behind them, it has more to say about the establishment of a relationship than about the exertion of influence within it. If they contribute to any reduction in criminal behaviour, it is as a by-product of their primary task of serving the client; most officers will hope that, in the course of their work, they do indeed bring about such changes, but most will also remain fully aware of their own limitations in the face of heavy odds.

(2) The second factor is simply that there is, as yet, insufficient evidence to support the notion that differential treatments currently in use vary in their effects on separately diagnosed offender groups. . . . As we now know, prediction studies have fallen on lean times[7] and some differential treatment experiments, despite limited success among juveniles, have suffered from their own organisational complexity, from a general lack of conceptual clarity and perhaps from an understandable desire to travel a long way in a short time.[8] . . . Streatfeild's enthusiasm for a science-based sentencing system is not only a reflection of where the individualised approach naturally leads, but is a reminder to penologists of the need for immense caution when claiming positive results in their research.

(3) The range of treatments available is extremely limited, and new forms tend to be introduced in response to 'felt need' rather than because it is known that they will certainly reduce the likelihood of recidivism; moreover, when innovations are made, they are rarely designed so as to facilitate experimental evaluation of their effectiveness in reducing the crime level. . . . In the present state of knowledge, with the range of treatment tools available, the best we can hope for from individualised sentencing is to match treatment to offender (as distinct from 'punishment to crime') in a commonsense sort of fashion, without making unwarranted assumptions about its probable reformist effect on criminal behaviour.

Decision-making and the Organisational Context

But who decides what is 'commonsense'? Even though we may legitimately doubt to what extent the sentencing process influences an offender's future criminal behaviour, it certainly can affect his immediate position; and it is obviously important to examine the decisions arrived at by both probation officer and court, and in particular to explore the relationship between the two. . . . To what extent then do recommendations to the court reflect the personal attitudes and the social situation of the workers? What is the effect of the relationship between probation officer and decision-maker on determining (a) the recommendation, and (b) the decision? . . .

One major problem which most research to date has tended to ignore is that the situation almost certainly varies enormously from one court to another, and that therefore merely to describe the influences at work in one court setting is not necessarily to explain the decision-making process in general. . . . In order to understand and analyse the decision-making process, it is accordingly necessary first to see it in the context of the relationship between each officer and court (including its local traditions, the role of the chairman, the effect of the presence of different individual magistrates, the role of the clerk, and so on). Moreover, the generally high level of agreement between officers and Bench, already referred to, demands that some attempt be made to disentangle the interacting relationship between the two parties: 'probation and other specialists may tailor their recommendations to suit the judge'.[9] This is known as a closed loop system of influence, common enough in economics but not yet sufficiently explored in sociology.

In theory one could find any one of three extreme situations: an entirely static one in which the officer knew precisely what the magistrate would do, and recommended accordingly; one of total influence, where the officer ignored the magistrate's opinion totally but the magistrate sentenced according to the recommendation; and one of total conflict in which the PO again ignored the magistrate's opinion, but the magistrate similarly ignored the recommendation. Situations approximating to the first would reflect a process of symbolic communication in which (despite the 100 per cent agreement) the notion of influence in any single case would be virtually meaningless when seen in the context of the total process. Situations approximating to the second would reflect a process of real influence, in which the PO was seen as a technical expert in an area of limited knowledge and in which the sentencer recognised his own limitations. Situations approximating to the third would indicate a process of non-communication arising from role conflict or open hostility arising from differences of opinion about the purpose of decision-making. . . .

The probability is that, for most of the time, most courts now tend towards the first situation, but that in any analysis of the decision-making process in such courts, it becomes necessary for the researcher to be able to differentiate between run-of-the-mill decisions in which only symbolic communication occurs and other decisions in which the probation officer attempts to exert influence over the Bench. Depending partly on how committed he appears to be to the recommendation the court might respond either positively or negatively. . . . In other words, the steady process of symbolic communication indicates, as we have said, a static situation in which each understands the other's role. But each time a positive reaction is made by the Bench to one of the PO's more radical recommendations, so the officer's influence in the total sentencing process grows; in the event of a negative reaction (and in particular in the event of a whole series of negative reactions) the officer's low status in relation to sentencing is emphasised.

In Conclusion

. . . We have argued that the growth of social inquiry work has developed alongside the concept of individualised sentencing: once the primary decision has been taken not to impose a tariff sentence, the Bench and/or the probation officer determine where, on a continuum of need, the offender stands: if the need is minimal, then a residual tariff element is used to determine whether the offence warrants a fine or can be dealt with by a discharge; if problems exist, within a very wide range of circumstances, then a probation order is made and whenever possible the residual tariff is applied again to impose a financial penalty;[10] where personal or social problems are more severe, or perhaps (though not always) where probation has already failed, a number of alternative measures may be employed — hostel training, medical treatment or imprisonment. The introduction of intermediate treatment under the Children and Young Persons Act, 1969, and of the various experimental schemes offered by the Criminal Justice Act, 1972, merely adds to the range of alternatives available along the continuum of social need.

The recent Criminal Justice Act, in particular, lends support to the concept of individualised sentencing by providing new forms of treatment for offenders: it implicitly recognises the probable further growth of social inquiry work and the increased involvement of the probation service in penal decision-making; and the Home Office has lent further emphasis to the scientific connotations of sentencing by providing for the evaluation of each new process by research. The introduction of facilities such as day training centres and community service orders, however cautious official spokesmen may be in committing themselves, nevertheless lead the public to have reductivist expectations; and those who prepare the social inquiry reports are presumed to be able to identify the offenders most likely to be reformed in such specialised treatment settings. But here, as elsewhere in sentencing, we are faced still with the ambiguity of penal aims, and with the sad fact that almost all reputable evidence leads to pessimistic conclusions concerning our ability to influence future behaviour as a direct result of penal policy: hence, the notion of effectively reductivist social inquiry reports is, to say the least, premature. The use of reports nevertheless represents one of the most important penal developments of the twentieth century, and reflects a crucial change in the balance of sentencing authority. If, during the next decade, treatment research begins to pay dividends, there seems little doubt that the role of the probation officer as a sentencing adviser will become even more significant than it is now.

Notes

1. R. G. Hood and R. F. Sparks *Key Issues in Criminology* (London, 1970) p. 142.
2. D. A. Thomas, *Principles of Sentencing* (Heinemann, 1970) p. 3.
3. Home Office Circulars 84/1963, 138/1963, 188/1968, 189/1968, 190/1968, 59/1971.
4. See Thomas, op cit. p. 320.
5. Home Office Circular 188/68 (para. 4) particularly emphasises the individualised nature of sentencing women 'since it is widely recognised that the social consequences of imprisoning women tend to be more severe and background enquiries are therefore particularly valuable'.

6. Thomas, op. cit. p. 201.
7. See, for example, F. H. Simon, *Prediction Methods in Criminology* (HMSO, 1971).
8. S. Adams, *Inquiries Concerning Kinds of Treatment for Kinds of Delinquents* (California Board of Corrections: Monograph Number 2, 1961); T. Palmer *et al.*, *Community Treatment Project: Research Report No. 9* (California Youth Authority, Sacramento, 1969).
9. Hood and Sparks, op. cit., p. 168.
10. M. Davies, *Financial Penalties and Probation* (HMSO, 1970) pp. 3—4.

20. Inner Circle

by DAVID BARTLETT and JOHN WALKER

Reprinted, with permission, from *New Society* (19 April 1973), p. 139.

There are over 19,500 magistrates in England and Wales. They try more than 98 per cent of all criminal offences. With growing crime rates and increasing concern about justice they are clearly crucial people but little is known about them. This article is a study of 43 of them who form the bench in the county borough of Rochdale, a town of some 90,000 in Lancashire.

Research was difficult to carry out. To start with, some magistrates, who regularly require those who appear before them to supply the most personal details, were strangely reluctant to provide such basic information as age, marital status and number of children. But the most complicating factor was not so much magistrates' personal desire for secrecy as the official insistence on secrecy about the identity of those who select magistrates.

Appointments to the bench are technically made, in Lancashire, by the Chancellor of the Duchy of Lancaster (elsewhere it is the responsibility of the Lord Chancellor). In practice, however, the effective choice is made, in every area, by a Magistrates Advisory Committee. The identity of those who form it is officially a secret, 'in order that they may be shielded from undesirable and unwanted influence'. It is arguable that, far from being a guarantee of objective selection, this results in at least the suspicion of more subtle, hidden influences.

Certainly, the identity of the three men who comprised Rochdale's advisory committee was known to some people. They are: Norman Woolfenden, aged 69, a Liberal, a rotarian and a mason, magistrate since 1950, chairman of the bench and also chairman of the hospital management committee; Albert Golland, aged 65, a Conservative, a rotarian and a mason, magistrate since 1952 and a local accountant; Derrick Walker, aged 56, leader of the Labour group, magistrate since 1963, self-employed. The committee is virtually self-perpetuating as it nominates a successor for any member retiring.

The magic round-about: JPs' social connections in Rochdale

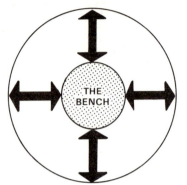

Rotary

100 members in two Rochdale groups. 21 are JPs, of which at least 11 are also Masons and 4 on the Hospital Management Committee.

Health Executive Council

15 strong. 6 are JPs, 3 have contacts with at least one of the other groups in this circle. One is a member of all four

THE BENCH

Masons

4 lodges with probably 100 in each. At least 12 are JPs, including 2 of the three members of the committee that recommends appointments to the Bench.

Hospital Management Committee

18 people. Their Chairman, Norman Woolfenden is also Chairman of the Bench and a member of the advisory committee. 7 of this group are on the Bench, of which 3 are also members of both Rotary and the Masons.

The committee's final recommendations must be unanimous. It would, therefore, appear likely that two broad categories of people are the more likely to emerge from this process: (a) those who are so unexceptionable as to have offended none of the three members, (b) those who get through as the result of a kind of sophisticated horsetrading. Cyril Smith, possibly Rochdale's best known citizen and now the local MP, has never been appointed to the bench.

Closer investigation of the bench does little to dispel such fears. The official Central Office of Information booklet (*The British Legal System*) makes two positive statements about the composition of benches, neither of which Rochdale's complies with. One is about age of JPs: 'It is desirable that all benches should contain a proportion of younger magistrates, men and women in the thirties and forties.' This bench has only one member under 45. Their average age is 54, and 20 of them (47 per cent) are 55 and over. The average age on appointment was 47. Only three (all women) were appointed in their thirties. Seven were already over 55.

The bench should also be 'broadly representative of all sections of the community which it has to serve'. In Rochdale's case, there are at least three crucial omissions: (a) only one employed manual worker is a

JP, (b) not one of the town's 6,000 Pakistanis is a JP, (c) Rochdale has a large Catholic population — 6,000 attend church each Sunday — but none of them is a JP.

On the other hand, some sections are over-represented. Our research shows four organisations, and the status of 'director', to have close associations with the bench: 21 JPs (49 per cent) are members of Rotary or its associated Inner Wheel; twelve (28 per cent) are members, or wives of members of the masonic movement; six (14 per cent) are members of the hospital management committee; seven (16 per cent) are on the health executive committee; 13 (30 per cent) are directors, or their wives.

Obviously, there is a considerable amount of overlapping. In all, 29 (67 per cent) have contacts with at least one of these groups; 19 (44 per cent) have contacts with at least two of them; and 13 (30 per cent) with three or more. The result is that a large proportion of the bench are closely allied with other establishment groups. To take just one more detail: eleven of them are members both of Rotary and the masons, including two members of the advisory committee. So the bench appears part of a mysterious old-boy network.

It may well be, as the chairman of the bench assured us, that this is entirely unconscious. But the fact remains that the whole system of lay justices is questionable enough, without it suffering the imbalances revealed by this research. If Rochdale is at all typical, there is a strong case for considerable democratisation of the process of selection. Two simple and inexpensive possibilities have been suggested: (a) to increase the size of the advisory committee, with the majority not being members of the bench and with some regular changes in its composition; (b) advertisements in the local press of the times when nominations are being considered, which advise people of their right to make such nominations.

In a society that increasingly insists on justice being seen to be done, the present system is a dangerous anachronism.

21. Sentencing the Motoring Offender: Towards an Explanation of Disparity

by ROGER HOOD

Reprinted, with permission, in abridged form from *Sentencing the Motoring Offender* (Heinemann, 1972), pp. 138–53.

It is now clear [from this study of sentencing the motoring offender] that fines vary most for the more serious kind of offence and that there is greater disparity in deciding on disqualification than on the appropriate fine. Earlier it was suggested that these differences in practice may be accounted for partly by differences in magistrates' personal and social backgrounds and their varying approaches towards, and perceptions of, the problem posed by the motoring offender, and partly by whole benches tending to develop rather special policies, either through the informal influences of the chairman, senior magistrates and clerk, or through the more rigid application of some system of 'starting points' or 'basic penalties' set out in a schedule and available as a guide whenever sentence is passed. It is now time to see to what extent variations in sentencing for motoring offences can be explained by these three sets of variables: namely, personal and social attributes; perceptions and attitudes; the bench.

The Influence of Personal Attributes of Magistrates

The basic purpose of the analysis was to discover which factors were associated with the imposition of *relatively* severe sentences. . . . One of the most important findings is a negative one. There were very few consistent associations over a variety of different types or kinds of offence between any of the attributes describing social, political, personal background, magisterial or motoring experience and relative severity in fining, imprisoning and disqualifying. Thus in this sample of magistrates disparity could not be accounted for simply by differences in their personal backgrounds. . . . Obviously a magistrate's background has an influence on the sentence he passes, but from this analysis it is impossible to ascribe any particular weight to the importance of any single attribute or group of related attributes over all kinds of case.

It is important also to note that whether magistrates came from the north, midlands or south, from urban or rural courts, or from large or small benches had no *consistent* effect on the size of the penalty. Different practices cannot be explained therefore by these kinds of environmental factors.

How Serious is the Case? – The Importance of Perception

The connection between the perception of the seriousness of offences and severity in the punishment imposed is a complex one, but one point stands out. These variables were not significantly associated with the severity of the decision in absolutely every one of the cases, but they occurred so frequently – often at a one per cent level of significance – that it is reasonable to generalize about their effect on sentencing. The rating of an offence as 'serious of its kind' and the severity of punishment were statistically associated in just over half the cases dealt with. Also, we found that the other more general measures of seriousness – the relative ranking of a motoring offence in relation to eighteen other offences, and the magistrates' stereotype of the kind persons who commit offences – were both more frequently associated with the penalty than any background or personal attributes of magistrates. The seriousness with which the offence was generally viewed was particularly associated with relatively high fines for two offences: failing to stop after or report an accident, and neglect of pedestrian-crossing regulations.

There is, then, general support for an explanation of sentencing which sees differences in the way magistrates perceive and categorize offences as an important factor in producing disparate penalties. The caveats to this general conclusion are, however, extremely important. They are: first, that the association is strongest in relation to the decision to imprison or disqualify; it is quite strong as regards the decision on the amount of fine; and hardly exists where the relative *length* of disqualification is being considered. . . . Secondly, seriousness rating was *not* associated with the penalty imposed in just under half the cases, and therefore magistrates who *agreed* to rate an offence as 'very serious' or 'serious' gave different sentences for some other reason. Thirdly, as with background personal factors, seriousness ratings were associated with decisions in some kind of cases but not others. . . .

We tried to see if there were any consistent associations between the attributes of magistrates who perceived the same circumstances differently: whether there was, for example, a relationship between political background or attitude and a tendency to consider cases more or less serious. The analysis failed to find any consistent relationships between social, political, motoring, personality, magisterial experience or any other attributes of magistrates and both their perception of the seriousness of a case and the severity with which they sentenced it. This does not mean that no associations exist, only that we found none in this sample.

The Pervasive Influence of the Bench

. . . The bench a magistrate belonged to had a highly significant effect on the amount of fine imposed for all eight kinds of offence and on the decision whether or not to disqualify or to imprison. It also had an effect on the length of disqualification given for dangerous driving but *not* for either drunken driving or driving while disqualified. There seem to be good reasons for this. In drunken driving cases there is general agreement that disqualification will normally be for the statutory minimum period of 12 months. In four of the five cases sent to magistrates, two-thirds or more imposed this statutory minimum. At the nine courts with local starting-points for this offence, six suggested 12 months, one simply said 'consider disqualification', and two recommended two years. The minimum seems to have become hardened into 'the usual', and this may of course be due to the increasing distrust of long periods of disqualification. . . .

Where all other offences are concerned, why does the local bench have such an important and pervasive effect on the size of the fine and on the use of disqualification? The association between bench membership and the sort of penalty given is all the more remarkable because it will be remembered that magistrates 'sentenced' the cases at home, and alone, and not in groups in the atmosphere of the court. . . . Before going further, though, we should warn the reader that we are *not* saying that all members of a bench do the same thing, only that they are more *likely* to do something similar to their colleagues than we would expect by chance. . . .

It would seem therefore that the development of a common policy on a bench is a subtle process brought about through the influence of clerks and senior magistrates becoming embodied in a tradition. Where the conditions for this do not exist – for example in benches with a number of strong personalities with differing views, or in large courts with magistrates divided into 'rotas' which rarely change or where the clerk plays little part in trying to advise on sentencing – the publication of a schedule may have little impact. . . .

There was some evidence to suggest that certain assumptions about penal policy are shared by magistrates on the same bench. For example, we found that magistrates who said they would give the same fine in serious cases regardless of the income of the offender tended to be concentrated in particular benches. At ten out of the twenty-four larger courts 36 per cent or more of the magistrates shared this view, while at seven courts more than 80 per cent completely rejected it. Similarly, the view that fines should not be affected by the costs in a case was associated with bench membership. It is interesting to note that holding either of these views was not confined to those benches without basic penalty schedules. . . .

Altogether these findings strongly suggest that 'bench constraints' and individual differences in the perception of the seriousness of cases act independently in affecting the sentence. Indeed, they suggest that while there is such diversity of views among magistrates the problem of disparity should not be solved simply by imposing a system of tariffs.

Implications and Conclusions

The results presented [in the previous chapter] suggest that, while benches may tend to agree in general on the appropriate fine, there is less agreement when cases present 'unusual' features. Our analysis seems to indicate that disparities in these cases may arise out of too great a reliance on systems to achieve uniformity in 'ordinary' cases. The Magistrates' Association has repeatedly denied that its list of 'suggested penalties' is a tariff, because that implies a rigid sentencing procedure. Yet in practice it must work rather like a tariff, for the vast majority of cases will be like the 'average' and the penalty will be the norm suggested or a slight variation on it. I am inclined to believe that disparities were due to lack of discussion about the principles which should be used in deciding what weight should be given to various aggravating circumstances in 'out of the ordinary' cases. This is supported by two findings — first, the lack of association in some of the complicated cases between their perceived seriousness and the size of the fine and, secondly, the variation in response to the introduction of 'complicating factors' in the information game. Leaving aside these 'complicated' cases, there is less cause for concern about fines, but there is a great deal of variation in the use of disqualification. Obviously here it is not a question of agreeing on a 'price' but of weighing up basic questions of penal philosophy. . . .

The danger is that attempts to achieve uniformity in sentencing through booklets, scales or more informal methods (such as the steady influence of the clerk) may well inhibit change — whether it be adapting present methods, or experiments with new approaches towards disqualification or traffic attendance centres.[1] One of the prices of uniformity is stagnation, and it is certainly not clear that the courts are so correct in their solution to traffic offences that they can afford a standard approach rather than pursuing a more dynamic experimental policy. This would admittedly be less uniform but perhaps more in line with a modern penal philosophy based on individualization of punishment. Clearly many people would regard this as inappropriate because they believe that motoring offenders are unlike 'real criminals', and that therefore so-called treatment aimed at attitude change is inappropriate. The wealth of studies in recent years, including Willet's[2] and Parry's[3], has done something to shatter this illusion, and it is clear from this research also that a considerable minority of magistrates now share the view that the problem is more complex. It would be a pity to stifle this new-found perspective, this concern to re-examine some basic assumption about the problem posed by the dangerous, drunken or careless motorist (not to say the defiant one!) in too rigid a system of local or even national agreements on 'basic penalties'. The fears of 'computer justice' are a natural outcome of too great a reliance on tariff principles.[4]

At the same time, one must recognize that there is a complete absence of information about the impact of a fine on motorists' attitudes and driving performance and that magistrates do not, and cannot, act in a vacuum. They are bound to reflect some of the common assumptions about the causes of driving behaviour and the view that, with certain exceptions, such offences are not properly classed as crime. Unless evidence changes the social evaluation of these offences, the fine will continue as the main type of sentence employed. But there is obviously a need to consider the principles underlying its use — whether as a 'penalty' or a deterrent punishment — and to evaluate critically the purposes of disqualification — especially in those cases which are clearly 'out of the ordinary'. Without such consideration there can be no common acceptable policy. . . .

As far as motoring offences are concerned, it appears that less attention needs to be paid to the question of 'balancing' appointments — for different backgrounds as such were not clearly associated with different sentencing practices or points of view.[5] Conversely, more attention should be given to the way in which magistrates learn their sentencing trade and local benches develop their policies. The organizational aspects, including the roles occupied by senior members, and clerks in particular, need to be studied in depth. There is sufficient evidence to suggest that research can as usefully concentrate on 'becoming a magistrate' as on 'becoming a marihuana user'.[6] How one learns to intepret information, accommodate one's views to those of the group, and develop an understanding of those who present cases to the court from either a prosecution or a defence standpoint are all part of a socializing process, the study of which has been too long neglected.

Notes

1. Report of the Advisory Council on the Penal System, *Non-custodial and Semi-custodial Penalties* (HMSO, 1970) para. 10, pp. 35—8. The Committee, in particular, noted the lack of diversity in the sentences imposed for traffic offences, including the serious ones.
2. T. C. Willett, *Criminal on the Road* (London, Tavistock, 1964).
3. M. H. Parry, *Aggression on the Road* (London, Tavistock, 1968).

4. Editorial, 'Consistency in sentencing', *Law Society Gazette*, 67(1970) p. 366.
5. Although of course this may have been due partly to the relative homogeneity of our sample. It is conceivable that a wider range of people on the bench would affect sentencing practices in these cases. And, of course, it may well be that different social backgrounds discriminate between sentences imposed for other types of offence.
6. See the well-known article by Howard Becker, *Outsiders* (Glencoe, Ill., Free Press, 1963). There is, of course, a large literature on socialization into occupational groups. See, for example, Howard Becker, *Sociological Work* (London, Allen Lane, Penguin Press, 1970) Chs 11—14.

22. Severe Sentences: No Deterrent to Crime?

by ROBERT BAXTER and CHRIS NUTTALL

Reprinted, with permission, from *New Society* (2 January 1975), pp. 11–13.

The idea of general deterrence — the belief that people will not commit an offence because of fear of punishment — has an important place in criminal justice. It also attracts strong support from many members of the judiciary and the general public. There are frequent demands for its efficacy to be measured by research, but this would create enormous difficulties. So, using a small-scale study, we have tested one particular proposition about general deterrence that is sometimes advanced — the idea that individual sentences can deter criminal activity.

During 1972, mugging — i.e. attacks on, and robberies from, individuals in the open — attracted much public anxiety. There was concern that, in some of the major cities in England, this crime was running at a significantly higher level than in previous years and both MPs and the press reflected public disquiet. The Home Office consulted chief constables and later issued an advisory circular to them on the problem. By late 1972, the police forces in the most seriously affected cities had already started to take special measures, and in March 1973 a dramatic decision came from the judiciary when the Crown Court in Birmingham sentenced Paul Storey, a 16-year-old youth, to 20 years' detention while his two accomplices got ten years. Storey was charged with attempted murder and robbery, but the offence was popularly seen as mugging. It produced banner headlines in most national papers such as 'Twenty years for the mugger aged 16' (*Sun*) and 'Boy of 16 gets 20 years for mugging' (*Guardian*). The court decision attracted enormous publicity from press and television — indeed it was probably one of the most publicised sentences in recent years.

Though the sentence was seen in many quarters as being intended to have a deterrent effect, the trial judge, Mr Justice Croom-Johnson, made it clear in passing the sentence that he was primarily concerned with individual factors, as was the Court of Appeal. Lord Chief Justice Widgery, commenting on the offenders, said:

> 'No trace of mental illness is discoverable in any of these three young men, and absolutely no kind of motivation or reason at all in their background, history or any other source is to be found. If they can do acts of this kind in those circumstances once, obviously there is a danger they will do them with equal lack of excuse again, and the safety of the public and the protection of the public from similar incidents is a factor which has to be in the forefront of the sentencing exercise.

He went on to discuss at length the problem of predicting the future behaviour of the offenders, especially Storey; and expressed his view, in confirming the sentence, that 20 years was justifiable on the understanding that the Home Secretary would consider the possibility of early release. He also expressed the hope that the Home Secretary would not feel bound by the practice, normal in adult cases, of reviewing the possibility of release only after one third of the sentence had been served. The Home Office gave the court an assurance on this point.

Despite the judges' views, the sentence was widely presented to the public by the press as an exemplary sentence which was meant to have a general deterrent effect. Some members of Parliament and representatives of the police saw it in this light and their views were publicised. The *Daily Mirror* headlined such a view from a spokesman for the Police Federation; and the *Daily Mail* reported similar views from a police officer ('If this doesn't frighten them, nothing will') and from a member of Parliament ('We must have sentences of this sort to strike real fear into the young thugs and criminals'). In an editorial under the headlines 'A terrible deterrent', the *Mail* went on to comment that,

> Only as a deterrent can society contemplate such terrible punishment. Mugging, the trendy term for a crime as old as sin itself, is in vogue with young thugs. The law should make it known, by every propaganda means at its disposal, that deterrent sentences are in vogue too.

The *Daily Telegraph* adopted a similar attitude in its editorial. Virtually every newspaper, from the *Financial Times* and the *Guardian* to the *Daily Mirror* and the *Sun*, headlined the 20-year sentence for mugging.

From the terms used, the 20-year sentence was obviously presented as a general, rather than an *individual* deterrent.

If the sentence was effective as a general deterrent, one would expect the mugging rate to decline after the trial. Because of the publicity, the impact might reasonably be expected to be immediate, even if it declined after memory of it faded from people's minds. Judging from the public concern at the time, the mugging rate was popularly supposed to be running at a high level (interestingly, the level of robbery offences in 1973 was below that of 1972 — in some cases the drop was very substantial). However, no matter what was happening to the rate before the trial, one might anticipate that it would drop significantly after the sentence on 19 March 1973 and perhaps rise again as the effects of the sentence began to wear off. It was to find out whether this did happen that we examined the robbery rate for 1972 and 1973.

No satisfactory definition of mugging exists and as the Home Office police department's request for information in October 1972 had produced figures from chief constables based on differing definitions of the crime, the only way of obtaining consistent information was to collect figures of offences categorised as 'robbery or assault with intent to rob'. This created the problems that crimes other than mugging were included within the category, but the benefit of having comparative and reliable figures seemed reasonable compensation.

Mugging is generally regarded as a youthful exercise; around half of all offences in the robbery category are committed by people under 21, and around three-quarters by people under 25. Information was sought only from the large, completely urban police areas outside London as the offence is almost entirely a city crime. Six authorities were approached — Birmingham, Bristol, Liverpool and Bootle, Manchester and Salford, Sheffield and Rotherham, and the West Midlands. Leeds and the two London forces were not included because of problems in collecting data. The information which was obtained — weekly breakdown of the offences reported for 1972 and 1973 — showed that only in Liverpool and possibly in Manchester were there sufficent numbers to suggest that the comparative incidence of this offence was exceptionally high.

Although the 20-year detention sentence was passed in Birmingham as a result of a crime there, that city's robbery rate remained relatively low throughout the two relevant years (the average number of robberies was 4.8 a week in 1972 and 4.4 a week in 1973). The neighbouring West Midlands police area, with weekly averages of 4.0 for 1972 and

2.4 for 1973, and Sheffield, whose weekly averages for 1972 and 1973 were 2.3 and 2.0 respectively, experienced similarly low offence rates. In Bristol, the mumbers of such crimes were also very low (less than 1.3 in 1972 and 1.0 in 1973).

In none of the police areas studied did the sentence have the anticipated impact on the number of reported robberies. In Birmingham, where the original offence was committed and the sentence passed, the pattern in the offence rate continued uninterrupted — the number of offences had already started to rise and reached a peak a few weeks after the trial (see Figure 1). This is similar to the two previous peaks, which also lasted about five weeks. In Manchester there was no particular pattern (see Figure 2). The offence rate had begun to increase shortly before the sentence, as it had in Birmingham, and it continued to do so afterwards though it remained below the level of January 1973. The level remained constant in Liverpool (Figure 3) and, again, does not seem to have been influenced by the sentence.

Lack of any apparent general deterrent effect of severe sentences was predictable from various studies carried out in both Europe and the United States. In his research, *Deterrents and Incentives to Crime among Boys and Young Men aged 15—21 Years*, H. D. Willcock found that punishment for an offence was rated only fourth by his respondents as a consequence of committing a crime. Ten per cent placed it first, whereas 49 per cent thought that the reaction of their family would be their chief worry. Professor Johannes Andenaes said in

Sentencing as a deterrent: number of robberies by week, 1972–73

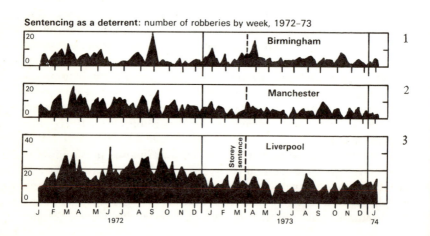

his historical review (*The General Preventive Effects of Punishment*) that fear of apprehension was considerably more important as a deterrent than any possible punishment. Indeed, the California Assembly Committee on Criminal Procedure has taken the same view, remarking that 'there is no evidence that more severe penalties deter crime more effectively than less severe penalties' and that 'we can find no evidence that crime can be reduced by increasing time served.' The committee agreed with the view that the severity of punishment was less significant as a deterrent to crime than the certainty of detection. This opinion was shared by some members of the British police with regard to mugging.

One chief constable pointed out the effect on deterrence of the low risk of apprehension, when he responded to Home Office inquiries about the problem in his city. He remarked that muggers did not have to be very bright to realise how low the chances of detection were and that only an obvious police presence was likely to deter them. This is quite a serious objection to the imposition of deterrent sentences and it was made in November 1972 – some months in advance of Storey's trial. The robbery rate in this chief constable's area was very high; and he put down the low detection rate of around 26 per cent to factors such as the surprise nature of an attack, the darkness making identification by the victim difficult, and the random element brought about by the attacks being motivated by hooliganism. It was hard for the police to obtain reliable evidence that would lead to an improvement in detection, but it was open to them to take preventive steps.

By March 1973, several police forces had already began to take measures in this direction. The Liverpool police force estimated that the monthly average for mugging in their area had risen from 78 for July to December 1971, to 130 for January to June 1972. They noted that this coincided with a substantial growth in all recorded crime during the blackouts caused by the electricity power cuts during the industrial conflict early in 1972. The power cuts may well have aided criminal activity but, at least with regard to robbery, the association between visibility and the crime rate did not last long. The rate continued at a high level throughout the summer and began to fall in autumn, despite the darker evenings. The Liverpool police were fairly specific in the information they gave about the measures they introduced to combat mugging. On 1 August 1972 a number of special patrols were set up, divisional commanders were encouraged to take action, and a crime prevention campaign was begun. The Manchester police also reported that they had introduced special measures, such as plain clothes patrols, during 1972 (though they gave no exact date). In Birmingham, similar changes were introduced, including uniformed and plain clothes patrols sometimes using dogs (again, no exact date was given).

Although the trial of Storey in March 1973 had no apparent impact on the level of robbery offences, there was a significant change (in Liverpool and Manchester, at least) in this rate during the two-year period. In Liverpool it began to drop substantially in October 1972, the decline accelerated during December 1972 and early January 1973; and the rate remained reasonably level thereafter. Once the offence rate had stabilised early in 1973, there were few significant variations in it. Manchester bears some similarity to Liverpool, though the crime rate was substantially lower in both years. The level began to fall slightly in late September 1972 and again at the end of January 1973; and the overall decline from 1972 to 1973 was of a similar proportion to Liverpool. The rate was 44 per cent lower in 1973 than in 1972 in Manchester while it was 43 per cent lower in Liverpool. The pattern in Birmingham differs from the two northern cities. This was partly because the robbery rate was never as serious and partly because it did not fall substantially in 1973 — the decline was only 12 per cent below 1972. Apart from an undulating pattern, there does not seem to be anything particularly remarkable in the movement of the robbery level in Birmingham.

It is difficult to measure the impact (if any) of a single deterrent sentence and the problem must be approached cautiously. When we looked more closely at Liverpool, however, and divided the two-year period into three parts at 1 August 1972 (the date when special police measures were introduced) and at 19 March 1973 (the date of the Storey sentence), the offence rate showed a very clear pattern. It was rising slightly between the beginning of the year and 1 August 1972; it then fell sharply, and after the court sentence remained level. Analysis established a remarkably close statistical relationship between the introduction of police measures and the decline in the offence rate and also demonstrated that the court sentence had no statistical impact at all.

Judging from when the crime rate did begin to fall in Liverpool and Manchester in the autumn of 1972, it looks as though the chief constable of Liverpool was right when he commented, in November 1972, that: 'Recent figures show a slight reduction for robbery offences but this is probably due to increased police activity rather than the publicity given to certain recent sentences.' His opinion seems supported by the probability that if the sentences had had an impact, there would have been a decline at that time in all the cities we looked at, and not just in Liverpool and Manchester. It is interesting to note that the police forces of Birmingham, Liverpool and Manchester told the Home Office in November 1972 that they had already introduced special measures to combat mugging; and that by the time the Home Office circular was issued on 1 May 1973 to encourage police measures in this field, the crisis had already passed.

The sentence given to Storey was not intended by the courts to be exemplary or to operate as a general deterrent. It is apparent from our study, however, that the employment of a severe sentence as a general deterrent is of questionable use. Storey's sentence appears not to have had any effect on the rate of robbery, as other research such as the work of the California Assembly Committee on Criminal Procedure might have led us to expect. There is no evidence in our study that the sentence had any impact at all; but a strong suggestion that the police measures did.

23. Towards More Effective Treatment Evaluation

by R. V. G. CLARKE and I. SINCLAIR

Reprinted, with permission, in abridged form from *Collected Studies in Criminological Research* Vol. XII (Council of Europe, 1974), pp. 55–82. The original paper was commissioned by the European Committee on Crime Problems.

The Strategy of Evaluative Research

If it is to make progress, we believe that penal evaluation will have to take account of difficulties arising from two sources. The first source of difficulty stems from a growing recognition of the inappropriateness of the medical analogy of penal treatment; we call this the 'medical myth' and argue below that it has heavily influenced previous evaluative research. The second source of difficulty, which is closely associated with the first, derives from the predominantly negative findings of the previous evaluative research.

The Medical Myth

According to the medical myth, delinquency or crime is a symptom of pathology in the individual person. The 'illness' is most commonly thought of as a disturbance of personality or attitudes which should be dealt with by subjecting the delinquent to a character-forming 'treatment'. This treatment is expected to act like an antibiotic or a course of radiotherapy. As in medicine, the main objective is thought to be 'cure' of the individual and careful experimentation and assessment are seen as ways to enable the more effective techniques to be identified and consequently adopted on a wider scale.

The medical myth can be attacked on a number of counts. First, the differences between delinquency and illness are being increasingly recognised. Broken ribs or septic tonsils exist irrespective of how others define them and hence can really be said to be a matter of personal pathology. In the case of delinquent behaviour, however, actions which are defined as deviant in one culture are often not so defined in another and, even within a single culture, large sections of the population can be out of sympathy with some of the standards of behaviour prescribed by the law. Secondly, self-report studies (e.g. Christie *et al.*, 1965; Gold, 1970) have shown that serious delinquent behaviour is quite common among people who have never appeared before the courts and is, statistically speaking, not all that abnormal. Bias, witting or unwitting, by the law enforcement agencies against certain sections of the populace (working class youths, for example) has a significant part to play in determining who becomes officially designated as criminal or delinquent.

In addition, the powerful influence of environmental and situational factors on the commission of acts that are deemed delinquent has been demonstrated on a wide scale since the pioneering studies of Hartshorne and May (1928). For example, studies that we have undertaken of offending by residents in probation hostels (Sinclair, 1971) and of absconding from approved schools (Clarke and Martin, 1971) have shown that these actions are much more a function of the institutional environment than the personalities of those involved. It is unlikely that these effects are confined to the institutional situation since Davies found (cf. Davies and Sinclair, 1971) that boys who succeeded on probation were dealt with by their parents in a manner strikingly similar to that in which the successful probation hostel wardens dealt with their charges.

In the light of these and similar findings it is not surprising that several decades of careful research have seen little success in establishing clear-cut personality differences between those who commit crimes and those who do not. Some differences indeed have been found, but these are not marked and can often be explained by the effects of incarceration. . . .

Previous Evaluative Research and the Medical Myth

The penal research undertaken by evaluators influenced by the medical myth has had two broad characteristics: in the first place, it has been concerned almost exclusively with the ability of penal measures to 'cure' the offender of his delinquent 'illness' while it has paid very little attention to other objectives. In the second place, it has handled penal treatments as though their characteristics were precisely known, analogous perhaps to an antibiotic or a course of surgery. In this way it has largely ignored the complexities of treatment itself, the interaction between those treating and those being treated, and the effects of the environment on the offender. It has thus sought to *demonstrate* the effects of particular treatments (probation, prison or fines) without making a systematic attempt to understand or explain how these effects could be achieved.

It would, of course, be untrue to suggest that all penologists have ignored the environment in which treatment takes place since there have been a number of sociological studies of the workings of prisons and other institutions (e.g. Clemmer, 1940; Morris and Morris, 1963; Polsky, 1962; Sykes, 1958). This research, however, has not been much concerned with the long-term effects of the institution, let alone with connecting these with precise aspects of treatment. And from the point of view of evaluation, these studies often have the further defect that, although they are usually concerned with a single institution, their findings are nevertheless generalised to cover all institutions of that type.

There have thus been two streams of penal research: an evaluative stream which has aimed to compare the effects of treatment which it did not describe, and a sociological stream concerned to describe treatments it did not compare. Our recommendations are directed towards bringing the two streams together and also with remedying a defect present in both; the lack of any attempt to relate specific treatment process to specific results.

Previous Evaluative Research and Negative Findings

In one respect, however, the sociological and evaluative streams of penal research support each other. Sociologists have found little cause to think that any of the treatments they have studied would reform or rehabilitate and, equally, the main result of the evaluative research has been negative: *there is now little reason to believe that any one of the widely used methods of treating offenders is much better at preventing reconviction than any other.* This conclusion is based on a great number of studies carried out both in Europe and the United States and its importance can hardly be overestimated. On the one hand it has served to shake the complacency about existing treatments and, on the other, it has provided a proper check to the uncritical enthusiasm that usually greets the advent of new measures. What little cause for optimism exists, has arisen from research suggesting that relatively specific types of treatment can prevent reconviction among offenders with certain specific characteristics. Fundamentally, however, the research worker must start from the depressing realisation that he is in danger of looking for positive results where none are to be found.

Implications for Evaluation of Rejecting the Medical Myth and of Negative Findings

In considering the implications of the above, we should begin by spelling out some of the differences between penal and medical treatment. In the first place it is wrong to see a penal measure as being akin to a medical remedy, such as an antibiotic. At the risk again of over-simplifying, we see antibiotics as having a clear-cut objective — that of curing the patient's sickness. They are simple to administer and simple to understand (i.e. they have communicable formulae), they are relatively powerful and consistent in their effects, and they can readily be adopted for use in quite different medical settings. While these features make evaluation a relatively easy task, they are not shared by penal measures. In contrast, these must serve a variety of sometimes conflicting aims, including reform of the offender, humanitarian considerations, retribution, general deterrence, and protection of the public; they consist of many ill-defined and little understood elements interacting in complex ways, and, as shown by the previous evaluative research, their effects are at best weak and variable. Moreover, their complexity makes it very difficult to identify the essential elements in any success they may have and this, together with the multiplicity of the aims they serve, makes it difficult to extend successful experiments to other settings or to a wider range of the criminal population.

The implications of these facts for evaluative research are twofold. In the first place we hope that a wider recognition of the ineffectiveness of penal treatment and of rejecting the medical myth will direct attention to some of the broader aims of penal policy. It is likely that policy-makers in planning and resource allocation will increasingly expect research to provide answers to such questions as:

a. Does the measure deter from crime others who have not directly experienced it?

b. Does it satisfy public notions of justice and due process?

c. Does it afford adequate protection to the public from the activities of known criminals?

d. Does it serve a purpose in usefully extending the range of disposals open to the courts?

e. Is it economical in terms of the human and other resources required to implement it?

f. Does it cause avoidable harm to the offender and his family?

g. Does it afford the offender scope to develop his own potential and to be of use to the community?

Evaluative studies concerned with some of these new questions, as well as the traditional ones, would be better adapted to the realities of penal practice and should produce findings more capable of influencing it. . . .

A second reason for a more analytic approach arises from the need to reproduce successful treatments. Even if previous results had been more positive, they would still usually have been of limited use. . . .

We are arguing, therefore, that evaluative research needs to become more analytic in the sense of asking what elements in treatment lead to what precise changes in the offender and how in turn these changes make him more law-abiding. Since it will be looking for rather small effects, it will have to employ research designs adequate to detect these. In addition, it will need to become more concerned both with the treatment environment — which might enable the offender to change in certain respects — and with the offender's home environment which works either for or against treatment. Only in these ways will we learn how treatment may work and so be able to improve existing treatments and reproduce the more successful ones elsewhere. . . .

Research Design

If evaluative research is to become more concerned with explanation and the development and testing of theories, it will require a different style of research project. The usual 'monolithic' project by which we mean a large study based on a single design and directed to answering only very few questions (usually of the sort, 'Does treatment X work better than treatment Y?'), will be too uneconomic an approach. Instead, research enquiries will need to take the form of a series of small-scale studies focused on particular aspects of the treatment process. Successive stages of the research will build on what has been learned earlier, hypotheses will be formulated and tested, and gradually a valid theory of the treatment will evolve.

In the early stages of the work it is important that the researcher adopt a flexible, free-wheeling approach to the problem. He should examine it quickly from a variety of different perspectives, analysing any information that is readily available, but being careful to avoid data-gathering exercises that will tie up his resources for too far ahead. Gradually as he becomes more familiar with the subject matter, this scavenging, opportunistic, approach might be replaced by deliberate attempts to get information that is thought to be valuable. Even at this stage he should avoid the more formal evaluative designs discussed at some length below, but might instead make use of quickly executed surveys or participant observation studies. Once he has got the 'feel' of the situation he might consider more structured exploration, perhaps in the form of a cross-institutional study. Still later (probably much later) he may find it worth while (within the limitations we discuss below) to mount carefully controlled experimental studies of particular aspects of treatment process.

The strategy outlined above is rather like the grounded theory approach to the development of classification systems in criminology that has been advocated by Bottoms (1972), though in the present context more importance would be attached to the testing and validation of theory. By and large this strategy is more appropriate when the operations of existing systems are being monitored; when new treatments are being evaluated, there may only be one or, at best, very few examples of the treatment and the underlying theory may be more closely explicated. In these circumstances a 'rationale' type research (see below) may be needed in order to give some quick indication of likely effectiveness, or it may even be found appropriate to launch an experimental design at a relatively early stage (so long as this does not run the danger of ossifying the development of the treatment).

It follows that the research worker must be more alive to the potentialities of the situation as well as to the constraints of working in a treatment setting. He should be prepared to undertake a much wider variety of research enquiries and, instead of relying so heavily upon formal design to confer scientific respectability upon his work, he should be guided by an analysis of the situation, intuition sharpened by experience, and the readily observable facts. In short, he should be prepared to think much harder. . . .

Conclusion

It is convenient here to relate our discussion of research design more closely to our main theme, that is, the need to achieve an understanding of how treatment works. This theme in fact underlies most of the points about methodology that we have tried to make. In the first place we have argued that formal, comparative, designs should not be attempted until the research worker has at least a minimal understanding of how the treatment may work. Rationale research either examines treatment processes in terms of the way in which they are assumed to operate, or else attempts to create some kind of understanding of the treatment situation. It does not, however, attempt to measure treatment outcome. Prediction, matching and experimental methods which do measure outcome, do not themselves readily permit a close analysis of the treatment process. This means that they do not usually lead to the kind of understanding that we believe is necessary to improve treatments or to reproduce successful ones elsewhere. By contrast, cross-institutional studies seem to be well suited to producing this sort of understanding and we believe that a wider use of these designs is appropriate at the present stage of treatment research.

Implementation of Findings

We began by pointing out that the introduction of research was not followed by rapid improvements in penal practice, and that in fact too much had been expected. Change is not readily brought about in a system as diverse and complex as that being dealt with, or in one whose separate parts (the courts, prisons, borstals, and probation service) enjoy so much autonomy. Moreover, a good deal of inertia is built into the system in terms of the physical plant and entrenched staff attitudes (cf. Mathiesen, 1967). Because a variety of objectives is being served and because the staff in different parts of the system vary so much in training and outlook, research carried out in one part may not be readily transferable to another. Administrative control is often weak and indirect, knowledge is in short supply, beliefs are strongly held, and emotions run high. In short, anyone who wishes to introduce change must be prepared for a slow and complex road to success.

We feel that the type of research we commend is suited to the complex situation just outlined. As we see it, administrators should seek from research less a prescription for action and more an understanding of how treatment works, since this should make possible more flexible policies. But if research directed towards explanation makes it easier for administrators to act flexibly and rationally, it also requires them to think harder about which of a number of possible courses they might wish to take. At the moment there may be the hope that research could produce a 'best buy' among penal treatments and that its implications will be quite precise. This hope is rarely, if ever, fulfilled. . . .

If research yields only understanding and not concrete recommendations, it is important that administrators and practitioners should see the need for this type of research and should make their own efforts to relate it to other research, and supplement it with their own political and practical expertise. Only in this way can effective action result. Unfortunately it is easy for the wrong research to be demanded or carried out, for communications between researchers and practitioners to be defective, and for research results to be unused because nobody has thought through their implications. We examine below some of the ways in which things can go wrong.

At present, research is often demanded in response to urgent practical problems or a new treatment innovation. This feature works against 'explanatory' research and gives a rather patchy appearance to research effort, which switches from one topic to another too quickly to follow through earlier findings, but too slowly for the practitioners and administrators who wish to direct its course. For research is often demanded even though its conclusions must follow rather than antedate the decisions it is supposed to inform. This may be done without a full discussion with the researcher of what these decisions could be, and on the false assumption that only a new research project can help with a fresh problem; previous research and research from other countries is not seen as having any relevance. Often a short intensive look at a problem, combined with a literature survey carried out in the light of the decisions to be made, would provide guides for administrative action far more quickly and at far less cost than would a lengthy piece of evaluative research.

And once results are obtained, there still remain problems of communicating them. The researcher tends to present his results for an academic audience — as, indeed, he must if his conclusions are to be adequately assessed. Some practitioners and administrators have had social science training but many lack the background, time or inclination to read this all too frequently indigestible material. They may find research irrelevant or naive, and may argue that it tells them only what they know already, or gives them information too late to be of any use. . . . The important point is that the whole process of 'selling' research requires as much thought as the research itself and on occasion more resources.

So far, our examples have been concerned with the application of specific research findings. It goes almost without saying that the situation is no better in relation to formulating an overall penal strategy based on research. We have already argued that much treatment is founded on what we have called the 'medical myth' and that this must be replaced by a more situational view of offending. If we are right, this has profound implications for the whole range of existing treatments and for the development of new ones, as well as for the kind of research that needs to be done. It is rarely anybody's job to consider this sort of issue and to make appropriate recommendations.

The process of thinking through the applications of research requires the kind of sustained attention to detail that neither administrators nor researchers usually have the time to give, and it may be that research will only be properly used if *special provision* for doing this is made. At the central government level, as well as at other administrative levels in the system, a planning and development unit may meet this need. Besides bridging the gap between research and action, the unit would have a number of other roles. First, it would take practical problems that arise in the system, examine them in the light of available research knowledge (perhaps undertaking full-scale literature surveys and commissioning more research), and formulate practical strategies for dealing with them. Secondly, it might survey basic knowledge about the system, point to obvious gaps (in knowledge about the general deterrent value of penal measures, for example) and try to fill them with appropriately commissioned research. Thirdly, and perhaps most importantly, it might undertake a continuous review and analysis of the means of bringing about change in the system. These include statutory powers, financial controls and incentives, rights of inspection, training courses, demonstration projects, staff selection boards, provision of basic statistics about such things as absconding and reconviction, and persuasion and propaganda. The object would be to discover ways of strengthening administrative control over the system in such a way as to make its operations more rational and more solidly founded on knowledge, and at the same time to make administrators more responsive to feedback from research and from the field.

References

Bottoms, A. E. (1972). 'Methodological aspects of classification in criminology' in *Collected Studies in Criminological Research*, Vol. X (Strasbourg, Council of Europe, 1973).

Christie, N., Andenaes, J. and Skirbeck, S. (1965). 'A study of self-reported crime' in *Scandinavian Studies in Criminology*, Vol. I. (K. O. Christiansen, ed.) (London, Tavistock).

Clarke, R. V. G. and Martin, D. N. (1971). *Absconding from approved schools* (London, HMSO.).

Clemmer, D. (1940). *The Prison Community* (New York, Rinehart).

Davies, M. and Sinclair, I. A. C. (1971). 'Families, hostels, and delinquents: an attempt to assess cause and effect', *Brit. J. Crim.* 11, p. 213.

Gold, M. (1970). *Delinquent Behaviour in an American City* (Belmont, Brooks-Cole).

Hartshorne, H. and May, M. A. (1928). *Studies in the Nature of Character* Vol. I: *Studies in Deceit* (New York, Macmillan).

Mathiesen, T. (1967). 'Resistance to change in correctional institutions', in *Collected Studies in Criminological Research*, Vol. I, (Strasbourg, Council of Europe).

Morris, T. and Morris, P. (1963). *Pentonville: A Sociological Study of an English Prison* (London, Routledge & Kegan Paul).

Polsky, H. W. (1962) *Cottage Six* (New York, Russell Sage).

Sinclair, I. A. C. (1971). *Hostels for Probationers* (London, HMSO).

Sykes, G. (1958). *The Society of Captives* (Princeton, University Press).

24. The Failure of Penal Treatment – Where Do We Go From Here?

by A. KEITH BOTTOMLEY

Original contribution, specially prepared for this volume.

Evaluation Research Reassessed

A good example of the 'pendulum theory', applied to trends in penological theory and research, is the way in which the great popularity during the 1960s of evaluation studies of the effectiveness of penal treatment has given way in the mid-1970s to a rash of critical reviews of the results of such evaluation research, with calls for a complete reappraisal of this aspect of penology. In the United States the earlier negative conclusions of the surveys of research by Bailey (1966) and Logan (1972) were followed by the much more polemical claims of Martinson (1974, 1976), supported by the full weight of the finally published report by Lipton, Martinson and Wilks (1975). The stir created by Martinson and his team provoked a lively debate in the academic journals, with stout rejoinders being made particularly by Adams (1974, 1976) and Palmer (1975). In England, on the other hand, just as the evaluation research has been on a much smaller scale, so the recent reviews of treatment evaluation and the effectiveness of sentencing have been typically more muted (Clarke and Sinclair, 1974; Brody, 1976); the authors of these reviews have not ruled out the value of further research in penal evaluation, but have suggested rather different and broader objectives.

Practitioners in the penal services have necessarily been involved, directly or indirectly, in the evaluation studies that have been carried out in the last decades and they have a natural concern to learn any lessons that may emerge; but on the whole it has been the academic criminologists and researchers who have been at the centre of these developments. Both groups can be seen to have personal investments in the continued attempts to discover more 'effective' penal treatment — practitioners because it affects their day-to-day work, academic criminologists because of the intellectual challenge inherent in research of this kind. These vested interests may help to explain why evaluation research proceeded for as long as it did without major questions being asked of the kind that are now beginning to emerge. There are, of course, many other groups in the community, both among the general public and among those more directly involved in policy formulation, law enforcement and sentencing, who are vitally interested in the issue of, in Martinson's phrase, 'What Works? — questions and answers about prison reform'; the growing impatience of this much wider audience for clear-cut answers to their questions may well have contributed in an important way to the current reappraisal.

On the surface, it would appear that the answer to those who ask the question, Has penal treatment failed?, must be an unequivocal 'Yes'. The conclusions of all the recent surveys of the effectiveness of penal treatment seem to be more or less in basic agreement on this. Martinson, for example, summarised the outcome of the mammoth review for the New York State Governor's Special Committee:

> With few and isolated exceptions, the rehabilitative efforts that have been reported so far have had no appreciable effect on recidivism. [Martinson, 1974]

Similarly, in their review of the literature for the Council of Europe, Clarke and Sinclair concluded:

> There is now little reason to believe that any one of the widely used methods of treating offenders is much better at preventing reconviction than any other. [Clarke and Sinclair, 1974, p. 58]

Inevitably, such apparently sweeping rejections of so much earlier research effort have not been allowed to go unchallenged. Martinson has been criticised for ignoring or underplaying the importance of numerous positive findings from what he termed 'few and isolated exceptions', and for setting up as an unrealistic objective the discovery of a *single successful method* of reducing recidivism for all kinds of crime and criminals (Palmer, 1975). Much previous research has also been faulted on technicalities or substantial weaknesses in methodology, or criticised for failing to ask the right questions about what aspects of treatments may or may not be responsible for particular effects.

Many of these criticisms do contain important elements of truth: there *are* certain 'positive' findings which ought not to be thoughtlessly swept aside with the mass of negative findings; research methodology has been far from faultless, and ought to be improved before we can claim to have properly tested the limits of what might be discovered; and just as there are now few criminologists who seek or hope to find single 'monolithic' theories of crime, so in penal evaluation the most that perhaps ought to be aimed at are answers to Palmer's questions, 'What methods work best for *which* types of offenders, and under *what* conditions or in what types of setting?' (Palmer, 1975). This means that there may still be some justifications for continuing to improve research methods, and for framing research objectives in a more precise if more limited fashion with regard to investigating specific types of offender in specific 'treatment environments' (see Clarke and Sinclair, 1974 pp. 228–37 above); but see also Bottoms, 1973a). However, before indicating some of the changes of approach that now seem to be necessary a few comments are needed about the broader context of penal objectives within which research takes place.

Effectiveness and Objectives in Sentencing

The origins and impact of social research cannot be understood properly without paying close attention to the context in which the social behaviour or institutions being studied actually exist and operate. The most definite conclusions of penological studies may have very little impact, not because of any ambiguity or methodological flaws in the research itself but because certain basic assumptions may not be shared by researchers and policy-makers. Thus, the findings of parole prediction studies or projects such as the Mannheim and Wilkins (1955) Borstal studies may fail to have the expected impact because the parole or Borstal institution board members use a different frame of reference; similarly, in the case of comparisons between the effectiveness of open and closed Borstals, or short versus longer prison sentences, there are invariably other external or internal considerations to be taken into account by the executive decision-makers which have not been incorporated — and often indeed cannot be — into the research design.

There is a need, therefore, that seems to be gaining increased recognition in Britain, to review the whole field of evaluation research from a wider perspective than that which has tended to inform past research; there is a need to question the purpose and relevance of evaluation studies of penal treatment, and to attempt to answer at least some of the questions that are in the minds of magistrates, judges and members of the general public, as well as those of the researchers themselves. Such a review should start from a basic consideration of sentencing objectives of the kind outlined by the Streatfeild Committee (above pp. 194—201) and progress to an even broader assessment of objectives in penal policy.

As long ago as 1961 the Streatfeild Committee described how the trasitional reliance by sentencers upon the 'tariff system' was giving way to a new set of objectives, including deterrence, the protection of society and the reformation of the individual offender. It recommended new procedures and new kinds of information for sentencers that should be reliable, comprehensive and *relevant to what the court was seeking to achieve*. These recommendations gave added impetus to the provision of social inquiry reports on offenders and brought about a dramatic change in the role of probation officers in the sentencing process (see Davies, 1974, pp. 202—10 above). Another specific result of the Report of the Streatfeild Committee was the provision of an official handbook for courts on the treatment of offenders, *The Sentence of the Court* (Home Office, 1964, 1969) — a publication, however, that fell sadly short of the high ideals of the Committee to which it owed its origin, being narrowly descriptive and legalistic in form and content. Nevertheless, tucked away in an Annex was a report of the results of evaluation research in Britain which hinted at an important change of perspective. After summarising the rather meagre findings of previous research, it outlined a new comparative study by the Home Office Research Unit to evaluate sentencing effectiveness *from the point of view of the court making the sentencing decision.* The preliminary findings of this study are well enough known: it was claimed that fines and discharges were followed by fewer reconvictions than expected (when certain limited background factors had been allowed for), that probation and approved schools seemed to have better results with recidivists than with first offenders, and that detention centres had slightly worse records than borstals. Unfortunately much greater significance and weight has been attached to these findings than they deserved, even in their own terms, as the careful

critique by Tony Bottoms in the *Criminal Law Review* has made clear
(Bottoms, 1973b). Relatively few and crude factors were controlled,
leaving it very probable that the apparent efficacy of fines and the
apparent lack of success that probation enjoyed with first offenders was
due to a failure on the part of the research to take account of the way
courts may select from within groups of offenders those that appear to
them most suited to particular measures — thereby going a long way
towards 'explaining' differential success and failure rates. Even so,
whatever justified scepticism we may retain about these much-quoted
findings, of equal interest at the time were the concluding comments
about their admitted limitations: together with the usual methodological caveats about the virtual impossibilty of researchers being able
to control for *all* the factors that may be considered relevant by
sentencers, and other warnings about the dangers of courts interpreting
the results of the research too simplistically, they concluded:

> To study reconviction rates is, of course, to assess the effectiveness
> of sentences from one point of view only; some kinds of sentence
> may have fewer disadvantages for society even though they do not
> give better relative reconviction rates. [Home Office, 1969, p. 72]

Although there is little evidence that the implications of this message
were taken to heart by many researchers at the time, at least it was not
completely forgotten, but reappeared in the recent review by Brody
(1976). The first part of his review focused on the intentions of the
sentencing court, and started from the important premiss that 'the
effectiveness of a legal penalty has to be judged according to what
purpose it is intended to serve' (p. 1), which admittedly sounds rather
obvious but needed reiterating nevertheless. Even with an individualised
approach to sentencing, Brody indicated that a sentence needs to be
chosen 'which will best satisty the demands that justice be done, that
public opinion be appeased, that no harm or undue suffering be caused
and that as far as possible any reoccurrence of criminal behaviour be
prevented' (p. 3). When consideration is given to whether sentences are
fulfilling other aims besides individual reformation, the questions often
cannot be answered because of the lack of and inherent difficulty of
collecting the relevant evidence. Despite the fact that the major part of
this report then proceeded to assess the results of research with a
narrow focus upon individual reform, this fundamental issue was
restated in the conclusions:

Reformation is not the only aim behind a sentencing decision, and sentences can equally well be evaluated according to how far they satisfy demands of humanity or demands for retribution or public protection, or simply in terms of more or less sophisticated analyses of relative expense or social cost. [Brody, 1976, p. 66]

Clarke and Sinclair reached very similar conclusions in their Council of Europe paper (see above, pp. 228—37) and felt that the increasing recognition of the apparent ineffectiveness of penal treatment ought to lead to closer attention being paid to some of the broader aims of penal policy, with future evaluation research proceeding on a wider front:

> Instead of needing to pay so much attention to reformative aspects, the researcher will be far more free to compare penal measures with respect to such things as their economic and social costs, their capacity for general deterrence, the protection afforded to the public, from the activities of known criminals, and the extent to which they satisfy requirements of justice and humanity. [Clarke and Sinclair, 1974, p. 83]

Future Directions: Justice and the Rehabilitation of Punishment

The last decade has seen a great increase in the amount of research into the deterrent effects of criminal sanctions (see for example Zimring and Hawkins, 1973; Gibbs, 1975; Andenaes, 1974), and there continues to be considerable public and political debate about the ethics and practical feasibility of protecting society against certain violent and recidivist offenders, if indeed such can be identified in advance of sanctions (see Working Party on the Dangerous Offender, 1977). What is needed at this stage, to capitalise on these developments, is a strategic plan for a broader based analysis of the aims and effectiveness of penal policy and sentencing decisions. In England a recent paper by Steven Folkard (Home Office Research Unit, 1977) is one of the most encouraging signs yet of a new sense of direction along these lines within official circles:

> If the general meaning of penal treatment is accepted then the concept of evaluation needs to be correspondingly broadened. Reconviction rates, or any other criteria based on the therapeutic

model, are inappropriate, and objectives other than rehabilitation need to be considered. These might include retribution, containment, deterrence, or reparation. . . . Given the complex nature of the public response to crime it would probably be unrealistic to stress any one objective to the exclusion of others. However, bearing this in mind, it might be suggested that one of the central concerns is to ensure that justice is done. [Home Office Research Unit, 1977, p. 38]

We have seen that the methodological problems of evaluation research based on the traditional individual treatment model have been complicated enough, as have the different problems involved in attempts to measure the deterrent effects of sentencing. Part of the attractiveness of these approaches, as far as the researcher is concerned, is that global assumptions are made (which are then put to the test) whereby *all sentences* of certain types are assumed to be aiming at changing the individual offender, or deterring potential offenders. However, a very different set of problems faces any one who wants to assess the extent to which sentences satisfy criteria of retributive appropriateness or notions of justice: in particular, these include the conflicts of values and interests in most modern societies, and the problems created by the general lack of openness and specificity in sentencing decisions. The whole history of the sociological study of sentencing behaviour has been bedevilled by the almost universal reluctance of judges to spell out the objectives and reasons for particular sentences; for as long as judicial objectives are not clearly identified there can be no proper evaluation research. Even if a situation could be envisaged in which reasoned decisions were always given by the court, the task for the empirical researcher to follow up each specific case in terms of stated objectives would still be more than daunting.

It may well be that more valuable progress could be made, not along traditional 'empirical' lines at all, but rather by instituting new structures for greater public and social accountability of judicial decisions, of the kind so forcefully advocated by Roger Hood in his 1974 NACRO lecture in the House of Lords, *Tolerance and the Tariff* (see below, pp. 296–307). This may be the only way to influence sentencing policy, as it seems clear that the use of imprisonment by the courts has been little affected by the negative findings of most traditional evaluations of penal treatment, despite the fact that prisons (apart from being no more 'effective' than other measures) are certainly more costly in both economic and human terms than virtually any non-custodial alternative. It is high time to examine the implications of Hood's new approach with renewed seriousness:

> The new approach addresses itself directly to the moral evaluations of these judges, and the way they interpret the gravity or dangerousness of various offences in modern society. It does not take judicial opinions for granted and would also aim to bring the judiciary into a critical debate over how our society should define its deviants and what systems of punishment are justifiable in a social order, still full of inequities and injustices. [Hood, 1974, p. 14]

Empirical evaluations of the traditional kind, based on questionable assumptions about the primacy of individual treatment, should give way to new moral and social evaluations of old concepts such as punishment, responsibility and justice. In this way new connections might emerge between the criminal justice process, penal policy and the wider concerns of social policy and social justice, which are inextricably linked with the problems of crime and social control in contemporary society.

References

Adams, S. (1974). 'Evaluative research in corrections: status and prospects' *Federal Probation* 38, pp. 1, 14.
—— (1976). 'Evaluation: A way out of rhetoric' in *Rehabilitation, Recidivism and Research* (Hackensack, N.J. National Council on Crime and Delinquency).
Andenaes, J. (1974). *Punishment and Deterrence* (Ann Arbor, University of Michigan Press).
Bailey, W. C. (1966). 'Correctional outcome: an evaluation of 100 reports' *Journal of Criminal Law, Criminology and Police Science* 57, p. 153.
Bottoms, A. E. (1973a). 'Methodological aspects of classification in criminology' in *Collected Studies in Criminological Research*, Vol. X (Strasbourg, Council of Europe).
—— (1973b). 'The efficacy of the fine: the case for agnosticism' *Criminal Law Review*, p. 543.
Brody, S. R. (1976). *The Effectiveness of Sentencing* Home Office Research Study No. 35 (London, HMSO).
Clarke, R. V. G. and Sinclair, I. (1974). 'Toward more effective treatment evaluation' in *Collected Studies in Criminological Research*, Vol. XII, (Strasbourg, Council of Europe).

Davies, M. (1974). 'Social enquiry for the courts' *British Journal of Criminology* 14, p. 18.

Gibbs, J. P. (1975). *Crime, Punishment and Deterrence* (Amsterdam Elsevier).

Home Office (1961). *Report of the Interdepartmental Committee on the Business of the Criminal Courts* Cmnd 1289 (London, HMSO).

——(1969). *The Sentence of the court* (London, HMSO).

Home Office Research Unit (1977). *Research Bulletin No. 4.*

Hood, R. G. (1974). *Tolerance and the Tariff* (NACRO Reprint No. 11).

Lipton, D., Martinson, R. and Wilks, J. (1975). *Effectiveness of Correctional Treatment: A Survey of Evaluation Studies* (New York, Praeger).

Logan, C. H. (1972). 'Evaluation research in crime and delinquency' *Journal of Criminal Law, Criminology, and Police Science* 63, p. 378.

Mannheim, H. and Wilkins, L. T. (1955). *Prediction Methods in Relation to Borstal Training* (London, HMSO).

Martinson, R. (1974). 'What works? – questions and answers about prison reform' *The Public Interest*, Spring, p. 23.

——(1976). 'California research at the crossroads' *Crime and Delinquency*, p. 180.

Palmer, T. (1975). 'Martinson revisited' *Journal of Research in Crime and Delinquency*, 12, p. 133.

Working Party on the Dangerous Offender (1977). *The Dangerous Offender: A Consultative document*

Zimring, F. E. and Hawkins, G. J. (1973). *Deterrence: the Legal Threat in Crime Control* (Chicago, University Press).

PART VI

Judicial vs. Executive Discretion in Criminal Justice

Introduction

Many of the readings in earlier sections of this volume have been concerned with the problems that are raised by informal or 'low visibility' decision-taking. In this final section, we turn to consideration of an area – that of executive or administrative discretion – in which these problems are seen in perhaps their sharpest focus. Recent years have seen the increasing erosion of the sentencing discretion traditionally vested in the criminal courts and its gradual transfer to administrative, non-judicial bodies of one kind or another. In the United States one of the major themes of the emergent movement in favour of the so-called 'justice model' in corrections is the urgent need to review the indeterminate sentence and to control the excessive discretion allowed to judicial and executive decision-makers (see, for example, American Friends Service Committee, 1971; Von Hirsch, 1976). Even in England indeterminate custodial sentences, for which the actual date of release is set by the institutional authorities rather than by the courts, have long been used, though on a much more limited scale than has been the case in the United States. Obvious examples exist in the form of sentences of 'life' imprisonment and Borstal training, and an element of indeterminacy has been present for virtually all prison sentences since remission was introduced in England in 1898. The introduction of parole in England under the 1967 Criminal Justice Act as well as the enormous reduction in the powers of the Juvenile Court under the 1969 Children and Young Persons' Act have considerably accelerated this trend. As a future indication of current thinking in this regard, the Advisory Council on the Penal System (1974) in their report, *Young Adult Offenders*, recommended what amounts to an extension of the parole system to the age group seventeen to twenty years, though with a much greater degree of discretion vested in the custodial authorities than is the case with the present system for adult prisoners. The Home Secretary, in a parliamentary written reply (February 1977), has indicated that adoption of this measure for young adults should be the 'eventual objective', though, because of financial considerations, it is not currently feasible.

Nigel Walker (himself a distinguished member of the Advisory

249

Council) has for a number of years stoutly defended this transfer of discretion from the courts. He and Roger Hood (part of whose brilliant critique of indeterminacy is reproduced here) have engaged in a vigorous, yet lucid and provocative, debate about the acceptable limits of administrative discretion. The principal argument in favour of such decision-making is that it allows the possibility of reconsideration of a sentence imposed by the courts by a body of experts in the light of new information and changed circumstances of an offender, including his response to the custodial regime. This is a compelling argument, on the surface at least, though, as has been seen repeatedly in the contributions in this volume, the advantages that accompany informal and out-of-court justice may well be greatly outweighed by the real dangers that such a system necessarily introduces. David Thomas succinctly marshalls the counter-arguments as follow:

> It is a sound general principle . . . that power over the personal freedom of an individual should be exercised subject to all the safeguards broadly encompassed in the concept of due process of law, and consisting at least in publicity of proceedings, the specification of allegations, the requirement of the production of evidence to establish relevant facts to a high degree of probability, and the right of the subject of the proceedings to challenge the evidence against him and to call his own witness. These requirements are substantially satisfied by existing judicial sentencing procedures and are generally absent from existing administrative decision-making procedures affecting offenders. [*Criminal Law Review* 1974 pp. 691−2]

The exercise of administrative discretion fails to satisfy the requirements of a just system as outlined in our introduction to Part I: more specifically, the exercise of this discretion tends to be arbitrary and unpredictable, or at least to be viewed as such by those subject to it; it tends to be secret, and those affected by the decisions are only exceptionally informed of the reasons for them; the critera taken into account are far from clear and are not as a rule precisely specified; the decisions are rarely open to scrutiny or appeal. In short, justice is not open and public.

Further Reading

Advisory Council on the Penal System, *Young Adult Offenders* (HMSO, 1974).

American Friends Service Committee, *Struggle for Justice* (Hill and Wang, 1971).

Bottoms, A. E., 'On the decriminalisation of English juvenile courts' in R. Hood (ed.) *Crime, Criminology and Public Policy* pp. 319—45 (Heinemann, 1974).

Cavenagh, W. E., *The Changing Face of Juvenile Justice* (Eleanor Rathbone Memorial Lecture, 1976).

Harrison, P., 'The Children Act under attack', *New Society* (12 June 1975) p. 642.

Home Office, *Children and Young Persons Act 1969: Observations on the Eleventh Report from the Expenditure Committee* Cmnd. 6494 (HMSO, 1976).

Hood, R., 'The case against executive control over time in custody: A rejoinder to Professor Walker's criticisms' *Criminal Law Review* (1975) p. 545.

———, Steer, D. and Hawkins, K. O., 'Young adult offenders: Comments on the report of the Advisory Council on the penal system', *British Journal of Criminology*, 14, (1974) p. 388.

May, D. R., 'Rhetoric and reality: The consequence of unacknowledged ambiguity in the children's panel system', *British Journal of Criminology*, 17, (1977) p. 209.

Nuttall, C. P., *Parole in England and Wales* Home Office Research Study No. 38 (HMSO, 1977).

Thomas, D. A., (ed.) *Parole, its Implications for the Criminal Justice and Penal Systems* (University of Cambridge, Cropwood Round-Table Conference 1973).

Von Hirsch, A., *Doing Justice: the Choice of Punishment* (Hill and Wang, 1976).

Walker, N., 'Release by executive decision: A defence' *Criminal Law Review* (1975) p. 540.

West, D. J. (ed.) *The Future of Parole* (Duckworth, 1972).

25. Juvenile Justice: Where Next?

by ALLISON MORRIS

Reprinted, with permission, from *Howard Journal of Penology* XV, 1 (1976), pp. 26–37.

The juvenile court has always performed a variety of functions, assumed a variety of roles, and expressed a wide range of values. Not surprisingly, perhaps, these functions, roles and values are not always consonant and frequently conflict. As a result, juvenile courts since their inception have been beset by ambiguities, dilemmas and conflicting expectations. Should the court, for example, regard the individual before it as a child who may be in difficulties or as an offender who has committed an offence? Should it look to the interests of the individual child or to the protection of society? Should it protect the child from its environment or the environment from the child? Should it protect the child from its environment or protect its liberty? Should it protect the child from the stigma which may result from a court appearance or use it to assert society's values? The choices before the court in actual situations are, of course, rarely as clear-cut as this, but a consequence of these varying demands has been that our courts have been confused by constantly shifting objectives. The primary objective in one instance may be the interests of the child; in another, the interests of the community. Or, in any one case there may be a number of demands, but these demands may not be reconcilable – they may conflict. Winifred Cavenagh (1967) an experienced juvenile court magistrate, suggested that it does not matter which sort of system for dealing with children we have as long as the public are protected, civil rights and liberties are preserved and the young offender gets the treatment he or she needs. But, in fact, these criteria call for the application of different standards. For example, the last is best served by what could be described as a welfare model which looks to the needs of the child rather than to the nature of the offence, and which requires flexibility of treatment, wide powers, the dominance of professional judgments and a preference for administrative decision-making. The first and second are probably best served by what could be described as a justice model, but this requires a tariff system, some proportion between the disposal and the offence, and stresses notions of individual responsibility and punishment, justice through legal rules and procedure, the offence as the sole justification for intervention, and the protection of society through sanctions. These two models involve different assumptions, attitudes, procedures and objectives, and the setting and structure of the juvenile court has come to exhibit the conflict between the two. Elements of both exist at a statutory, procedural and operational level.

Unresolved Dilemmas

Recent changes incorporated in the Children and Young Persons Act, 1969, far from resolving these dilemmas, have made them more apparent, and it is these unresolved dilemmas that are the source of many of the current frustrations and tensions experienced amongst those involved in the operation of the Act. The solution to these difficulties does not lie in the provision of more resources, more secure institutions, and so on. It is not simply a matter of 'give us the tools and we'll do the job' for we do not know what tools to give and we are not very sure what job we are trying to do. We could certainly place more children in institutions and we could reduce the case-loads of social workers, but current difficulties have far deeper roots.

Many of the difficulties now experienced existed, of course, before the implementation of the Act. For example, the number of absconding from approved schools increased each year reaching nearly 9,000 in 1968 despite the fact that from 1964 onwards the number of boys actually in approved schools at any given time was dropping. Neither probation nor approved schools had high success rates, and children continued to commit offences during the currency of such orders. There was also general criticism before the implementation of the Act over the lack of facilities. The Act did not create these difficulties.

What is more important in trying to understand present criticisms — for example, that children who are the subject of care orders can commit further offences with impunity — is to realize that the Act is essentially a compromise between these two different approaches: the welfare model and the justice model. This is clear when one considers the philosophy underlying the legislation.[1]

The White Paper, *Children in Trouble*, endorsed a treatment or caring philosophy. The model set out in paragraph 20 was one of assessment of the needs of the child, diagnosis and treatment. Delinquency was viewed as possibly symptomatic of underlying disorders and the offence *per se* was not to be a ground for intervention (Home Office, 1968). Reference was to be made rather to whether the child required care which he was unlikely to receive unless he was referred to the court, or to whether the child was beyond parental control. The basic aim was to provide help and guidance – primarily on a voluntary basis; and the child's home background was to be considered before taking the decision to institute court proceedings for an offence.

But the White Paper also acknowledges other interests – those of society in protecting itself against crime. Paragraph 7 states that an important object of the criminal law is to protect society against the social consequences of delinquency; the same paragraph recognizes the importance of caring for those who are too young to protect themselves. The report argues that these two distinct grounds for action by society have been moving steadily together.

> It has become increasingly clear that social control of harmful behaviour by the young, and social measures to help and protect the young, are not distinct and separate processes. The aims of protecting society from juvenile delinquency, and of helping children in trouble to grow up into mature and law abiding persons, are complementary and not contradictory.

But these aims are contradictory,[2] or at least there is a tension between the two, and this tension is reflected in the operation of the Act. Police, magistrates and social workers alike are uncertain about their proper roles with respect to child offenders

Conflicting Ideologies

The Act challenged traditional ideas on justice and the law. It was an attempt to introduce a caring system based on our supposedly greater understanding of the causes of problem behaviour in children. It involved therefore, a radical shift in values – it required changes in court procedure and in the conduct of those dealing with children. But to what extent has this occurred? Only very slightly, it seems (Priestley, 1975). Paragraph 18 of the White Paper suggested that one of the major effects of the proposals would be 'to encourage and strengthen consultation and co-operation between the juvenile court magistrates, the police, the local authority services concerned — including the schools and the probation service'. But can consultation really take place? The White Paper assumed a common philosophy or ideology amongst these groups on the appropriate way of dealing with child offenders. This does not seem to exist.[3]

Each of the above groups has a specialist function. They perhaps share a common long-term objective — let us say the prevention of delinquent behaviour — but each group has its own more immediate objectives. For example, the police are primarily concerned with the identification of suspects, the probation officer or social worker with the investigation of needs, and the magistrate with maintaining the dignity of and respect for the law. Individual policies are developed to achieve these particular objectives. These may already conflict but, in addition, others may be added — the investigation of the needs of the child by the police (as in the police juvenile bureaux), control of the offender by the probation officer or social worker (as part of the probation or supervision order) and the need for the magistrate to have regard to the welfare of the child (in making his decision as to the appropriate disposal for the child). Traditional role boundaries accordingly become blurred, and this leads to strains both within each agency and between the various agencies. For example, the central duties of the police are the prevention, control and detection of crime, and the normal end product is to take the individual to court. The job of the juvenile bureau officer is to recognize and refer to the courts the child who needs skilled treatment and to keep others out of them, essentially a social work role. This can create a conflict in the various roles of the individual officer, but it can also lead to conflict with his colleagues and with other agencies. The police refer a child to the court when, according to them, action is necessary, something should be done. The court is aware of this and may be susceptible to pressure for certain kinds of decisions. If these strains become severe it may not be possible to reach the major objective — the prevention of delinquent behaviour.

To some extent this is what happened in England. For the Act to work there needs to be confidence and co-operation — yet many of those involved in the operation of the Act are poles apart in their thinking and in their professional ideologies. This creates tension amongst the various groups and this in turn affects the operation of the system. For example, magistrates since the outset have been concerned with the issue of equality before the law. They felt that the legislation was unjust in that it was class-biased and discriminated against children from 'a bad home'. It does this, of course, to the extent that we rely on our own values to determine 'good' or 'bad' homes, and to the extent that we assume that middle-class children come from good homes. But it seems that the magistrates' real intention was an attempt to retain the offence *per se* as a ground for intervention and this was, of course, at cross-purposes with the whole conception of the White Paper and the subsequent legislation with requires that, *in addition* to the offence, the child must require care which he cannot otherwise receive. Recently, the Magistrates' Association in its memorandum to the Sub-Committee òf the House of Commons Expenditure Committee asked for an order stronger than a care order to show that 'in the last resort the law has teeth'. They argued that children were escaping the law and committing crimes with impunity, that the law was no longer respected, that the public were not being protected and that public confidence in the courts was being undermined.[4]

Much of the magistrates' concern about the operation of the Act has become transmuted into indignation at the real or imagined defects of social workers. They are seen as keeping children out of court and out of institutions. But although social workers are probably not in favour of a child appearing in court just for the sake of the experience of a court appearance, they are clearly not in favour of children continuing to commit offences. Their professional aim is to use their skills to prevent this. I may be accused at this stage in my argument of creating stereotypes, but this is exactly what each group does of the other. It is often asked of social workers (and this is a quotation from a magistrate) 'How can these young people fresh from university departments of sociology, but otherwise completely untrained and inexperienced, possibly understand the needs of a delinquent child from a deprived home in one of the city's slums?' (Berlins and Wansell, 1974, p. 85) But reverse this — 'How can these middle-aged, middle-class, professional people, virtually untrained, who customarily sit in adult courts meting out punishment, possibly understand . . . '. Neither picture is real, but often what people think is happening is more important than what is actually happening. It is this that shapes their attitudes.

The Care Order: A Case Study

The debate centring on the implementation of care orders highlights this basic conflict – is the care order a punishment for the offence committed or a measure for the protection of society? Or is it to provide care to the child who is not cared for at home, to provide him with a breathing space so that he might develop as an individual? Mr Callaghan in introducing the Children and Young Persons Bill set out how care orders were intended to work. 'They rest on the principle that it is for the court to decide the nature and extent of the compulsory powers to be exercised and that within specified limits the responsibility for decisions on treatment in individual cases should be placed on those who undertake the treatment.' (H. C. Deb. vol. 779 col. 1176) It appears from this that the magistrates' proper functions are firstly to determine whether or not there are grounds for intervention, and secondly to set the limits to any intervention. It was intended, therefore, at the outset that care orders would not necessarily involve the child's removal from home – all they did was to give the social worker *power* to do so. In practice, however, it seems that the bases for decision-making and for action by magistrate and social worker differ – the child may be sentenced by the magistrate on the basis of the offence he has committed, but the order is implemented by the social worker on the basis of the child's needs. In discussing the functions of juvenile court magistrates, Cavenagh (1973) states that these are to define compulsory powers in relation to care, or to regulate the imposition of sanctions – she stresses that the decision is judicial rather than clinical, and that the question is whether the proposed grant of powers or the suggested sanction is justified by the gravity of the situation as revealed by the evidence in the reports. She emphasizes that this is not the same as the question of what is in the best interests of the child on welfare grounds. If this is how magistrates see their role, then conflict with a social work-based decision seems inevitable.

Yet one of the stereotyped pictures presented is that social workers are frustrating the desire of magistrates to commit certain children to institutions by arbitrarily allowing them to stay at home. I have tried to show how this type of situation may well arise, but how true is this anyway? According to a survey by the Department of Health and Social Security, (1973) local authorities in general did not send fewer children to residential institutions after the implementation of the Act than previously. Some authorities did place fewer children in approved schools in 1971 than the courts had in the previous system, but other authorities placed more. The number of children in care who are in fact living with parents or relatives has increased considerably: from 6% to 17% in 1973 (Harrison, 1975). Some of these are children whom it has not been possible to place in community homes, as headmasters are now free to take or refuse particular children; there is certainly a need for a greater degree of specialization in community homes. But it would be wrong to give local authorities the power to direct headmasters to accept children whether they want them or not. This negates the whole notion of specialization and assumes that headmasters are acting unprofessionally. In the main, this 17% involves children for whom *at this point in time* home is felt to be the best place. Information from one assessment centre shows that in 1973 only 48 out of 667 were returned to their parents, and this was after full assessment (Roycroft 1973).

There has also been much criticism of the number of children committing offences while on care orders, but again there is little evidence that the picture is as bad as it is presented. The Department of Health and Social Security survey showed that of 538 such children appearing before the court in March 1973, 240 were, at the time of the offence, in the charge of their parents.[5] The initial inference made from this was that the children had been allowed to remain at home. But if the length of time which had elapsed between the making of the order and the finding of guilt in March 1973 is considered, we find an average period of 26.6 months between the making of the earlier order and the later court appearance.[6] Most of the children, therefore, could have spent an average length of time in a residential establishment and then returned home. Alternatively, if the children had been at home throughout the period, 26 months without a court appearance indicates that the decision to leave the child at home was reasonably successful.

Suspicion and its Consequences

These feelings of suspicion and lack of trust have led to a number of consequences. Firstly, there has been an increase in 15 year-olds being sent to Borstal and detention centres.[7] The non-punitive ethos of the Act has largely been ignored. Secondly, remands to penal institutions are both increasing[8] and appear to be being used punitively. A survey by London Boroughs Children Regional Planning Committee covering six months from October 1972 until March 1973 found 219 juveniles remanded to prison. Forty-three were not dealt with during the survey period, but of the remaining 176, 43% received *non-custodial* sentences. Of 14 girls sent to prison, 9 received non-custodial sentences (Bamford, 1974). Of course, we do not know the full facts of individual cases, but these statistics at least raise the question of why such children were sent to prison.

What Alternatives?

So far I have suggested that the difficulties experienced in England are more fundamental than can be resolved by additional resources. Basic dilemmas in this legislation, as in previous legislation, have remained unresolved, and conflicting expectations amongst those operating the system have created confusion. Are the dilemmas resolvable? What alternatives are there?

The system in Scotland is different from that in England. When the Kilbrandon Committee report (Scottish Office, 1964) — the report which led to the Social Work (Scotland) Act, 1968 — was published, the Scottish branch of the Howard League stated that this would place Scotland in the mainstream of world penal reform. Certainly it would be foolish for England to change its legislation without looking at the experience of other countries, particularly Scotland. In Scotland the juvenile courts were abolished and were replaced by welfare tribunals staffed by lay people. Children's hearings, as these are called, are concerned only with the disposal of the child. There is a complete separation between judicial and disposal functions. If the child or the parent denies the commission of the offence, the case is referred to the sheriff court for the offence to be proved. If the child or parent objects to the decision made by the children's hearing on the disposal, they may also appeal to the sheriff court. In both these instances the parents and the child are entitled to legal aid. The key figure in the new system is the reporter. It is his function to decide, on the basis of reports, whether the child referred to him by the police, social worker or education department is in 'need of compulsory measures of care'. If he believes that this is so, the child is then referred to the children's hearing. The new system applies to all children under the age of 16. Where the child enters the system before 16 he remains within it until the age of 18 unless the hearing terminates its jurisdiction. The hearing can discharge the referral or impose a supervision order – the latter may be with or without conditions and can include residence in a List D school (that is, a former approved school). The hearing specifies the school to which the child is sent and also has continuing jurisdiction, that is, the case must be reviewed annually by the hearing. The hearing has no power to fine, to send the child to detention centre, or to remit to the sheriff court for a Borstal sentence.

There are important differences in detail between the two systems, primarily the role of the reporter and the powers and continuing jurisdiction of the hearing. But they share a number of common characteristics: both systems endorse a child care philosophy; the major source of referral continues in both countries to be the police; the majority of children plead guilty or accept the ground of referral, and thus in both jurisdictions the main question is what to do with the child; the children appearing before the courts and hearings come from similar backgrounds and present similar problems; both countries have expressed concern over resources; both systems have been the object of criticism; and in both countries the juvenile crime rate has continued to increase. It is because of these similarities rather than the differences that an evaluation of the Scottish system can be of some relevance to the current situation in England. How well, then, is the Scottish system working? The Scottish system, like the English, endorsed a child care or welfare model, but, as I have argued in more detail elsewhere (Morris, 1974), the welfare model cannot readily be applied to delinquency. Briefly, such an approach assumes the pathology of deviant behaviour, that deviants are different from other people and have a special set of problems which explains their deviance. But delinquency is more complex than this. Such an approach also assumes that we have sufficient knowledge about the causes of delinquency and its effective treatment to make an assessment of a child's needs and to arrange an appropriate treatment programme for him. But there is little agreement at any precise level about the underlying reasons for delinquent behaviour or about the most satisfactory way of dealing with it. Information presented to the hearing to aid its decisions tends to concentrate on personal and familial factors which are often both subjective and irrelevant. There is a lack of objective criteria for assessing the needs of a child and, consequently, decisions are related to social conformity as much as to the child's needs. It was also hoped by the Kilbrandon Committee (Scottish Office, 1964) that the movement away from a court to a welfare tribunal would solve this problem of the conflict between the welfare of the child and the protection of the community. The new system, therefore, hoped to abolish delinquency — all that would remain would be children in need of care. But delinquency cannot be abolished so easily. Society's attitude to children who offend cannot be isolated from society's attitude to offenders in general — they expect something to be done about the delinquent behaviour. Political and community pressures have, accordingly, shaped the hearings' behaviour and they are concerned as much with control and with the protection of the public as with the care and welfare of the child. The Scottish system, therefore, has not resolved this particular dilemma. But it has, to some extent, reduced it. The system is geared towards keeping children out of the formal control system, towards distinguishing the child 'at risk' from the casual offender. The crucial question has become not whether action is justified, for example on the basis of the offence, but rather whether action is necessary in the light of the total circumstances.

More children were, in fact, referred to the reporters by the police in 1973 than were formerly referred to the procurators-fiscal in the court system.[9] (The procurators-fiscal are in charge of prosecutions in the Scottish courts.) But the majority of children referred in this way to the reporters are *not* subsequently referred by them to the children's hearing. They refer only about half of those referred to them to the children's hearing; the fiscals in the court system referred about 95%. The reason for this difference lies in the changed nature of the discretion involved. The fiscal's task was primarily to assess whether prosecution was in the public interest and whether there was sufficient evidence to establish the commission of the offence. The reporter, on the other hand, arranges a children's hearing only when it seems to him that the child who has committed an offence is also in need of compulsory measures of care. It is his role to determine whether or not the referral is justified and necessary. Voluntary care may be arranged for the child, and thus care is available in appropriate cases without the stigma associated with contact with formal social control mechanism. As a result, fewer children reach the formal social control agencies in the children's hearing system than in the former court system.

It might be suggested that the juvenile bureau officer in England plays a role similar to the reporters' in Scotland. Although there are wide regional variations in the number of children referred to the court by the police, in the cities it is about 50%. But there is at least some evidence that it is the behaviour of the child *per se* which leads to this decision. Few children are cautioned more than once (this varies from area to area) and it was only recently that a group of children involved in the same offence could be dealt with on an individual basis. It is not yet known whether the juvenile bureaux operate as a sift or whether they widen the net. Evidence from the operation of Youth Bureaux in the USA suggests that the latter is likely (Howlett, 1973), and research on the former juvenile liaison schemes suggested that few of the children dealt with in this scheme would have been brought before the court even if the alternative of a juvenile liaison scheme had not existed (Taylor, 1971). Certainly there has been no reduction in the number of children reaching the juvenile courts in England.[10] The reporters, on the other hand, operate very much as a visible sift between the police and the hearing.

The children's hearings themselves are, unlike English juvenile court magistrates, concerned only with the appropriate disposal for the child and they continue to sift out on the basis of further information those who do not need compulsory measures of care; 34% of the children referred to the hearings in 1973 had their referrals discharged. List D schools, however, are full; although only 12% of the hearings' disposals are supervision orders with residential requirements, there are now 40% more children in List D schools than in approved schools in 1970. There has also been an increase in the use of compulsory supervision by a social worker, from 3,529 probation orders in 1970 to 7,069 supervision orders in 1973. Once the child reaches the hearing, therefore, the level of intervention is greater than in the juvenile court. It is also possible for the child to remain within the children's hearing system for longer than in the court system, but hearings are willing to terminate their jurisdiction at the annual review and to say that this child *no longer* needs compulsory measures of care. In 1972, jurisdiction was terminated in 32% of the cases reviewed by the hearings.

Thus, the children's hearing system, though based on an inadequate treatment model, may be moving towards a 'non-interventionist' model. Edwin Lemert (1967) set this out as an ideal model for the juvenile court. He suggested that children should be referred to the court only when all other attempts (for example, by parents, schools, etc.) to resolve their difficulties had failed. He argued that if the juvenile court is to become effective, its function must be reduced to the enforcement of the ethical minimum of youth conduct necessary to maintain social life in a pluralistic society. . . . It can then proceed to its secondary task of arranging the richest possible variety of assistance to those special disadvantaged children who come under its jurisdiction.

The benefits of such a system are numerous; for example, it reserves limited resources for the more difficult child and it encourages the development of criteria for identifying such children. There is also some evidence that intervention by formal social control agencies can be harmful, both with respect to the child's self-image and to future employment opportunities, that children may commit further delinquencies because of intervention (Farrington, 1977) and that there is some advantage (in terms of the juvenile's attitudes and self concepts) in intervention by agencies which are not associated with the courts. One criticism which has been made of such a system is that it prevents the stigmatisation of only the marginally deviant, but that the hard core delinquent will continue to experience stigmatisation. Emerson (1969), for example, writes 'the principle of judicious non-intervention would seem not to change the juvenile court's handling of such hard core, discredited delinquents most in need of salvaging'. This is true, but it is not an argument against non-intervention and increased voluntary and community care as such. At least the instances in which formal stigmatization can occur are reduced.

A more thorough-going and expanded version of 'judicious' non-intervention — leave the kids alone. Proponents of this approach (Schur, 1973) aim at diverting children from the court, but they also oppose intervention by social work agencies. They argue that collective action programmes are necessary rather than those that single out specific individuals, the socio-cultural change will reduce delinquency problems, and that, therefore, we must change the structure and values of our society rather than the youth. This approach argues in favour of voluntary treatment, of decriminalization, of narrowing the scope of the juvenile court jurisdiction, and of unmasking 'euphemisms'. But some of these can be achieved within the 'judicious non-intervention' model, and others cannot, in reality, be achieved. Few crimes, for example, can be decriminalized. As Cohen (1974) argues, crimes of property and personal violence cannot be dealt with by 'laissez faire liberalism'. Also, although the notion of coercive care is problematic, this approach wrongly assumes that there are no children for whom compulsory measures of care or control may be necessary in the child's own interest and in society's interest.

An alternative perspective is that suggested by Sandford Fox (1974). He argues in favour of the child's right to punishment, for a system in which there is no individualization of disposals, no indefinite periods of control, no official discretion. Professor Fox writes: 'the paramount virtue of the idea of punishment is that it seems to suggest remedies for the most blatant abuses of a treatment-orientated system ... punishment implies limits to what is officially done, whereas treatment does not.' The basis of Fox's suggestion is that punishment is a 'necessity for the body politick ... a necessary evil'. Such an approach certainly remedies many of the defects of a treatment system; it also solves one of the dilemmas that we have been discussing — whether disposal should be determined by the needs of the child or by the nature of the offence committed. It probably also brings the system closer to the way in which children and their parents see it. Peter Scott's (1958) work shows that boys consider themselves on trial in a criminal court and expect punishment if found guilty; their idea of justice is retributive. Similarly, Voeckler (1960) found that by far the most popular interpretation by parents of the way in which the court disposes its cases involved the concept of graded punishment and they were surprised if the court did not fit this pattern. But while there may be merits in this approach when dealing with adult offenders, as an end in itself it is socially unacceptable to most people in this country who are dealing with children and who see their role as a helping one. Nor does this approach limit the number of children who would appear before the court.

Yet another approach in the United States has been to grant the child procedural protections. This began with the Supreme Court decision *in re Gault* (1967) 387 U.S. 1, which held that the due process clause of the 14th amendment applied to proceedings in state juvenile courts. The child, therefore, was given the right to be represented by counsel and was warned that he need make no statement, that he was privileged against self-incrimination. A survey (Lefstein *et al.*, 1969) since then, however, suggests a high level of non-compliance in the juvenile courts with these instructions. The lawyers' major contribution was their ability to mitigate the severity of dispositions. Lawyers in the United States have also become increasingly involved in 'right to treatment' suits (e.g. in *re Elmore* 127 U.S. App. D.C. 176). This is litigation on behalf of children, usually in institutions, which argues that the constitution guarantees these children 'individualised treatment appropriate to their needs'. The cases call on the courts to order that public resources be applied to this end and that, if no treatment is offered to the child, the child be released from the institution.

Conclusion

Each of these various ways of dealing with child offenders has its advantages and disadvantages – probably what this review shows is that there is no perfect system. But it seems to me that any system dealing with child offenders should have as its major aim the integration of young people with difficulties *into* the community rather than separating them from it. We know that there is considerably more delinquency committed than is dealt with by the police or juvenile courts, and offences by middle class delinquents are often handled without reporting them to the police – parents or schools settle the matter with the victim informally, or the child may be referred to the psychiatric, social work or child guidance services. The behaviour of such children is often similar to those referred to the juvenile court, but in these cases care is afforded informally without the stigma of a court appearance. There is no evidence for the belief that a court appearance is a beneficial experience. This suggests that there is a strong case for making such resources more available to many of those currently appearing before our courts. It is also as well to stress that it is in the developments in the wider field of social policy – housing, education and so on – that we are likely to find means to reduce crime.

In the English context I would specifically argue in favour of full implementation of the Children and Young Persons Act so that an offence by itself is not a ground for intervention. There is also a case for the appointment of someone like the reporter in the Scottish system – an independent assessor of whether or not the child requires compulsory measures of care. The police should not be expected to fulfil this role. One could, in fact, go one step further and require formal evidence that the child requires *compulsory* care, or that the child could not get the necessary care without a court order. Children should be kept out of courts or hearings (there are no essential differences) wherever possible.

Notes

1. This is, of course, complicated by the fact that certain key sections have not been implemented because of ideological differences between the two major political parties. Thus, although the provision allowing more care proceedings was brought into effect in January 1971, there was no immediate ban on bringing criminal proceedings for any age group. This failure to implement sections of the Act shows in itself how divergent views are on the appropriate way of dealing with child offenders.
2. In fact, the Act acknowledges that these are contradictory. Section 27 (2) states: 'If it appears to a local authority that it is necessary for the purpose of protecting members of the public to exercise their powers in relation to a particular child in their care in a manner which may not be consistent with their general duty under S12 (1) of the (Children) Act of 1948 to further his best interests and afford him opportunity for proper developments, *the authority may, not withstanding that duty, act in that manner.*'
3. This is confirmed in the report of the subcommittee of the House of Commons Expenditure Committee (House of Commons, 1975).
4. Evidence submitted by the Magistrates Association to the sub-committee.
5. Quoted in *The Magistrate*, 30, (1974), p. 83.
6. Quoted in *The Magistrate*, 30, (1974), p. 173.
7. 1383 juveniles were sent to detention centre in 1969 compared with 2,315 in 1973, a rise of 67%. Sentences to Borstal training increased by 50% over the same period.
8. The number of 14–16-year-olds on remand rose from 2,947 in 1971 to 4,645 in 1974.
9. In 1969, 18,912 children under 16 were referred to the courts and in 1973, 22,176 such children were referred to the reporter (Criminal Statistics, Scotland, 1974, HMSO.).
10. In 1969, 63,830 juveniles were dealt with in the juvenile courts for indictable offences, in 1973, 70,710 were dealt with.

References

Bamford, T. (1974). 'Juveniles in prisons' *Social Work Today* s, 3, p. 82.
Berlins, M. and Wansell, G. (1974). *Caught in the Act* (Penguin Books).
Cavenagh, W. E. (1967). *The Juvenile Courts, the Child and the Law* (Pelican Books).
Cavenagh, W. E. (1973). Unpublished paper to European Seminar on 'Collaboration between the courts and the social services', Paris, 1973.
Cohen, S. (1974). 'Human warehouses: the future of our prisons', *New Society* (14 November) 407–11.
Department of Health and Social Security (1973). *Further Survey by Social Work* (5 October).
Emerson, R. (1969). *Judging Delinquents* (Aldine).

Farrington, D. P. (1977). 'The effects of public labelling' *British Journal of Criminology*, 17, p. 112.

Fox, S. (1974). 'The child's right to punishment'. Unpublished paper presented to Childrens Panel Training Summer School, Stirling.

Harrison, P. (1975). 'Children: who cares?' *New Society* (13 February) p. 391

Home Office (1968). *Children in Trouble*, Cmnd. 3601 (HMSO).

House of Commons (1975). *Report of the Subcommittee of the House of Commons Expenditure Committee on the Children and Young Persons Act*, 2 vols (HMSO).

Howlett, F. W. (1973). 'Is the Y.S.B. all it's cracked up to be?' *Crime and Delinquency* p. 485.

Lefstein, N. *et al.* (1969). 'In search of juvenile justice, Gault and its implementation', *Law and Society Review*, p. 491.

Lemert, E. (1967). *The Juvenile Court – Quests and Realities* (Presidents Commission on Law Enforcement and the Adminstration of Justice).

Morris, A. (1974). 'Scottish Juvenile justice – a critique' in R. Hood, (ed.), *Crime, Criminology and Public Policy* (Heinemann).

Priestley, P. (1975). *In the Interests of the Child* (unpublished monograph).

Roycroft, B. (1973). 'Children and Young Persons Act', *The Magistrate*, 29, Nob. 88.

Schur, E. (1973). *Radical Non-intervention* (Prentice-Hall).

Scott, P. (1958). 'Juvenile courts: the juvenile's point of view', *British Journal of Delinquency*, 14, p. 200.

Scottish Office (1964). *Children and Young Persons: Scotland*, Cmnd. 2306 (HMSO).

Taylor, M. (1971). *Study of the Juvenile Liaison Scheme in West Ham, 1961–65* (HMSO).

Voeckler, P. (1960). 'Juvenile courts: the parents' point of view, *British Journal of Criminology*, 1, p. 154.

26. Parole Decision-making in Britain

by ELIZABETH E. BARNARD

Reprinted, with permission, in abridged form from
International Journal of Criminology and Penology, 4 (1976),
pp. 145–59.

This paper looks at the short history of parole in Britain through an examination of the structure and practice of decision-making. Criticisms of the system have become louder and more numerous recently, but, in my view, these have often been off-target in failing to take account of the relationship between parole decisions and other processes within the criminal justice system. They have also, for the most part, concerned themselves solely with making the present system work more fairly and efficiently, rather than reconsidering the objectives of parole and its place in criminal justice.

There are two distinct conceptual models of parole decision-making: the judicial and the administrative. Concrete systems have elements of each.

In the judicial model, parole is seen principally as a sentence, and the criteria that govern decisions are as those of sentencing. Primary among these are the importance of maintaining equity in the treatment of offenders in respect of the seriousness of the offence, and the public interest in being protected from dangerous persons. The control aspect of parole supervision is stressed, and may well be reflected in the background of parole agents in law enforcement roles, such as prison officers. At the same time, justice demands the protection of the prisoner by due process; he should be permitted to speak and to call evidence on his own behalf; he should have legal advice and representation; there should be provision for appeal. Parole and revocation both involve a new sentence, so both should be covered by due process provisions. Decisions should be made by a body wholly independent of prison management, and it should give reasons for its decisions.

In contrast to this, the administrative model sees parole as no different, in decision-making terms, from allocation of a prisoner to a particular institution or a particular work assignment. The major objective is 'treatment'; it may be part of the rehabilitative needs of the offender to be discharged from prison under licence, with the help of parole supervision. Not so frequently referred to officially, but of considerable practical importance, is the usefulness of parole as a tool of prison management, particularly in controlling the size of prison populations and providing a powerful incentive to good behaviour. It is also attractive to governments in reducing the direct and indirect costs of imprisonment. Whether to parole and whether to revoke are ordinary decisions of the correctional agency, made by those with day-to-day experience of the penal system and the offenders within it. Legal arguments which have been employed in support of this procedure include the idea that parole is an act of grace, granted by a benign administration, but not a right; that parole is a contract, under which the offender agrees to certain conditions governing his behaviour, but not giving him the right to dispute if the administration withdraws the privilege; and that parole does not change the status of the prisoner, who remains in legal custody, but has been granted some measure of liberty.

The comparison of these two models is not just an academic exercise. The interpretation of the nature of the system by actors within it or in related systems is significant for its practice, as a few examples will show. If the judiciary see parole as a rival sentencing system, then they may vary their own sentencing policy accordingly, most probably by increasing prison terms, but if parole is seen as an administrative process, legitimately within the sphere of penal policy as exercised by the correctional agency, then sentencing will not be affected. Prisoners' attitudes to parole will also be likely to vary; if they think the process is or should be similar to sentencing they may expect elements of due process, as prevail in the courts, but if they see it as just another gimmick, like group counselling or colour television, that has been thought up by some distant, all-powerful authority, then their expectations may well be quite different.

To the best of my knowledge, neither of these ideal types exists in pure form. The very origins of parole show a combination of judicial and administrative aspects. With the shift in penal thinking from the offence to the offender, the inflexibility of the court's sentence was seen as a barrier to effective reformation of the offender and so an inadequate safeguard of the community. In many jurisdictions, parole and indeterminate sentencing were introduced together, as inextricably linked elements of a reforming correctional philosophy. Thus, in support of a 'treatment' objective, sentencing functions were removed from the courts and transferred, in most cases, to specially appointed 'expert' parole boards, closely allied to the penal agency itself. . . .

Assessment of prisoners' conduct is an important part of the paroling process, giving the administration at least some role in decisions. Even if such information is passed on to another body to make that decision, it is not to the ordinary criminal courts. Thus, however judicial the orientation of a particular parole system, the judicial role is not played by the ordinary judiciary. Powers of revocation are sometimes granted to the courts, but these are not usually exclusive and are used less than administrative recall powers.

The British System

As proposed in the white paper *The Adult Offender* in 1965 and in the Criminal Justice Bill in 1967, parole in Britain was intended to conform to the administrative model. No proposals were made to alter the sentencing powers of the courts. The intention was 'merely' to extend executive discretion in the allocation of prisoners, and it was clear from the parliamentary debates that parole was considered to be a modest measure, to be used sparingly, for fairly exceptional cases. For a long time, the final third of a prison sentence had been remitted, subject to conformity to prison discipline, and this remained untouched. Release on licence, after a third of the sentence had been served, and subject to supervision by a probationer officer, was to be made available to a selected few prisoners serving sentences longer than 18 months.[1]

The official objective was clearly rehabilitative; after some decades of optimism about the potential of training and therapy in the custodial setting, it was thought that further progress could be achieved by some flexibility on discharge dates and by supervision during the difficult period of transition to ordinary life. It was alleged that prisoners reached a 'recognisable peak' in their potential for good post-custody adjustment, and that if they were detained for longer, they may deteriorate . . . but the theory underlying the proposal to introduce parole to Britain rested on weak empirical foundations. . . .

The legislation as finally enacted provided a three-stage selection process. The prison committee was formalised as a Local Review Committee, comprising, at least, the Governor, or his Deputy, a probation officer other than a welfare officer, a magistrate from the Visiting Committee, and a wholly independent member.[2] Thus, prison officials were to be in the minority, and the 'outside' members were to include experts, including a judicial representative, and those whose only qualification was a concern for the public interest. The second stage, of Home Office officials, receded in importance, and a new stage, a Parole Board without civil service members, was created. By statute, judges were to be represented on the Board, together with 'experts', such as probation officers, psychiatrists and academics, and others. They would serve part-time and for quite short periods, and the Home Secretary could veto a positive recommendation but not overrule a negative one.

Although the creation of specialist bodies introduces a quasi-judicial element, the process as a whole is highly bureaucratic. Hearings are not held, so dependence on the file, or 'dossier', as it is usually referred to, is virtually total, especially at the Parole Board stage, thereby increasing the difficulty in coming to a different conclusion, as the information provided is identical. The adminstration's power rests in its control of the file. It contains reports of the trial, of prison conduct, of past, present and future home and work circumstances, and various prognoses, both clinical and actuarial. It is not surprising that considerable attention is paid to improving documentation, for this is the only input to the Parole Board. . . .

Due process is almost entirely lacking. The prisoner may make written representations and be interviewed by an independent LRC member, but he has no right to a hearing, to representation or appeal, and he is not given reasons for the decision. This issue is frequently raised, but the policy has not yet been changed. Not unnaturally, the Parole Board is seen as a collection of faceless men and women. The rejected prisoner is not entitled to know the stage at which he was turned down or the reasons, though the prison governor or welfare officer may hint, often from incomplete knowledge. It is normal practice to review cases annually, but each of the selection stages may recommend an early review. Thus, the prisoner is a passive participant in the selection process; only by exercising his right to decline consideration can he have much effect on the outcome. So, whereas one of the objects of parole is to improve the scope for good prison management, it has often served to increase anxiety and lower morale, particularly in institutions from which few get parole. Indeed, the independent agencies may serve to siphon off hostility from prison staff to some extent. Alternatively, their independence may be doubted, and prisoners may feel that they are being judged unfairly.

Parole Practice[3]

An examination of parole statistics lends weight to the argument that in a bureaucratic system, the first tier has greatest power and the final tier least. Decisions over five years, 1969 to 1973, have been examined and show this trend. The major policy changes were based on evidence supporting this contention.

During this period, there was little change in the proportion declining consideration; this remained at about 5% at first review and somewhat over 10% at later reviews. There is no published evidence as to whether disappointment at first review leads to opting out later or whether the figures represent a greater degree of non-involvement on each occasion by those serving longer sentences, who may also be the more criminal and more institutionalised inmates.

The major change has been that LRCs now recommend about 40% as suitable, compared with 33% earlier. There has been a rather smaller increase in the proportion of these recommendations accepted by the Parole Board, from 75% to less than 80%. Thus, overall, the Board has moved in step with LRCs. It may have played an exhortatory role in increasing the liberality of LRCs but it has not exceeded them. The actual proportions, as well as the changes, are of interest, as they indicate that the LRC is the crucial hurdle; once that is passed, it is a simpler matter to satisfy the Board. Over the whole period, the proportion of those thought 'unsuitable' by LRCs who have been paroled has remained at 5%, although the policy on which of these to refer to the Board has altered. . . .

Under the Criminal Justice Act, 1972, the Home Secretary, in consultation with the Parole Board, may designate categories of prisoners who may be paroled without their cases being referred to the Board. Research has shown that the Board rejected very few in some categories thought suitable by LRCs. At present, the designated category is under three-year sentence, without sex, violence, arson or drug-trafficking, and unanimously recommended by the LRC. This provision enables the Board to consider more cases without increasing further in size.

Over this period of five years, the proportion of eligible prisoners being released on parole at each review has risen from 25% to 30%. This is accounted for principally by the increased recommendation rate of LRCs from 33% to 40%. So is the complex selection machinery, which entails considerable expense and delay, really necessary?

Proposals for Change

Criticisms of the structure for parole decision-making and proposals for change may be grouped into three types, and they rest, often implicitly only, on differing conceptions of crime and the appropriate role of the state in crime control. I shall refer to these approaches as rehabilitative, reformist and radical.

Ironically, parole was introduced in Britain at the time when criticism of the rehabilitative model of penal treatment was increasingly voiced by 'progressive' thinkers. For the previous century or so, rehabilitation had been seen as the progressive objective for criminal justice systems. Its decline in esteem followed the decline in assumptions of a moral consensus, the realisation that it could lead to excessive punishment and the abuse of power by so-called expert rehabilitators, and its failures even within its own terms of reference, namely, to reduce recidivism. . . .

What I have referred to as the reformist position is concerned primarily with issues of justice, mainly in procedural terms; i.e., proposals have been made to introduce elements of due process, to shift the system from an administrative to a judicial one.[4]

What such reformers do not consider sufficiently is what effects these judicial bodies would have on the courts themselves. In discussion I have found judges who have been members of parole boards to have been strongly opposed to such a move, as diminishing the distinctiveness of the parole process from the sentencing process, and thence their own role. This leads one on to query whether there is a distinctive function for a parole selection process to perform. The independent effect of prison behaviour on future conduct has consistently been found to be slight, at most, in prediction and other studies, which is not surprising when one considers the peculiar nature of living within prisons. So cannot we simply leave it up to the courts to decide the lengths of prison terms and licence periods? This is central to Hood's[5] proposals, which would retain the Parole Board to consider the cases only of those serving long terms in which the trial judge had included a proviso that they shall not be released without Parole Board agreement, in the interests of public safety. Hood hopes that this policy would lead to a reduction in the lengths of prison terms, and it would seem that the universal provision of supervision on license is proposed to reassure the judiciary rather than out of confidence in its rehabilitative efficacy, although Hood is not explicit on this issue. Such a provision would change parole from a reduction in sentence to an addition to sentence, and we already have evidence that compulsory aftercare is often resented by ex-inmates of penal institutions.

The radical approach to parole is, quite simply, to abolish it. This line is taken by prisoners' rights organisations and some others. This may seem odd to those who see parole as being in the interests of prisoners. The aspects of parole stressed by the radicals are that it exerts control, including the threat of recall, over discharged prisoners; that it encourages judges to increase the terms of imprisonment ordered, and, as many do not get parole, this means more time spent in prison on average; that it increases the dependence and humiliation of prisoners by requiring them to 'earn' parole, not just by good behaviour, but by more positive adherence to the official value system; that it places prisoners and their families in an intolerable situation of uncertainty, with attendant anxiety; and that it gives the executive excessive power. Whereas they are concerned at the lack of due process, and the ineffectualness of the prisoner's participation in the decision, the radicals eschew reform of parole as only making it more effective and durable in its oppression. They see parole as the superficially human face of imprisonment, masking its true nature, and possibly retarding the move away from custodial penalties altogether.

Prospects for Parole

How realistic are these three types of proposals for change? What are the chances that any of them could actually happen? In attempting to answer these questions, I shall need to give more attention to the objectives of criminal justice and the environment in which it operates.

Parole decisions are affected by similiar criteria to sentencing decisions, and it is well known that objectives such as rehabilitation, social defence and general deterrence may be in conflict.

As I see it, there are five objectives of parole, and these are given varying emphasis in official statements of policy. They may be summarised as follows, and will henceforth be referred to by their key words.

(1) The long-term *rehabilitation* of the prisoner, to a crime-free life as an ordinary member of the community. Traditionally, this has been the dominant official goal, particularly at the introduction of parole.

(2) To modify the sentence of the court in the light of later behaviour, as a *reward* to the prisoner. This has been played down officially, but has been seen as influencing actual decisions.

(3) To give correctional agencies more control over their work, by

    (a) affecting the population of prisons;

    (b) providing an incentive to good behaviour.

In this respect, parole is a *management* tool.

(4) To reduce public *expenditure*, as keeping people in custody is considerably more expensive than other penal measures.

(5) For public *protection*, by providing controls over ex-prisoners, rather than discharging them absolutely, without supervision.

. . . I would divide the environment which affects the degree to which the realisation of such objectives, and of proposals made by critics to which I referred earlier can be achieved, into three circles of increasing distance from the parole system itself: the rest of the criminal justice system; the socio-political situation in Britain; and overseas experience of penal change.

There are three points at which problems within the system are highlighted: the selection process; management; and operating personnel.

I have considered the present cumbersome selection process at some length. As a new graft on an existing structure, it has affected the work load and environment of those involved.

The parole system exists between two largely separate sectors, the prison system and the probation and aftercare services. The traditions and values of the two bodies are radically different, and the management problem of co-ordination awesome. The prison service is centralised and disciplined, with hierarchical chains of responsibility and a distinctive officer corps. In contrast, in the probation service, the relationship of officer and client is central, and the pattern of supervision is primarily an issue of individual, professional judgment, with responsibility at local level, to the courts, and not to the Home Office directly. The weak co-ordination of these agencies may have advantages, such as letting the parolee feel he is free of prison pressures and motivating the supervisor against recommending revocation in all suitable circumstances.

Another aspect of poor co-ordination is between the courts and the penal system. Because the courts have offenders to deal with first, they determine the boundaries of penal action, and they are in a position to frustrate some plans of correctional agencies. For instance, in relation to parole, they could increase prison terms to ensure that parole did not bite into the sentence so quickly. Although Parliament has made available a greater variety of non-custodial measures in recent years, with the clear intention that fewer people should be sent to prison, the courts have tended to reshuffle the pack of non-custodial measures and to deal them out to the same players. . . . As courts are slow to change, it may be more profitable to proceed by reducing the minimum prison term, now one year, which must be served before parole may be granted, if one wishes to reduce the use of prisons.

The larger the non-custodial sector, the greater the need for trained, flexible manpower. Physical controls within institutions reduce the problems of managing people. In case of trouble, locking-up will usually provide at least temporary respite, though there is a long international history of prison riots and disturbances. The human relations skills required for less obvious forms of control are greater. . . .

There is undoubtedly a trend, supported by administrators and advocates for penal reform, if not the public at large, towards greater emphasis on non-custodial measures. The major influences on this trend are the lack of evidence that custody has any deterrent or rehabilitative effects, and, more importantly, perhaps, the considerable expense of custodial institutions, on capital and current account. Parole has political attractions as a stage towards removing the custodial element of many sentences entirely. If it can be shown to give the public as much protection from crime as custody, then why have custody?

In Britain and overseas, the methods of dealing with juvenile offenders permit considerable administrative discretion, including what is, in effect, immediate parole. For example, the English care order gives the local authority social worker extensive discretion, which may lead to the child remaining in the parental home. Some of the magistracy are unhappy about this arrangement, and a few notorious cases — such as the 16-year-old who admitted 87 offences within a week of being committed to care — have led to disquiet, but there have not been demonstrations and petitions from large sectors of the general public.

The Younger Committee proposals for young adults, particularly the major minority report, extends this principle of keeping the threat of custody in the background, as an option available to the supervisor as administrative action rather than a judicial order, within the terms of the sentence of the court.[6] So we may be witnessing a change of emphasis, in official thinking and among influential citizens, from custody, with supervised licence as an option, to supervision, with spells of custody as an option. . . .

Indeterminacy has been justified by the proposition that the judge at time of trial is not in a position to determine the most effective correctional career for each offender. However, these empirical foundations are unsound. Actuarial prediction studies have always found institutional behaviour to be a poor measure of later behaviour. This is supported by sociological and psychological studies of prison life, which paint a picture of exceptional circumstances requiring exceptional adjustments for survival, and bearing little relation to the skills required for ordinary living. Indeterminacy may also increase inmate anxiety and give correctional agencies excessive power to sanction non-conformity. The career of George Jackson is an indicator of this. It has become the first objective of the American prisoners' union to abolish indeterminacy. . . .

Notes

1. Prisoners serving sentences of less than three years are not eligible for release on licence after serving one-third, as a minimum of one year must be served in prison.
2. Under Criminal Justice Act, 1972, a fifth, independent, member has been added.
3. The following section refers only to England and Wales. In Scotland, the process is identical but separate.

4. K. Hawkins, 'Parole procedure: an alternative approach', *Brit. Jo. Criminology*, 13 (1973), pp. 6–25.
5. R. G. Hood, 'Some fundamental dilemmas of the English parole system and a suggestion for an alternative structure' (Paper presented to Cropwood Round-Table Conference on Parole, Cambridge, 1973).
6. Advisory Council on the Penal System, *Young Adult Offenders* (London, HMSO, 1974).

27. Control of Sentencing: the Balance Between the Judge and the Executive

by LORD JUSTICE SCARMAN

Reprinted by permission of the Howard League for Penal Reform, being the text of the address given at the AGM of the Howard League in September 1974.

With the publication of the Report by the Advisory Council on the Penal System upon Young Adult Offenders, our society may well be facing a turning-point in the development of the penal system. The report could prove as significant as its famous predecessor, that of the Gladstone Committee in 1895. It challenges assumptions upon which the present system is based and invites us to accept a diminishing role for the courts in the sentencing of young offenders. This challenge raises questions of sentencing policy which are not confined to young offenders. I propose, therefore, in the light of the report, to take a look at the sentence of the court: to what extent, if at all, should it control the future career of the person sentenced?

As you all know, the Advisory Council recommends the abolition of detention, Borstal training and imprisonment for young adults (seventeen to twenty-one years) and the substitution of a single generic sentence, the custody and control order. Its second major recommendation is that there should be a new and stronger non-custodial sentence for young adults, the supervision and control order to be operated by the probation service. I would expect that both these recommendations will prove to be acceptable; but I question whether the Council's detailed proposals for the operation of the custody and control order are sound. There are reasons, I suggest, for thinking that they are very dangerous indeed.

The proposals are these. Where a court has power to pass a sentence of imprisonment on an adult, it should have power, in the case of a young adult, to make a custody and control order. The sentence pronounced by the court would be for a determinate period during which the offender would be liable to either custody or control. But the court would not determine how long is to be the period of custody. The constitutional responsibility for decisions to release offenders from custody to serve the remainder of their sentence under control in the community would rest with the Home Secretary, acting in the case of shorter sentences on the advice of a local licence advisory committee and in the case of sentences of three years or more on the advice of the Parole Board. The licence advisory committee would consist of the governor of the establishment where the offender is in custody; a representative of the local probation service; a member of the Board of Visitors; and a member of the local community. This body would, in effect, decide the period of custody, i.e. the date of release, for the shorter sentences, and advise the Parole Board for the longer ones. By this means the function of the sentencing court would be limited to determining the period of social intervention in the life of the offender: but the executive would determine the period for which he is deprived of his liberty.

In submitting, as I shall do, that this is a dangerous step to take, I must at the outset emphasise that I do not challenge the wisdom of substituting for imprisonment, Borstal training and detention the single generic sentence of custody and control for young adult offenders. Nor do I challenge the view that such evidence as there is suggests that many types of offenders who have in the past been sentenced to custody might well be supervised in the community without any increase in the rates of re-offending. My challenge is solely to the proposal that the executive, not the court, should determine the length of the time spent in custody.

The argument adduced in the Council's report is largely negative in character and, so far as it goes, sound. The Council stress the inconclusive results of research, but say such evidence as there is indicates that 'the goal of helping, assisting and influencing the offender to live his life and manage his affairs without committing offences has a better chance of being achieved by supervision in the community than by committing him to custody'. They recognise that Borstal training, which since 1961 has become the medium-term sentence for young offenders, does not produce a success rate sufficiently high to challenge this proposition. They accept the general proposition that long sentences are damaging to the personality of the offender and, therefore, to his chance of rehabilitation: they accept also the relevance of international experience that there is no evidence to support the proposition that longer sentences mean less crime.

These are powerful reasons for introducing their new sentence of the court, designed to ensure that the young adult offender will spend the minimum period in custody before being released to control within the community. But do they support the further proposal that the date of release should be determined by the executive?

Roger Hood has recently restated with force the classical case against entrusting to the executive the decision as to the length of time spent in custody, and I do not intend to repeat it. But additionally he makes some telling points. After mentioning that research has failed to establish that rehabilitation occurs more frequently after treatment in a progressive institution than after serving a sentence in a less progressive environment, he analyses early release procedures employed by the executive, demonstrates that they rely largely on information (e.g. the social inquiry report) available to the court at the time of sentence, and concludes that the release decision is in truth a re-sentencing decision with this difference – far less emphasis on the offence and its circumstances. Another of his points, so often overlooked that I will repeat it, is that the court, being an open forum in which all the interests, those of society as well as of the offender, can be argued about, evaluated, decided and reviewed on appeal, is likely to be, and to appear to all, including the offender, to be, more just than the committee-style procedure of executive decision. Parenthetically, I would ask: why should not the prosecution be heard on sentence? This could help the court in its assessment of the public factors bearing on the sentencing problem.

Roger Hood also refers to the argument (now being increasingly advanced) against the 'indeterminate sentence' that it is damaging to the status and integrity of the offender. Why should an offender be under pressure to adopt the life-style approved by the director of his establishment, the probation officer and the Board of Visitors? Is he not being encouraged to conform rather than to reform? It is one thing to offer treatment: it is quite another to say that your liberty depends upon your acceptance of it. That conformity rather than the intention to reform is a common reaction when a prisoner realises his liberty depends upon the opinion of those who are responsible for his daily life in custody was well illustrated by a BBC-TV interview the other week of a young man released from custody to community service. He was concerned only to conform and chose what he thought would be the least arduous community service — work in a youth club. The desire to reform did come — as a result of his community service and contacts in the youth club. His case, if fully analysed, is very revealing: so far as he was concerned, institutional or custodial treatment was of little or no value as an influence for rehabilitation, but service in the community was. Were rehabilitation the sole interest to be served by the sentence of the court, this young man should never have been committed to custody: but it is an accepted principle of our law that before sentence is passed there are other interests to be weighed and brought into balance, interests that are not primarily or necessarily those of the offender's rehabilitation. Upon the assumption, which I will later examine, that these are genuine interests, is it really acceptable, the court having balanced all the interests and reached its conclusion, that the executive, upon the advice of those primarily concerned not with those interests but with the offender and his circumstances, should have the responsibility of determining the length of time he is held isolated by custody from the general life of the community?

The Advisory Council's report endeavours to meet these arguments. First, they say that the custody and control order is not an indeterminate sentence: secondly they emphasize the intimate and full degree of 'executive knowledge' possessed by or available to a local licence advisory committee or the Parole Board.

It is a determinate sentence, they say, because the court will determine the period of social intervention in and control over the life of the offender. But this is not what primarily concerns the public or the man: they want to know how long he will be incarcerated. And it is this period that the public and the offender see as of critical importance, and which under the Council's proposals is not to be determined by the court. It is, therefore, disingenuous to speak of a custody and control order in which the court does not determine the period of loss of liberty as a determinate sentence of the court: for the court does not determine that which matters most to the people affected — society and the man himself.

Their second argument — the fullness of 'executive knowledge' — collapses because, however well informed the representatives of the executive are about the offender, they are certainly not better informed about the offence, public opinion, and the sort of penalty needed to reassure and satisfy public opinion. Whatever the penologists may think, the law has to satisfy public opinion; for without public assent the law fails, and chaos ensues. As research has so far failed to establish the optimistic assumptions as to the rehabilitative consequences of penal treatment that are the basis of the attack upon the traditional principle that, subject to remission and parole, the court should fix the period of custody, it is not surprising that a penology based primarily on rehabilitation has not yet won public confidence. Until it does, it would be damaging to the rule of law to base sentencing on such a philosophy.

For these reasons I believe that, while we should welcome the custody and control order for young adult offenders, we should insist that the element of custody in the order be determined by the court of sentence – subject only to the entirely acceptable relaxations of remission and parole.

The report does, however, implicitly emphasise the need for a reappraisal of sentencing policy and law generally. One of the most baffling features of the deep and wide-ranging research into the causes and cures of criminal behaviour that is the mark of modern penology has been its sterility. We know nothing fundamental of the causes of crime save that, given certain environmental circumstances, instincts such as acquisitiveness, display, aggression and sexual passion, all of which have contributed to the dominance of the human species in the animal kingdom, stimulate conduct that society in self-defence condemns as criminal and treats accordingly; and nothing of the cure, save that imprisonment, which relieves us for a time of the distressing presence in our midst of offenders whom we fear, does little or nothing to reduce the volume of crime.

Without prejudice to what future research may expose, I submit that current sentencing policy and law must be based on existing knowledge – not on hopeful speculation. The state of existing knowledge, which, it seems to me, the Advisory Council apply when they advocate their two proposals of custody and control and supervision and control, but disregard when they recommend executive decision for release from custody, can be summed up in three propositions:

(1) there is no evidence that custodial treatment, however

sophisticated and humane, has yet produced a satisfactory rehabilitation result;

(2) there is little or no evidence to suggest that re-conviction, or the rate of recidivism, is much affected by difference of custodial regime;

(3) there is some evidence that suggests that allowing an offender to continue in society, albeit supervised and controlled, does operate directly to strengthen his resistance to the pressures and temptations that can lead him back to crime.

If this be, in brief, the sum of existing knowledge, certain conclusions can be drawn:

(1) that no offender should be imprisoned, or subjected to custodial treatment, unless it can be shown to be essential in the interests of society;

(2) that sentences of imprisonment should be as short as is consistent with the service of those interests of society that can be met only by the loss of his liberty;

(3) that there should be no expenditure of time, money and effort on elaborate institutional techniques such as allocation, Borstal training and detention;

(4) that priority in the allocation of our resources should go to the supervision, control, and treatment of offenders in the community.

The principle of the law should, therefore, be that loss of liberty is an evil to be accepted only for the minimum period required in the interests of society. This equation, for the reasons I have mentioned earlier, must be the court's problem. But I have to admit that the argument for retaining with the court of sentence the duty of fixing, subject to remission and parole, the period of loss of liberty rests upon the premiss that there are interests other than those of the rehabilitation of the offender that have to be weighed in the balance. I now ask: are there really any such interests? Or is it one of those untested assumptions which so often govern the public and private lives of human beings?

It is logically possible to turn the question by replying that there ought not to be any interest other than rehabilitation. But, as a matter of practical experience, we know that society does have other, and on occasions compelling, even overwhelming, interests in the sentence of the court. I suppose – and, speaking personally, I dare to hope – that supervision and control of offenders in the community, based upon a liberal provision of hostels, training and treatment centres, and a large, well-paid and highly qualified profession of probation officers to do the highly individual work of supervision and control, may one day provide the evidence of rehabilitation at such a rate of success that society sees in it its best chance of safety. But that day has not yet come – indeed, may never come: for it is possible that the new idea of supervision within the community may prove no more successful than the brave idea of Borstal, which we now see has helped some carefully selected offenders but not the great majority – certainly not enough to make it worth retaining.

Sentencing is an act of such great social importance that, to be acceptable, it must respond to public opinion and public feeling. The dilemma is how best to reconcile the demands of public opinion with the interests of the offender: the balance that is struck is called 'justice' and, to be seen as such, must be openly struck and then loyally adhered to. Society is, of course, interested in rehabilitation, but is frequently sceptical as to the chances. But it is also intersted in protection and punishment. The reasoning that lies behind these interests is often muddled: but the fear is genuine, deep, and not to be ignored if the law is to enjoy, as it must, the consent of the people. Deprivation of an offender's liberty is seen as both a protection and a punishment: while it lasts, the offender cannot offend and he loses the most valued of all our freedoms. Within its limits, and whatever its consequences, deprivation of the liberty of an offender does protect society and must exert a measure of deterrence: it also marks public disapproval of the offence committed. I neither praise nor condemn our society for expecting these interests to be met and balanced in the sentence of the court: but, as a working judge, I note them and know that the public acceptability of the law depends upon a fair balance being struck and kept between them and the interest of rehabilitation. And for the reasons I have given, the balance is best struck in open court, and, if public confidence is to be retained, must then be honoured by the executive in its treatment of the offender. A custody and control order, which removes from the court the power and duty to determine the period of custody, means that the executive, not the court, strikes the balance: it is, therefore, an innovation that could well undermine confidence in a vital branch of the law.

Once one accepts that the court must determine, subject to remission and parole, the time spent in custody, the way is open for reform.

Long sentences should become the exception — only to be imposed if it can be shown that an extended sentence is necessary for the protection of society. I would suggest that all maximum sentences allowed by law should be reviewed as a matter of urgency. Parliament should consider whether there is any justification for permitting a court to impose a sentence of more than five or seven years save in exceptional circumstances which should be specified by statute. Second, serious consideration should be given to whether courts of summary jurisdiction should retain their power to imprison. This would depend upon the availability of effective alternatives to a sentence of imprisonment: until they are provided, there can, of course, be no question of removing from magistrates their power to imprison.

It is in the provision of alternatives to imprisonment that we must make progress if we are to reduce the number of prisoners and the length of their sentences. Probation and community service need to be developed: and is it really necessary that the offender's consent should be obtained before either order is made? Attendance centres, day training centres, hostels — if money were spent in these ways, it ought to be possible to reduce the number and length of sentences of imprisonment.

Accordingly, my conclusion is that the true path of reform lies not in removing the power of decision from the courts but in law reform. The policy of the law should be to provide as many alternatives to prison, when effective, as ingenuity can suggest and our resources permit; when effective alternatives have been provided to remove from the magistrates' courts the power to imprison, and to set new, significantly lower limits to the terms of imprisonment the Crown Courts can impose.

Given a law that restricts imprisonment to the role of protection and punishment, we can set about more productive tasks than attempting to use loss of liberty as a means of rehabilitation. We can accept it as a punishment and then ensure that the only punitive element in it is the loss of liberty. We can make life in prison as pleasant, as dignified in human terms and as full as is consistent with the deprivation of liberty. We can, and must, as the Advisory Council suggests, put effort and money into strengthening and expanding the alternatives to imprisonment, especially the supervisory services and the establishment of a wide variety of hostels. All this can be done without depriving society and the offender of the decision of the court fixing the period of loss of liberty, taken openly, after argument, according to law, and consistently with principle openly reached and declared by the appellate courts. Public confidence in the penal system, and indeed, more generally, in the law, depends upon a socially acceptable division of function between the courts and the executive: and there is, as yet, no evidence to support a take-over by the executive of the traditional task of the court.

28. Indeterminate Sentences

by MARVIN E. FRANKEL

Reprinted, with permission, in abridged form from *Criminal Sentences* (Hill and Wang, 1972), pp. 86–102.

We are all amused these days by the mechanistic simplemindedness of the idea that the punishment should 'fit the crime'. It is part of our self-confessed greater sophistication that judgments far more subtle and detailed must be made in the specific case of each unique criminal. The sophistication has been developing, and reflected, during the last hundred years or so in the widespread movement toward 'indeterminate' sentences. The quoted word is not used uniformly. I shall use it here, rather loosely, to describe any prison sentence for which the precise term of confinement is not known on the day of judgment but will be subject within a substantial range to the later decision of a parole board or some comparable agency under whatever name . . .

The basic premise of the indeterminate sentence is the relatively modern conception that individualised rehabilitation is the paramount goal in sentencing. The idea is to avoid the Procrustean mold of uniform sentences to fit crimes in the abstract and to focus upon the progress over time of the particular individual so as to determine when it may be safe for society, and good for him, to set him free, at least within the limits of parole supervision. At the same time, the power given to a single parole agency may be expected to mitigate the disparities in sentencing caused by the unregulated vagaries of individual judges. While it has not been advanced as a primary justification for the indeterminate sentence, this seeming power of equalisation appears to be at least one among the conceptions of their functions entertained by parole boards.

The goals of flexibility and evenhandedness seem compellingly worthy. To the extent that these goals are pursued by giving power to parole boards, the result is a corresponding loss of effective authority by sentencing judges. And we all know the familiar habit of officials to cling to power. Despite that, judges have not lately been heard to oppose, but often extol, the indeterminate sentence. In part, this reflects a genuine distaste for the grim responsibility of sentencing. A related sentiment is a sometimes conceded sense of inadequacy, generating a relieved willingness to defer to the supposed expertise of parole officials.

The judges are by no means alone in such favorable sentiments. The movement toward indeterminacy in sentencing is broad and powerful. Scholars of the first rank have joined and propelled it . . . .

Until the last couple of years, the trend toward indeterminate sentencing has seemed irresistible. Just recently, from the prisons and elsewhere, some voices of dissent have been heard. I have come to believe that this minority position is sound and that indeterminate sentencing, as thus far employed and justified, has produced more cruelty, and injustice than the benefits its supporters envisage.

Before undertaking to particularize this position, let me state it with somewhat greater care. I do not condemn the indeterminate sentence always and everywhere. My strictures have nothing to do, either with such devices as 'good time' or 'industrial time' — the reductions a prisoner may earn for behaving well or working while confined. My thoughts, briefly capsulized here and spelled out below, are that:

— Vagueness and uncertainty in the law are (as I have urged earlier) prima facie evils, which does not mean they may never be tolerated, but does mean they call always for justification.

— There is no sound justification for a general and uniform system of indeterminacy, and the use of this idea across-the-board has blocked or concealed the need for concrete justification in specific cases where indeterminate sentences may conceivably make sense.

— In our easy adoration of expertise, we have given over power to people of dubious qualifications, subjected to little or no control.

— We have subjected the supposed beneficiaries of the rehabilitative process to a hated regime of uncertainty and helplessness, ignoring that a program of 'cures' thus imposed is doomed from its inception.

The case for the indeterminate sentence rests, initially, upon a laudable concern for each unique individual, coupled with a frequently baseless assumption that we are able effectively to understand and uniquely to 'treat' the individual. The offender is 'sick', runs the humane thought, and/or dangerous. He needs to be helped and 'cured'. Nobody, certainly not the sentencing judge, can know when he will be well and no more dangerous than the masses of us who are lucky enough not to have been convicted. Hence, those charged with 'treatment' must be left to decide the time for release.

This 'rehabilitative ideal', as a noted legal scholar has tagged and criticized it,[1] is genetically flawed and malformed. Its first dubiety is the fallacious — or, at least, far too broad — assumption that criminals are 'sick' in some way that calls for 'treatment'. Of course, if you say blandly that nobody commits a serious crime unless he is 'sick', the proposition is a useless tautology. To be meaningful in our context, the statement must be that (1) the person has some identifiable disorder apart from the mere biographical datum of his offense, (2) the disorder in some verifiable (or theoretically refutable) way is causally related to the offense, and (3) the penologists or judges or somebody in authority knows some way and place for treatment of the disorder. Formulated in this testable way, the theory fails on at least a couple of weighty grounds.

We sentence many people every day who are not 'sick' in any identifiable respect and are certainly not candidates for any form of therapy or 'rehabilitation' known thus far. Many convicted criminals fall within a class labelled in one lively, psychoanalytically oriented book as 'normal criminals'[2] . . . The 'normal criminal', whatever else he may need or merit, is not a promising candidate for any sort of treatment available in our prisons, our hospitals, or any other known institution.

Another facet of the case, abstractly separate but not easy to keep always separate in fact, is the severely limited character of our ability to treat the supposedly sick criminal. As to the theoretical separability of this point, there is no strain in distinguishing the idea of disease from that of cure. We know of identified diseases, some deadly, for which we know no cure. In the field of criminology, however, where ignorance reigns so nearly absolute, the distinction is blurred. The apostles of rehabilitation and indeterminate sentences posit 'sickness' without identifying its character and then urge 'treatment' no better defined or specified. The absence of treatment or facilities is by itself a fatal defect for purposes of the present discussion. However useful it may be elsewhere to identify incurable diseases, there is no justification for a regime of rehabilitation through indeterminate sentences unless we have some substantial hope or prospect of rehabilitating. Our subject is, after all, the confinement of people for long and uncertain periods of time. It is an evil to lock people up. There may be compensating goods that warrant it. But a mythical goal of rehabilitation is no good at all . . . .

It is not disagreeable for people 'in the community and in the field of criminal justice', assuming they have no more pressing things to do, to devote their energies to the attempted proof or accomplishment of universal redeemability. What is disagreeable – and vicious – is to cage prisoners for indeterminate stretches while we set about their assured rehabilitation, not knowing what to do for them or, really, whether we can do any useful thing for them.

Having imported the supposed model of sickness-and-cure with a simpleminded lack of discrimination, the proponents of indeterminate sentences actually misconceive the medical analogy. The physician, when he undertakes a cure or treatment procedure, is usually not indeterminate to any large extent in forecasting the time required. When you check in for an appendectomy or brain surgery, or for hepatitis or mononucleosis, it is generally possible to predict within reasonable limits how long before you will be out, one way or another .... With indeterminate prison sentences, however, the approach to time predictions is neither sought nor attainable. Having in view no genuine programme of 'treatment', the sentencers and parole officers cannot say how long it will take ....

In this state of blissfully ignorant cruelty, we dump into our generally huge prisons unsorted varieties of prisoners – the few who may need treatment we know how to supply, the many we don't know how to treat, whatever they may need, and the many more who evidence no perceptible need for treatment, existing or imagined. This is the macabre but not astonishing culmination of an indeterminate-sentencing process that rests mainly upon fiction and absentmindedness. The sentence purportedly tailored to the cherished needs of the individual turns out to be a crude order for simple warehousing. The prison characteristically has no treatment facilities of any substantial nature. The means for rehabilitation, undefined and probably unknown, are not at hand. How could they be if they have not been identified, let alone supplied?

Thus, while we pour increasing numbers of people into prisons for the serving of uncertain sentences, the most basic of asserted justifications, the programme of rehabilitation, is absent. In a host of cases, then, when somebody says a prisoner must stay locked up because he is not 'ready' for release, the ultimate Kafkaism is the lack of any definition of 'ready'. Facing the facts, we know that 'treatment' is mostly an illusion in our prisons. There is powerful evidence that the majority of prisoners deteriorate – become poorer risks and lesser people – rather than improve in prison. This is certainly the case for sentences dragging on beyond four or five years, which includes a huge number, especially among highly indeterminate sentences. It is bracing doctrine, of course, whether or not it makes sense, to insist, as many do, that our prisons must be improved to make rehabilitation a reality. Assuming that is feasible — assuming we can on any scale rehabilitate people while keeping them locked up — the point of transcending consequence at the moment is that we are not doing so. Because we are not, the main prop for indeterminate sentences is a hollow reed. Unless we mean to make sadist jokes, we cannot fairly send people away for 'as long as it takes' to be rehabilitated, then merely hold them until a whimsical release date, doing nothing meanwhile that pretends to be rehabilitative.

The quality of horrid joke manifests itself in more than one way. It appears every time we impose an indeterminate sentence on a defendant who is patently not a subject for any kind of rehabilitation . . . .

The reference in this connection to parole boards spotlights another gruesome aspect of the indeterminacy regime. It is widely believed, in prison and out, that parole boards operate without orderly and uniform criteria for judgment, often moved by 'political' pressures or the winds of public opinion, without the benefit of mature and organised wisdom. There are grounds for such beliefs, based upon what parole officials and scholars have told us, and perhaps even more upon the heavy blanket of silence and mystery under which these agencies carry on . . .

It would be unfair and inaccurate to conclude that the major ill in this quarter is the inferiority or bad disposition of parole officials. Taken all together, they are — like judges and others — merely human. Because their roles are vaguely defined, their qualifications are inevitably uncertain. Many of them, assigned without guidance to answer unintelligible questions, work hard and earnestly for small rewards. But the system is unworkable. Given the foggy terms of their mandate, parole boards give us no less than we have a right to expect. We charge them to make indeterminate sentences determinate, but we give them no conceptual or other tools to work with. We set them lofty goals of rehabilitation, but with no directions or means of achievement . . . .

And what of the alleged beneficiaries of the rehabilitative ideal, the prisoners? How do they respond to the boon of indeterminate sentences? A former Attorney General of the United States has extolled the indeterminate sentence as an attractive incentive, contrasting favourably with the grey inexorability of a fixed term.[3] A United States Attorney, who has since become a Federal District Judge, put the same point this way:

> Inherent in the indeterminate sentence procedure is the stimulation of an offender's incentive towards rehabilitation. He is aware that under the programme designed for him there will be periodic revaluations of his potential for parole, and that he will return to the community only when his attitudes and patterns of behaviour have been sufficiently modified.[4]

However good 'stimulation' and 'incentive' may sound to prosecutors and others on the outside, it does not detonate echoes inside prison walls. The growing evidences of prisoner sentiment — which introspection and conversation lead me to find persuasive — indicate that the inmate experiences as cruel and degrading the command that he remain in custody for some uncertain period, while his keepers study him, grade him in secret, and decide if and when he may be let go. I think this should not surprise us. Harking back to a point made early in this book, it is pertinent again to recall how deeply we prize certainty and predictability in the workings of the law. We want to be able to plan our businesses and family decisions by knowing in advance just how painful the tax will be, what the zoning laws promise, how long an employment contract will endure. It may be imagined that knowing the actual length of a prison term might serve similar, though much more searing, needs.

At any rate, prisoners and students of their plight so testify. The uncertainty of the indeterminate sentence is experienced as a steadily galling affliction. There is a sense of helpless rage which is enhanced by a prevalent disbelief in the reality of rehabilitation as a goal. 'How', writes one rehabilitee in California, 'do you rehabilitate a cat who has never been "habilitated"?'[5] Brooding and skeptical, wondering when he will be released, the same prisoner writes: 'He can only guess. And this guessing game only infuriates him and increases his distrust of the penal system.'[6] As to the absolute control of California's Adult Authority over the actual time to be served, he says: 'No such power should be in the hands of a few men.'[7] . . . .

For those wondering when the miracle may happen, there is a desperate sense of mystery about what the rules are, most centrally about what will 'work' toward the tensely focused goal of release. There is a bitter, and seemingly growing, conviction that a craven conformity is the key. The silence surrounding parole-board decisions nurtures cynicism among the prisoners — a belief in the arbitrariness and essential corruption of those in power. A pervasive sense of helplessness generates frustration and rage.

These sentiments are important data in themselves. Even if we knew much about how to rehabilitate, the hostility of those invited grandly to be 'redeemed' would be a countervailing force of some magnitude. The trouble is compounded if, as I believe, the hostility responds to a system that is misconceived, harsh, and oppressive in its operation . . . .

It is not my claim that rehabilitation is always and everywhere impossible. Nor do I argue that an indeterminate sentence could never be wise and fair. The great evil in current thinking is the pair of false assumptions that (1) rehabilitation is *always* possible and (2) indeterminate sentences are *always* desirable. I urge that the shoe belongs on the other foot. Most importantly, my contention is that the presumption ought always to be in favor of a definite sentence, known and justified on the day of sentencing (and probably much shorter than our sentences tend to run). There should be a burden of justifying an indeterminate sentence in any particular case — a burden to be satisfied only by concrete reasons and a concrete programme for the defendant in that case. The justifications, I tentatively suggest . . . would consist of identified needs and resources for effective rehabilitation or for incapacitation of a dangerous offender, or both.

To be slightly more concrete, there are specific kinds of defendants for whom we have plausible, if by no means certain, hopes of rehabilitation. It appears, for example, that there are some meaningful hypotheses about 'treatment' for some drug users, some sex offenders, and, most hopefully, some of our numerous young offenders. Even as to these, the hopes must be modest, scaled to the meagerness of our knowledge and our niggardliness in allocating resources to such concerns. Other kinds of specific cases could be added . . . .

Moreover, having railed against the airy nonsense that everyone can be rehabilitated, I would not insist that certainty of success be a precondition for the attempt. In the field of drug abuse, to illustrate in terms of what may be our most harrowing problem today, there are competing ideas about treatment, with no clear case of efficacy made for any of them. So here, as in several kinds of more purely 'medical' effort, programs of treatment go forward in what ought to be seen candidly as courses of trial-and-error testing. But the uncertainty is not grounds for abandoning the effort. Unlike grand inanities about universal redemption, narcotics programs center upon a reasonably well-identified and defined species of pathology. The several modes of treatment are describable in terms that have meaning and tolerable limits, including, importantly, limits upon the time required for achieving success or admitting failure. It is significant, too, that the subject admits of intelligible discourse about 'success' and 'failure'; it is possible to identify results or their absence with a decent approach to precision. Finally, programs for treatment of addicts are characteristically, though not always, built upon the patient's acquiescence. The willing participant seeking a shared objective is a pole away from the subject of an indeterminate sentence ostensibly justified by rehabilitative objectives for which he has been shown neither the need nor the means of achievement. . . . .

Subject, then, to more wisdom later, let me reiterate my basic thoughts about indeterminate sentences: they are usually evil and unwarranted, but they may be suitable upon detailed showings in specific cases involving (1) demonstrated needs for rehabilitation and incapacitation and (2) rationally organized means for serving those needs. Otherwise, and for the great majority of cases, sentences ought to be stated with maximum certainty, based almost entirely upon factors known on the day of sentencing, and determined with the nearest approach we can make to objective, equal, and 'impersonal' evaluation of the relevant qualities of both the criminal and the crime.

Notes

1. Francis A. Allen, *The Borderland of Criminal Justice* (Chicago University Press, 1964), pp. 25—41.
2. Franz Alexander and Hugo Staub, *The Criminal, the Judge and the Public* (Glencoe, Ill., The Free Press, 1956), pp. 81—2, 96, 107, 139—49, 209—11.
3. Ramsey Clark, *Crime in America* (New York Pocket Books, 1971), p. 203.
4. Matthew Byrne, Jr., 'Federal sentencing procedures: need for reform,' *Los Angeles Bar Bulletin* 42 (1967), pp. 563—567.
5. Prisoner Alfred Hassan in Eve Pell, (ed.), *Maximum Security — Letters from California's Prisons* (New York, Dutton and Co., 1972), p. 22.
6. *Ibid.*, p. 31.
7. *Ibid.*, p. 33.

29. Tolerance and the Tariff: Some Reflections on Fixing the Time Prisoners Serve in Custody

by ROGER HOOD

Reprinted, with permission, in abridged form from NACRO Reprint No, 11 (1974).

Introduction

In the last few years some attention has been switched from the problems of avoiding short-term imprisonment to the problem of the lengths of sentences imposed on those whose crimes are so serious or criminal careers so extensive that a period of custody seems inevitable. Those who receive medium and long terms of imprisonment form the major body of the prison population, and it is now widely felt that a substantial decline in the numbers in prison can only be achieved if the terms of incarceration they serve can be considerably cut. There are, of course, various ways in which this can be achieved. First, the courts could impose shorter maximum penalties, thus affecting all prisoners whether released on parole or not. Second, the present parole system itself could be expanded to release more men under supervision. Third, a period of statutory release on licence at an earlier period than the present two-thirds date could be introduced for nearly all prisoners. A fourth alternative would be to introduce, first for young adults and perhaps later for all offenders, the scheme proposed in the Advisory Council's Report on Young Adult Offenders (the Younger Committee) whereby most prisoners could be released by the licence advisory committee at any stage of 'a custody and control order'.[1] Under such a scheme it might be possible to reduce the length of time spent in custody by the exercise of executive discretion without there being any changes in judicial sentencing practice in setting maximum penalties. Indeed it is significant that there is no discussion in the Younger Report of appropriate lengths of the sentences to a custody and control order set by the courts. . . .

I want to challenge what has become a basic element of modern policy, namely the doctrine that the actual period of a custodial sentence served should be fixed by review boards of various kinds advised, in the main, by the penal authorities who have been responsible for containing and 'training' the offender. The sole function of the judge is seen as fixing the maximum period of custody, to reflect the limits of public reaction to the crime and at the same time to protect the offender from abuse of the discretionary power of the authorities. Such a system of 'indeterminate' sentencing has been part of the reformers' platform for so many years, and the arguments against it have been so readily dismissed as 'reactionary' or 'retributive' in the worst senses of these pejorative terms, that few in this country have thought to raise them. But I hope to persuade you that the arguments do have substance. They are 'reactionary' in the best sense of returning to some fundamental liberal principles, and they are 'retributive' in the best sense of attempting to place clear limits on the State's control over offenders. But they also involve matters of principle relating to the purposes of punishment; of theory, in so far as they rest upon challenging assumptions about criminal behaviour; and of practice, to the extent that they appeal to the empirical reality of our knowledge about the treatment of offenders rather than to what we wish we knew or could do. I do not wish to be dogmatic about it, but it seems to me that the present trend in policy as enunciated in the parole scheme, to a greater extent in the recommendations of the Younger Committee and in the even more far-reaching proposals for the future of the minority of that Committee (Mr Blom-Cooper, Mr Stirling, Professor Trasler and Lady Wootton), may be no more effective and almost certainly less just in reducing the amount of time prisoners spend in custody, than what can be achieved by adopting a determinate sentencing system in which the proportion of a combined order for custody and supervision actually spent in custody is fixed by statute. Thus, the actual period served would be decided by the judge in court and all offenders would have a period of supervision subject to recall. There would, of course, be exceptions to this determinate system — indeterminate sentences can probably be justified for a minority of long-term dangerous offenders . . . My argument is that, instead of abandoning the judiciary as incompetent to set the actual time served by most prisoners in the hope that some other body can undertake the task without creating even greater problems, we should seek to ensure that the values and knowledge implicit in judicial sentencing practice are made more explicit and so subject to public debate and where necessary to statutory control.

The Decline of Positivism and the Re-Emergence of a Liberal Doctrine

There is a perennial tension in penal philosophy between basing the sentence on the one hand upon an assessment of the gravity of the offence and the culpability of the offender, thus maintaining a scale of punishments reflecting a moral evaluation of past behaviour, and on the other hand upon an assessment of the likely effects of penalties on the future conduct of the offender and of potential offenders. In recent years there is no doubt that the latter approach has been in the ascendancy in England: it is the basis of Juvenile Court legislation; it received official approval for adults in the Streatfeild Report, it lies in principle behind the selective processes of parole (even if in practice that system has not endorsed it entirely) and the Younger Committee proposals. It is the cornerstone of what many would regard as the progressive minority report of Mr Blom-Cooper and his colleagues who state categorically that they think that

> the courts are mistaken when they assume that sentences can be adjusted to degrees of criminal responsibility, so that the graver the crime, the longer the period during which the offender should be deprived of his liberty: we find this idea inappropriate if applied to the penal system as a whole. . . .

So naturally they feel that the sole concern of the courts should be to decide on whether 'some form of social intervention is called for' and to fix the maximum duration of such intervention 'in the interests of personal liberty'[2] — although they do not say what criteria other than the offender's actions could be used to decide this maximum. They believe that as far as the rights of the offender are concerned this is sufficient protection and they would welcome custody being 'viewed as a method of treatment for buttressing the non-custodial situation, and the decision to use it as part of ongoing supervision in the community should be made at leisure by those who have the day-to-day care of the young offender'.[3] Indeed, the principle that 'the date at which an offender can safely be returned to life in the community can only be properly assessed by those who are in day to day contact with him while he is in custody, and that no court at the time of sentencing is in a position to determine this in advance' is a penological dogma which seems to get stronger by its very repetition. But it is none the less sheer dogma — unsupported by any empirical evidence, based on a shaky foundation of penal philosophy, in conflict with contemporary opinions on the moral basis for intervention in the lives of citizens and through the anxiety and sense of injustice it creates perhaps more, rather than less, likely to alienate prisoners from the system of criminal justice.

The reaction to this dogma has come mainly from the United States and the Scandinavian countries. Ten years ago Professor Francis Allen attacked with vigour and incisive logic what he called the 'rehabilitative ideal'.[4] Recently, Federal Judge Marvin Frankel, a leading proponent of sentencing reform, has joined the battle. . . .

The lawyers have been joined by radical critics of the penal system. Among the most trenchant attacks is the Report published by the American Friends Service Committee called *Struggle for Justice*,[5] which employs a number of arguments also used by many Scandinavian criminologists. These arguments are as follows.

First, the claims for rehabilitation being related either to the length of incarceration or to the type of facilities offered to the offender are not substantiated by any empirical evidence. Indeed, the major research including that on the most progressive institutions shows no difference between offenders who have undergone treatment there or have served sentences elsewhere.[6] Thus it appears extremely difficult to justify altering the length of sentence served by a prisoner on the basis that his future behaviour has been greatly affected by the regime he has undergone and that those who observed his response to this regime can add to the predictive power of estimates of his likely behaviour in the future. We know this not to be the case; the prisoner's chances of reconviction can be better predicted by data already available at the time of sentence. Early release procedures by and large reconsider much of the information available to the court at the time of sentence and either further mitigate the penalty as unnecessarily long in relation to his past and likely future behaviour, or do not: in either case it amounts to a re-sentencing decision. The only difference, and a fundamental one, is that institutional authorities often know little about the circumstances of the offence and the defendant's involvement in it — it is sometimes almost regarded as irrelevant. They therefore reach judgements based on perceptions of the person as a whole rather than on his offensive behaviour — and this may subtly reinforce differences of social status, personality and life-style which, the critics complain, amount to a further scapegoating and alienation of the powerless who may consequently feel that authority continues to discriminate against them.[7]

If the courts consider that the risk of reconviction — based largely as it is on the offender's previous record, his dependence upon institutions, his isolation from associates in conventional sectors of society — should be an aggravating factor in the assessment of the length of penalty to be served then it would be better to make this explicit in sentencing policy. But, as we know, the Court of Appeal has evolved the principle that a man's previous conduct if good should count in mitigation, if very bad should result in no mitigation from the appropriate penalty for the offence.[8] Thus previous record is already taken into account in the sentence length imposed. The dogma of 'executive knowledge' leads to the same factors being taken into account yet again at a later stage, thus increasing the disparity in the penalties originally imposed. Is that just? And should not the decision be made in the courts where the policy can be properly evaluated, appealed against and argued about, for what it is, rather than disguised under a false rhetoric?

The second argument put forward by the critics of indeterminacy relates to the status and integrity of the prisoner. They would argue, as Professor Anttila of Helsinki does, that 'the fundamental principle of socio-legal treatment arrangements should be that the non-conformist is offered the possibility of receiving care. It is up to the individual to decide whether he will make use of that possibility or not."[9] There are two related issues here. On the other hand, they are aware of the unhappy truth that methods of behaviour modification and electronic surveillance and control are being developed which are potentially extremely effective, but which are also a thick edge of a large wedge that could threaten individual liberty.[10] On the other hand they are aware of the advantages of a determinate system where 'opportunities for treatment are provided by agencies that have no power or effect upon the duration of the prisoner's term and can, therefore, serve his interests with undivided loyalty': and I would add, unaffected by expediency or their own punitive reactions to those who do not accept the goods on offer. If this approach is right, then release should not depend upon the treaters' interpretation of the willingness of the inmate to accept the treatment:[11] all that does is to leave the door open for conformity to be the main criterion of change (as all prison staff know) and in some cases makes a mockery of the idea of consent to treatment implants – for example, in the use of drugs and hormone implants to control sex offenders. The indeterminate sentence system puts the prisoners so much in the hands of those who have the responsibility for this care and treatment that it not only may distort his response, but perhaps more importantly it acts as a system for institutional control which in reality is a recipe for denying the inmate individually, and collectively, the power to challenge the institutional structure without fear of affecting his liberty, and is likely both to neutralise one pressure for radical change and to block one avenue for the release of frustration and tension. This argument seems particularly important at a time when prisoners are becoming more conscious of their legal rights and less ready to take on a derogated status as people to be changed rather than given the opportunities for change.

Third, the critics point to the possibilities for the abuse of discretionary power as the margins between the minimum and maximum sentences increase, and argue cogently that the game of 'cat and mouse', of hope deferred, at best produces a quickly learned series of strategies to 'make parole' – sometimes the very antithesis of making constructive use of the time spent in prison – and at the worst a chronic anxiety about time, which is a morally unjustifiable extra burden to place upon the prisoner and his family.[12] The system which appears treatment-orientated and humane, it is claimed, may turn out to be neither, sacrificing a large proportion of inmates for the early release of others whose length of incarceration could have been set at a shorter level at the time of sentence (as happens, indeed, in the present parole system).

Behind all these criticisms there is of course a political point, namely that the State should not use its powers to punish in order to stifle diversity in life-styles; that it should not use the power to punish in order to deny the offender's view of his social situation as unjust or as uncaring if indeed it is; that the penal system cannot act as a major instrument of social change, and that if it attempts to do so it is in danger of adopting a stance whereby social deviation is attributed to individual pathology which can be 'corrected' by a 'treatment' service. . . .

What emerges from these views is that any decisions to reduce the lengths of deprivation of liberty should be made not in terms of their effectiveness but by a clear decision to re-draw the 'crime–punishment equation' (a term which would have been anathema to Enrico Ferri): in other words, to examine the kinds of behaviour which are regarded as sufficiently serious to justify incarceration, to reconsider the concept of dangerousness, to re-assess the degree of tolerance which we should show towards offenders — an example of which can already be seen in the changing definition of old lags into petty persistent offenders, minor property offenders into 'nuisances', the Lord Justice James's welcome proposals to deal with more of these categories outside of the criminal process,[13] as happens now in Holland. On the other side of course there must be a similar reappraisal of the nature of custodial sentences as punishments, and the degree of such punishment which is justified for particular criminal actions. . . .

What weight should be given to harm done? to previous record? to poor environment? to cultural differences in the interpretation of challenges to personal status or integrity? to marital stress or inadequate income? Which offences should be regarded as the most socially injurious? Have we placed serious traffic offences in their right order compared with most petty thefts and common-or-garden assaults? This is surely the proper area for judicial pronouncement on sentences, instead of being taken for granted, or dismissed as unanswerable or sidetracked by vague talk of individualisation of treatment. I do not believe those values on which a system of punishments should be based are easily deduced from a 'common morality', but by forcing judges to evaluate social behaviours we shall put them in the position of articulating the most important social principles. We shall, for example, be more easily able to evaluate the penalties awarded to individuals in different social situations. The 'reductivist' philosophy undoubtedly has led to greater punishments for the lower social classes, leaving many sociologists to wonder whether the criminal justice system is not simply a means of scapegoating those with little social power.[14]

But, of course such a sentencing system can only be put into effect if the judiciary are willing to state more specifically than they do, how their judgements on sentence length are reached. This they seem singularly unwilling to do. Speaking on the question of giving reasons for sentences of imprisonment, in the House of Lords in 1972, the Lord Chief Justice said:

> in nine cases out of ten, I am confident that the answer would be that the gravity of the offence itself requires the imposition of such a sentence and very little is to be gained by requiring as a matter of law, that these words should be included as part of the formula of sentencing.[15]

I am not of course saying that judges fail to take culpability into account (the example of a suspended sentence for rape recently on the grounds of the offender's penitence, drunkenness and marital difficulties springs to mind),[16] but I am saying that by forcing judges to articulate the moral judgements on which their sentence is based is the only sure and just way of reassessing and perhaps reducing in the long run the length of time many offenders spend in custody. . . .

The Younger Report's Proposals

It should be clear from what I have said that I would be hard-put to find arguments in favour of the proposals in the Younger Report on Young Adult Offenders in so far as they refer to the system devised for setting the period in custody. Let me say straight away that I most strongly support the general intention to reduce the use of custody for this age group — which has remained constant over the last 15 years while the proportion of adults going to prison has been steadily falling. I am also in favour of the abolition of the separate sentences to detention centre, Borstal and imprisonment and of the new supervision and control order. However it seems to me that when the Report comes to the custody and control order it exhibits an uneasy marriage between, on the one hand, the desires of the minority I referred to above (Mr Blom-Cooper, Mr Stirling, Professor Trasler and Lady Wootton), wedded as they are to the principle of indeterminacy, and on the other the majority who, while accepting the principle of executive control over release, give more weight to the general criticisms I have already mentioned. This is evident in the recognition that the former flat-rate maximum of the Borstal sentence imposed to allow time for training should be replaced by a maximum tailored to each offender 'to enable the court to express its judgement upon the offences on behalf of the community' (para. 26). The Report also devised a system of 'target dating' by which an offender will be given a date to aim for soon after his reception into custody, presumably to take some of the sting out of the indeterminate element. In addition it provides for a local licensing board, again to ensure some degree of assessment of suitability for release independent of the institution's own staff. And in order that the courts may in the more serious cases indicate their concern to ensure that the offender is not released too early the majority recommended that the courts could order that at least one third of the sentence must be served.

It seems to me that the Committee simply has not learned from the dilemmas and conflicts experienced by the parole system in reaching its decisions, nor has it taken note of the widespread demands for a system which would provide an element of due process such as reasons for refusal to release and a hearing before the tribunal. It has even added the wholly novel power to the Governor to recall an offender, after consultation with the probation service, during the first two months after his release 'on any reasonable grounds' (para. 229).

The Committee have accepted the 'basic principle' that the judge cannot know at the time of sentencing how long an offender needs to be in custody. But at the same time they said that they 'did not believe that custody as such will confer any particular benefits upon the offenders, but it does nevertheless present opportunities which might not otherwise be available to them and of which they might not otherwise take advantage' (para. 327). Does that mean that time in custody is to be tailored to the needs of various treatment or training programmes? Should not the programmes be tailored to the time in custody, if custody as such has no benefits? The Committee suggests that it is taking the latter view, but the use of terms such as the offender's 'needs and prospects' (para. 33) and 'progress in custody' (para. 212), make one wonder how it will work in practice. Apparently, 'the treatment authorities' will determine the degree of control to be exercised over the offender at each stage of his sentence, primarily with a view to his 're-integration in the community' (para. 26). The seductive use of the word 'control' so easily obscures the difference between custody and supervision out of custody: it is not just a matter of degree, but a fundamentally different status. Yet the Committee seemed to recognise this in another context when they said 'What counts with the offender is the length of time which he suffers loss of liberty, not the type of establishment in which the sentence is served' (para. 166). Surely this dictum must apply with greater force to the question of whether he is in an institution or not?

Is it true that because the judge cannot know how a man will look at the world in the future his liberty should depend upon other men's interpretation of his state of mind? The problem of assessing future dangerousness should not be confused with future reformation. No research on the Borstal system has shown that either the period of incarceration or the type of regime to which the offender is subjected affects the probability of reconviction. Indeed, one of the main planks of the Report's argument against a system of classification and allocation to institutions offering separate regimes, and in favour of 'community institutions', is that the ability to make such distinctions between offenders does not exist. But why then is the proposed system attempting to outline a programme for each offender based on a target date for release? Although it is claimed that the decision will rest on a full assessment report made within one month, it is difficult to see on what basis this assessment can recommend a particular period for training or control, and even more difficult to see what extra information will be forthcoming that will enable those concerned to reach a judgement, that could not be made by a court on the information available at the time of sentence after suitable enquiries. As the target date is in effect a quasi-sentence, it will become inevitable that it will come to bear some relationship to the length of sentence imposed by the court. If it does not and, for example, two offenders entering the institution on one day are given different dates although they have received the same maximum, a sense of injustice will be created. It will be even greater if someone given a longer sentence by the court is given a target earlier than that given to a prisoner given a shorter sentence. This element of proportionality has always been of concern to the Parole Board, although there it is less of a problem because all adults serve a standard period before eligibility. The Younger Committee do not discuss how their proposed system will deal with it, except to say that:

> The Court's view of the seriousness of the offence — as expressed in the length of the order — would clearly be one consideration, which would be relevant though not decisive. Public confidence in the operation of the system is, after all, an obvious condition of its success. [para. 35]

One might add, which the Report did not, that the prisoner's confidence in the operation of the system is just as important. The anxiety suffered in the 'cat and mouse game' of indeterminacy should not be heightened by a sense of injustice. The idea of target dating is, therefore, simply passing the decision on the actual length of custody from the courts to other agents who have no more expertise without any pretense that this decision is based on a belief that the time element is crucial to the reform of each individual.

Of course, the reason for this policy may be that members of the Committee distrusted the judiciary, believing that, left to them, the use of custody would not be reduced. They presumably believed that the authorities would be more likely to ensure early release into the community by fixing their target dates below the period a judge would fix if there were a fixed proportion of combined custody and control order which had to be served in custody. They may be right, but they may just as easily be wrong. Just as one meets insensitive and punitive judges, one meets insensitive and punitive psychologists, psychiatrists and social workers. The point is that judicial decisions made with reasons are open to review and debate, whereas decisions based upon 'clinical' diagnosis and having the status of 'professional expertise' are difficult to attack and hard to appeal against. The fact that one distrusts the personnel who make the decisions in a system of due process should not lead one immediately to seek a solution which gives power to others without due process. It is to confuse the issue of personnel with the more fundamental issue of procedure. If the personnel are at fault then the task becomes one of selecting, influencing and controlling them. I believe that in recent years the judiciary have shown themselves open to new ideas and I would rather build on that, coupled with more legislative control of the powers of the courts, than extend executive power over prisoners. In this respect the Younger Committee proposals go further than the parole scheme. Not only is there not an eligibility date, so that the prisoner can formally apply and state his case, but decisions are largely left to the local committee, except for those serving the longest sentences. In the parole system the well-known variations between local review committees are ironed out to some extent by ensuring that all cases which fall into a relatively good risk category, whether locally recommended or not, are seen by the National Board. Such a safeguard is not built into the Young Offender proposals.

I am for all these reasons convinced that, if the real aim of the proposed legislation is to cut the length of time spent in custody by combining a strict form of supervision with the institutional sentence, this would be better achieved by a fixed proportion being served in the institution set in relation to the maximum period of control ordered by the court. Only in those cases where it can genuinely be claimed that the offender's behaviour is unpredictably dangerous is there a case for administrative review. These of course, would only be the longer sentences and they could be dealt with by means of procedures which are fairer and more open. . . .

Notes

1. Home Office, *Young Adult Offenders* (The Younger Report). Report of the Advisory Council on the Penal System (HMSO, 1974).
2. Younger Report, Note of Dissent by Mr Louis Blom-Cooper, QC, Mr W. R. Stirling, Professor G. B. Trasler and the Baroness Wootton of Abinger, paras. 6 and 7.
3. Note of Dissent para. 1. It is interesting to note that these dissenters were opposed to the proposal in the main report to grant young offenders automatic remission of one-third of the maximum period on the grounds that it was 'logically incompatible with a *wholly indeterminate sentence*' (para. 13, my italics).
4. Francis Allen, *The Borderland of Criminal Justice* (University of Chicago Press, 1964).
5. *Struggle for Justice*, A Report on Crime and Punishment in America, prepared for the American Friends Service Committee (New York, Hill and Wang, 1971).
6. There are many references to support this. See, for example, Roger Hood and Richard Sparks, *Key Issues in Criminology* (London, Weidenfeld & Nicholson, 1970).
7. See *Struggle for Justice*, pp. 29 and 41.
8. D. A. Thomas, *Principles of Sentencing*, pp. 35–46.
9. Inkeri Anttila, 'Conservative and radical criminal policy in the Nordic countries' in *Scandinavian Studies in Criminology*, 3 (Oslo, Universitetsforlaget, 1971) at p. 21.
10. See Stanley Cohen, 'A futuristic scenario for the prison system' in F. Bassaglia (ed.) *The Crimes of Peace* (Turin, Einaudi, 1974).
11. See *Struggle for Justice*, p. 27.
12. This is the view now of Lord Hunt, the first Chairman of the Parole Board. See *H. L. Debates* 352, col. 530 (12 June 1974).
13. Lord Justice James, 'A new approach to the criminal process' The Riddell Lecture (1974).
14. See, for example, Denis Chapman, *Sociology and the Stereotype of the Criminal* (London, Tavistock, 1968).
15. *H. L. Debates*, 333, col. 581 (17 July 1972).
16. Reported in *Daily Telegraph* (19 June 1974).

Index of Names